COED PRISON

John Ortiz Smykla, Ph.D.

The University of Alabama
University, Alabama

HUMAN SCIENCES PRESS
72 Fifth Avenue   3 Henrietta Street
NEW YORK, NY 10011 ● LONDON, WC2E 8LU

Printed in the United States of America
0 987654321

Library of Congress Cataloging in Publication Data

Main entry under title:

Coed prison.

Bibliography: p. 273
Includes index.
CONTENTS: Pt. 1. General essays on coed prison: Ruback, B. The sexually integrated prison.—Ross, J. et al. Characteristics of co-correctional institutions.—Campbell, C. Co-corrections—FCI Fort Worth after three years.—Heffernan, E. and Krippel, E. A coed prison. [etc.]
1. Prisons, Coeducational—United States—Addresses, essays, lectures. 2. Prisons, Coeducational—United States—Bibliography. 3. Women prisoners—United States—Addresses, essays, lectures. I. Smykla, John Ortiz.
HV9469.C63   365'.3   LC 79-17202
ISBN 0-87705-410-X

FOR MY SON
JONATHON FRANCISCO

CONTENTS

FOREWORD

Criticism of the American Prison System is coming from every quarter. National and state study commissions, scholars and legislators, point to the system's apparent failure to rehabilitate, to achieve acceptable degrees of success in reducing crime or to break the cycle of recidivism among offenders. The liberal trend that dominated correctional policies during the past decade is being reversed. Pressure for a more heavy-handed, punitive law-and-order approach is gaining momentum. The new orthodoxy, fueled by rising crime rates, articulated by hundreds of editorial writers and politicians, and intellectualized by such academicians as James Q. Wilson, Ernest Van den Haag, and Robert Martinson, assures us that punishment works and that increasing imprisonment will reduce crime. This change in orthodoxy has already produced predictable results. The number of persons jailed or imprisoned has risen phenomenally since this reversal in trends in 1974, and institutions are burgeoning.

Yet before one embraces the new hard line, it will pay to remember that the history of corrections is full of fads, policies, and plans, which have failed to achieve their purpose and which have survived nevertheless. For 200 years, corrections has pursued inappropriate concerns and ineffective solutions. There is reason to think that this latest trend, too, is but another attempt to provide simplistic solutions to exceedingly complex problems. Strong evidence exists that incarceration, as we know it, contributes little in the national effort to reduce crime.

A brief look at an impressive, cumulative body of research explains why institutionalization is counterproductive. Clemmer's research finds that prisoners, through the process of assimilation and acculturation, tend to take on the criminal values, norms, customs, and general culture of the prison. Korn and McCorkle find that banishment to a prison represents the ultimate in social rejection, and that prisoners adopt antisocial values to "reject the rejector." Goffman reports that the processes of disculturation and dehumanization inflicted on inmates are not only destructive to the individual but also incompatible with practically every element of social life. Sykes, Cloward, and Schrag observe that prison subcultures tend to subvert even the most conscientious of institutional treatment efforts. Glaser, Wilkins, and Wolfgang, and more recently, Martinson, point out that favorable change seldom, if ever, occurs in prison or other incarcerative settings. When change does occur, the probability is strong that it takes place in spite of the experience, and not because of it.

In addition to the general ineffectiveness of prisons in terms of rehabilitation and crime control, those who have studied the prison system invariably observe that the "single-sex" social experience of correctional institutions contributes generously to the all-too-evident maladaptive behavior of inmates in those institutions. While assault, rape, and murder are more common in the United States than in most western industrialized countries, this tendency toward physical violence is even more concentrated in American prisons. Though there are no accurate figures on prison homicides, assaults, or sexual attacks, there are indications that these types of victimizations are intolerably high and rising. Unisex prisons exert a dehumanizing effect on those they contain. Individuals deprived of normal social (and not just sexual) interaction with members of the opposite sex, and in want of basic goods and services, adopt the prevailing inmate subculture more readily than those persons whose correctional environment is open and representative of community life. There is also general agreement among scholars and administrators that it is difficult for offenders (particularly young adults and juveniles) to develop positive, healthy relationships with the opposite sex in segregated correctional institutions. In addition, there are some indications that maladaptive behavior patterns acquired in unisex institutions tend to continue when offenders return to the community. Hence, such behavior decreases the likelihood that returnees will become productive and contributing members of society.

Such considerations, coupled with the amply documented failure of the conventional prison, have led some administrators and students of corrections to the assumption that coeducational correctional institutions could possibly provide a more normal environment in which inmates could serve out their sentences. Such environments, it was reasoned, would facilitate the growth of the individual inmate in dignity and self-respect, enable more effective program and work participation, and would be devoid, as much as this may be possible, of the destructive inmate subculture so pervasive in traditional institutions.

Yet in spite of the logic of these thoughts, there has been little information and research published on the subject of coeducational corrections up to this point. John Smykla's *Coed Prison* has begun to fill the void. What emerges from the various chapters is the best available thinking and research on the subject to date. We find, not surprisingly, that the movement toward integrating correctional institutions for men and women has been slow. Whenever it does occur, it is based on correction's traditional method of trial-and-error. Next to a thumbnail sketch of the characteristics of existing coed institutions, we are beginning to gain some insight into the "coed milieu;" institutional program offerings, extent and degree of program linkage to the community, staff attitudes, and security requirements of coed programs. We find that while the presence of men and women at the same facility appears to be a vital part of the basic thrust of such programs, coeducational arrangements do not make *eo ipso*, the difference between coeducational institutions and other, unisex facilities. More critical factors, voiced by those who have experimented with the concept and by inmates who have experienced such programs, seem to be: (1) extensive linkage between the institutions and the wider, surrounding communities, (2) extra-mural and intra-mural volunteer programs, which introduce non-correctional perspectives into the correctional settings, and (3) the general milieu and atmosphere of corrections built into such programs.

The last point pertaining to institutional atmosphere bears elaborating. Judging from the sensitive discussions by Campbell, Heffernan and Krippel, we find that staff's respect for their resident's human dignity is an important component in the correctional programs they either administered or evaluated. This consideration adds a new dimension to the usual choice between treatment and security in corrections. It does so by taking cognizance of the fact that commitments to correctional institutions not only reflect a great diversity of judicial philosophies, but also are a function of the vast number of criminal statutes, which, in turn, are violated for a wide variety of reasons. Finally, such an outlook views incarceration primarily as a social sanction rather than as the first step to either punishment or treatment, or both.

Within this context, two concerns seem to emerge: (1) the desire of progressive administrators to develop multiple approaches to programs, to assure that inmates spend their time in the least destructive manner possible, and (2) the desire to develop as many programs as possible, to assure that the problems which led to the individual's incarceration, whether personal or situational, may become mitigated.

Another key development in coed institutions, which seems to corroborate earlier hypotheses, appears to be the breakdown of expected role behavior on the part of residents and staff. Specifically, the well-documented roles of inmates as "cons," the role of the correctional officer as "turnkey," and the traditional chasms between inmates, line officers, and treatment staff seem to be reduced in coeducational institutions.

Since the existence of the traditional staff/inmate cleavage has been consistently identified in previous research as counterproductive to reintegration and rehabilitation, such early findings could be of considerable importance. Crucial to the much-desired breakdown of expected institutional role behavior appears to be, in addition to the coeducational variable, the great heterogeneity of staff and inmates in terms of age, race, religion, and social class.

The apparent changes in role definitions in coeducational institutions reported in this volume add new knowledge and additional dimensions to the existing research on the development of subcultures in prison. To wit, sociological literature on institutional adaptation suggests that males and females adopt markedly different organizational structures in incarcerative settings. While males tend to organize into an overall symbiotic structure characterized by a shared normative system epitomized in the "prison code," female inmates are characterized neither by overall cohesion nor by isolation. Instead, they tend to organize into pervasive primary relationships which involve, in many instances, dyadic homosexual attachments and extensive familiar relationships. We now have preliminary indications that coeducational institutions appear to produce yet another set of inmate adaptations based on role-definitions. Unlike unisex institutions in which social relationships tend to be structured by adaptive patterns to the deprivation of normal affective relationships, coed institutions provide opportunities for a multiplicity of relationships and even more importantly, "normal" relational opportunities, similar to those found in the community at large.

No doubt, the issue of coeducational corrections should be considered within the larger issues mentioned above. But even without unduly emphasizing the coed variable, it is noteworthy that the general atmosphere at coed institutions appears considerably more relaxed when compared to unisex facilities. While operational practices in the latter institutions are often dominated with custody and riot control considerations, coed institutions are concerned with the prevention of pregnancies. It is in this sense that coed institutions come close to resembling a "campus milieu," and differ pronouncedly from traditional prisons and jails, in which large proportions of aggressive and violent acts must be attributed directly or indirectly to homosexuality. There continues to be a preoccupation on the part of the individual authors with homosexuality and heterosexual relations in coed prisons. This fact is no doubt attributable to the precedent set by previous empirical ventures into the realm of women in correctional institutions, most of which have concentrated overwhelmingly on studying homosexual attachments within the prison setting (Giallombardo, Ward and Kassebaum, and Tittle). While the pursuit of such knowledge may be of intrinsic interest to some researchers, the ferreting out of ephemeral sexually delinquent behavior may serve to alienate (if not distract) the policy-minded legislator or administrator from an otherwise innovative approach and attempt to humanize corrections. While pimping and prostitution in coed institutions may be statistically infrequent events, the fact that they exist at all may suffice to pronounce the death knell for the nascent program, given today's punitive atmosphere.

Another key development which appears to be surfacing at some of the coed institutions studied in this book, concerns the unfolding of a new set of norms by inmates in their relationship to staff and to fellow inmates. While specific findings will require further study and corroboration, there appears to be a formation of a set of informal inmate norms to prevent the failure of coed programs and to control (at least to some degree) heterosexual relationships.

The informal role restrictions developed by inmates appear to be accompanied by formal role restrictions placed on women inmates by staff in some of the coed institutions reported on here. In other words, women seem to be more heavily restricted in their movements than men and may possibly be used to serve interests other than their own. The one highly negative chapter on the subject of coed corrections by Superintendent Crawford explores this issue further. Proceeding from the valid observation that women prisoners have historically been given last priority in correctional planning and programming, coed corrections is seen by this author as "destroying any separate programming for the female," and an attempt to force the small number of incarcerated women into programs designed to meet the needs of the much larger population of male prisoners. But I am dubious about a woman offender's need for confinement over a "protracted period of time," away from male exposure. It may well be, as Crawford argues, that many women offenders have been abused by men and are highly dependent personalities. But I hesitate to assume that such insecurity would have a better chance of being corrected in the highly abnormal setting of a unisex women's prison, with all its documented homosexual and pseudo-kinship relationships. While women, as well as other minority groups, have traditionally been exploited in our society, and current remedial steps should continue to rectify such abuse, we should not expect the corrections system to be in the vanguard of social reform. Considering that corrections has suffered decades, if not centuries, of neglect and wrong approaches, the pursuit of equity, justice, and just plain "normalcy," is surely more appropriate and realistic! Thus, we find that sex-role structures in coed institutions tend to duplicate and reflect the social divisions between the sexes in society at large. But there is also a definite "normalization" effect in such institutions, which can be defined as an alignment of the institutional milieu with life in the community at large. The documented decreases in disruptive behavior and concomitant humanization of coed programs surely fulfill many, if not most, expectations and hopes for finding some approach to reducing the destructiveness of prisons.

The Wilson study is particularly encouraging in this respect. Apparently, when men and women serve time in similar environments, the previously recorded differences in their styles of serving time in unisex institutions abate and a prisoner's sexual identity becomes less significant than his or her pre-prison identity. Thus, lower-class women seem more similar to lower class men than they are to other women, and less criminalized men have more in common with women of the same characteristic than with habitual felons.

No doubt, there will be a few who will object to some of the reported findings which indicate that some (but not all) women residents in coed institutions identify primarily with the family and focus their energies on the maintenance and expressive dynamics of coed relationships, while men identify primarily with work, leadership, and the initiation (as well as the control) of such relationships. The double standard of morality is apparently alive and well in coed prisons, as it is in society. Be that as it may, the question of whether women have needs and requirements so totally different from men that they cannot be met under the control of one multi-faceted and deliberately balanced program or facility, will ultimately be answered depending upon one's particular philosophy, value system, and political perceptions. Today, we continue to have a wide variety of views on this subject. These range from a mercifully few who think that biology is destiny, to ultra-feminists who cast all men as exploiters and scourges. But surely there is more than unites men and women through their humanity, than divides them because of their sexual attributes!

When we examine the various studies presented here from an administrative and prison management point of view, it can be said unequivocally that coeducational institutions seem to be more manageable than traditional institutions. They have less inmate and staff violence, fewer problems of homosexuality, better living conditions, more internal freedom, substantially reduced tensions, fewer grievances, and more "normalcy," than any other institutional modality in corrections.

I firmly believe that it is possible to create a fairer and less brutal penal system than we have now. Those who may be concerned about losing (or reducing) the deterrent effect of prisons by reducing their brutality, should realize that incarceration, even in benign settings, is still punishment— especially in a society (such as ours) that prizes freedom more than any other value in its social system. One caveat is in order. Coed institutions are not the cure for all the problems of correctional institutions. Since this approach appears to be intrinsically tied to heterogeneity of inmates and staff, extensive community linkage, openness, and multi-faceted programs, coed corrections would not be appropriate for highly criminalized, predatory offenders. While the identification of suitable candidates (of both sexes) has yet to be made by future research, we can state on the basis of past experience that we presently "select out" many individuals who would probably benefit from the experience. Improved classification procedures would significantly expand coed programs—at no increase in risk to society.

In conclusion, let me return for a moment to my starting point. Corrections is presently in an hiatus. Caught in an historical coincidence of high crime rates (largely but not exclusively attributable to a demographic bulge in the population at risk), and in the throes of neo-conservatism, the calls for increasing penalties and for making them harsher than ever are deafening. As a result, it could be said that *Coed Prison* arrives at an inauspicious point in time. But this latest fad will pass and reason will return once more to our criminal justice process. The public will come to realize that the gruesome system of punishment we are currently inflicting on those few who make it to the prison gates is essentially self-defeating. John Smykla and the contributors to his book will be joined by many others who collectively pursue a better way of dealing with this nation's crimes and criminals, and who will replace a harsh, arbitrary, and frequently dehumanizing corrections systems with a more coherent rationale and approach, as befits the civilized society we are.

Edith Elizabeth Flynn, Ph.D.
Professor of Criminal Justice
Northeastern University, College of Criminal Justice, Boston

PREFACE

"Deprivation of heterosexual relationships in prison may be one of the most destructive things about confinement," wrote Charles Campbell, Warden of the coed Fort Worth Federal Corrections Institution in 1971. Two years later a sense of excitement swept the country when the National Advisory Commission on Criminal Justice Standards and Goals recommended coed prisons as "an invaluable tool for exploring and dealing with social and emotional problems related to identity conflicts that many offenders experience." Several years later, a range of investigators are now finally beginning to explore the myriad and complex coed prison.

This book is the first of its kind, but I expect that many like it will follow. The essays in it are exciting as only important new discoveries can be. A sizable body of reasonably sound research literature does exist that can lay a foundation for a wide-ranging program of research in years to come. From the data that have been collected, researchers are providing important insight and thoughtful speculation. Many of us have been studying the coed prison since it reappeared in 1971. It has already proved to be a growing field.

Besides that, it's a field with implications for us all. Coed prisons are now in daily use by thousands of inmates, their families, and staff. And their social and economic benefits, which tend to reduce or help eliminate the problems that have plagued the prison systems for years, are paying off. But is all this, as one author speculated, happening at the expense of women?

We know enough about coed prisons to lay a foundation for a wide-ranging program of action, in addition to research. As one of many corrections professionals committed to human dignity, I hope this book will serve as a resource that will lead to the understanding necessary for change.

Coed Prison is divided into three parts. Part I is a collection of general essays on coed prison. They explore such important topics as the constitutionality of our segregated prison system, a legal evaluation of a coed setting, key characteristics of current coed prisons, the internal dynamics of a coed population, recidivism, a comparison of the way women and men in coed prison "do time," the assumptions about the normalcy, sexual behavior, and violence in the coed setting, and the instrumentation appropriate for research on the coed prison.

Part II draws together all that has been written on the female offender in coed prisons. Does the coed prison duplicate sexism? Does it provide the female offender the special assistance she really needs? Does it affect a woman's sexuality? What effect will the ERA have on our prison system? These and other issues represent the many questions now emerging in this field.

Part III is an annotated bibliography on coed prisons. It is as up-to-date as I could possibly make it at the time of publication. The sources in the bibliography are as enlightening as the articles in the book.

Coed Prison owes a great debt to women and men all over the country working in prisons, universities, and other institutions who kindly sent me copies of their materials, shared information with me, and generally have been most supportive. I thank Norma Fox, Vice-President and Editor-in-Chief at Human Sciences Press, for her support in publishing this book. I am also indebted to the University of Alabama for support services in bringing this book to completion, especially to the Criminal Justice secretaries, Moe Furney and Liliane Yudow, who undertook the voluminou typing required and admirably performed under the pressure of a tight publication schedule.

Most of all I thank Evelyn for her support and patience in the months of work that it took to bring this book to completion.

JOHN ORTIZ SMYKLA
Tuscaloosa, Alabama

CONTRIBUTORS

LINDA ALMY graduated from Boston University with a masters in social work.

RALPH R. ARDITI graduated from the Yale Law School.

VIKKI BRAVO (BRENER) is a social worker with the Anderson Hospital and Tumor Institute, Houston, Texas.

LESLIE BURD (IORIO) graduated from Boston University with a masters in social work.

CHARLES CAMPBELL retired as warden in 1975 from the United States Bureau of Prisons. He is now Director, Alaska Division of Corrections.

HELENE ENID CAVIOR is Research Administrator for the Western Region of the United States Bureau of Prisons.

PATRICIA CHIN graduated from Boston University with a masters in social work.

LINDA COHAN graduated from Boston University with a masters in social work.

STANLEY H. COHEN is Associate Professor of Psychology, West Virginia University.

JACQUELINE K. CRAWFORD is Superintendent of the Arizona Women's Correctional Facility.

FRANK GALLO is Director of Social Services, Lowell General Hospital, Lowell, Massachusetts.

ANTHONY GIORGIANNI is State Food Stamp Outreach Coordinator for the State of Rhode Island.

JEFFREY GOLD graduated from Boston University with a masters in social work.

FREDERICK GOLDBERG graduated from the Yale Law School.

M. MARTHA HARTLE graduated from the Yale Law School.

ESTHER HEFFERNAN is on a postdoctoral research grant at the Catholic University of America.

FORD JOHNSON is President of Koba Associates, Incorporated in Washington, D.C.

MARK JOSE is a social worker with the Kennebec Valley Mental Health Center, Waterville, Maine.

ELIZABETH KRIPPEL MINOR is employed at the Center for Women's Policy Studies in Washington, D.C.

JOELLEN LAMBIOTTE graduated from the University of California at Santa Barbara with a masters in sociology.

JOHN NOYES is a clinical social worker and retardation specialist with the Department of Mental Health, Massachusetts.

JOHN H. PETERS graduated from the Yale Law School.

WILLIAM R. PHELPHS graduated from the Yale Law School.

JAMES G. ROSS is a Senior Assistant with Macro Systems, Incorporated, Washington, D.C.

BARRY RUBACK graduated from the University of Texas School of Law.

JAMES SEVICK is a Research Associate with Koba Associates, Inc. in Washington, D.C.

JOHN ORITZ SMYKLA is Associate Professor of Criminal Justice, the University of Alabama.

NANCI KOSER WILSON is Assistant Professor of Crime, Delinquency and Corrections, Southern Illinois University (Carbondale).

ACKNOWLEDGMENTS

The Sexually Integrated Prison: A Legal and Policy Evaluation by Barry Ruback: Reprinted with permission from *American Journal of Criminal Law*, 1975, *3*, 301-330. Copyright 1975 by The University of Texas School of Law.

Characteristics of Co-correctional Institutions by James Ross, Esther Heffernan, James Sevick, and Ford Johnson: Reprinted from National Evaluation Program Phase I Report: *Assessment of coeducational corrections.* Washington, DC: U.S. Government Printing Office, 1978, pp. 18-29.

Co-corrections—FCI Fort Worth after Three Years by Charles F. Campbell: Reprinted with permission from the U.S. Department of Justice, Bureau of Prisons, 1974.

A Coed Prison by Esther Heffernan and Elizabeth Krippel: Reprinted from Interim Report on Research, Fort Worth Federal Correctional Institution (February 1973 to May 1974), pp. 23-26; and Final Report on Research, Fort Worth Federal Correctional Institution (February 1973 to March 1975), pp. 3-4, 25-26, 33-38, with editorial adaptations. Reprinted with permission of the authors.

A Study of a Coeducational Correctional Institution by Linda Almy (Stafford), Vikki Brave (Brener), Leslie Burd (Iorio), Patricia Chin, Linda Cohan, Frank Gallo, Anthony Giorgianni, Jeffrey Gold, Mark Jose and John Noyes: Unpublished Master's Thesis, School of Social Work, Boston University, 1975. Reprinted with permission of the authors. pp. 160-201.

Styles of Doing Time in a Coed Prison: Masculine and Feminine Alternatives by Nanci Koser Wilson: Originally presented at the 1975 meetings of the American Society of Criminology. From *Offenders and corrections* by Denis Szabo and Susan Katzenelson. Copyright © 1978 by American Society of Criminology. Reproduced by permission of Holt, Reinhart and Winston.

Problems with Research in Co-corrections by John Ortiz Smykla: A paper written especially for this volume.

The Development of a Scale to Assess Inmate and Staff Attitudes Toward Co-corrections by Helene Enid Cavior and Stanley H. Cohen: Reproduced by permission of the Society for Applied Anthropology from *Human Organization*, 1979, *38*: 12-19.

Cocorrectional Models by James Ross, Esther Heffernan, James Sevick, and Ford Johnson: Reprinted from National Evaluation Phase I Report: *Assessment of coeducational corrections.* Washington, D.C.: U.S. Government Printing Office, 1978, pp. 38-47.

Sex-Role Differentiation in a Co-correctional Setting by Joellen Lambiotte: Unpublished Masters Thesis, Department of Sociology, University of California at Santa Barbara, 1976. Reprinted with permission of the author, pp. 19-51.

Women in a Coed Joint by James G. Ross and Esther Heffernan: Reprinted with permission of the authors and the *Quarterly Journal of Corrections*, 1977, *1*: 24–28.

Two Losers Don't Make a Winner: The Case Against the Co-correctional Institution by Jacqueline K. Crawford: A paper presented at the annual meeting of the American Correctional Association, August 1975. Reprinted with permission of the author.

The ERA and Coed Prisons by Ralph R. Arditi, Frederick R. Goldberg, M. Martha Hartle, John H. Peters, and William R. Phelphs: Adapted from "The Sexual Segregation of American Prisons." Reprinted by permission of *The Yale Law Journal Company* and Fred B. Rothman and Company from *The Yale Law Journal*, 1973, *82*, 1264–1268.

INTRODUCTION

The articles in this book represent current inquiry into the practice of sexually integrating our adult correctional institutions. As usual, our research lags behind the implementation of innovation. Since 1971, there have been over 20 adult coed prisons. But lacking the guidance of evaluative studies, over half reverted to their original status as one-sex facilities. This is a sad commentary on the relationship between administrative expediency and research. Some have tried to fill this gap, but the problems are many. I hope that *Coed Prison* will fill part of the void by providing university and agency audiences the fascinating research that I found resting in obscure places.

Of the 13 articles in Parts One and Two, seven have been published before and six are published here for the first time. The authors represent many professions. Several are attorneys (Ruback and Arditi and his coauthors). One is a ranking Federal Bureau of Prisons research administrator (Cavior). Another is a former federal prison warden, and now Director, Alaska Division of Corrections (Campbell). Others teach university criminal justice (Heffernan, Wilson, and Smykla) and psychology (Cohen). One is a superintendent of a women's prison (Crawford), and three are criminal justice consultants (Ross, Sevick, and Johnson). Still others are social workers (Almy and her coauthors).

This diverse group of professionals employs a wide range of methods to explain co-corrections: case study and interviews (Ruback, Campbell, Heffernan and Krippel, Almy and coauthors, Wilson, Lambiotte, Crawford, and Arditi and coauthors); a national assessment of coed prison (Ross, Heffernan, Sevick, and Johnson); questionnaire development and survey analysis (Cavior and Cohen); and legal analysis (Ruback and Arditi and colleagues). What they all discover should be our immediate concern.

Ruback opines that coed prisons may withstand a challenge under the equal protection clause of the Fourteenth Amendment. Ross, Heffernan, Sevick, and Johnson describe how 10 coed prisons operate in terms of policies on facility arrangements, inmates, staff, programs, and policy on physical contact. Campbell recounts his three years of experience as warden of the first coed adult federal correctional institution. He gives us rich detail on the program's history, early implementation plans and problems, and what he believes is necessary to make the coed program work.

Heffernan and Krippel explain social relationships at the coed Fort Worth FCI during their two years of fieldwork there. Almy, Bravo, Burd, Chin, Cohen, Gallo, Giorgianni, Gold, Jose, and Noyes tell us about inmates' perceptions of the social climate, the coed aspects, and selected programs at the coed adult facility at Framingham, Massachusetts. They conclude that the Framingham program is an effective and worthwhile correctional enterprise. Wilson's observations and interviews support the theory that the way felons do time is a function of their pre-prison identities. She finds that a felon's sexual identity appears to be less important than her or his "felonious identity."

In a paper I prepared for this book, I review problems with evaluation, especially with evaluation of implementation. Before there can be valid evaluation data and planned implementation, these problems must be considered and planned for.

Cavior and Cohen develop a scale to assess inmate and staff attitudes toward co-corrections. They find a significant sex-by-status interaction indicating that male staff are less positive toward co-corrections than the inmates are. A second paper by Ross, Heffernan, Sevick, and Johnson identifies programmatic and non-programmatic models of co-corrections. They find that program models are seldom articulated and in any given institution more than one model was operative resulting in divergent policies and expectations which "wreak havoc" with institutional life.

The last four papers focus on women inmates in coed prison and raise powerful questions about sexism in the coed environment. Lambiotte finds at the coed FCI in Pleasanton, California, that sex-role structure duplicates and reflects the social division between the sexes in society both by behavior and behavioral norms and adherence to traditional sexual standards. In their national assessment of women in coed prison, Ross and Heffernan find that co-corrections has fewer positive features for women than for men in terms of institutional changes and the relationship aspects of the lives of women.

Looking at the historical development of the coed prison in relation to the special needs of incarcerated women, Crawford argues that "going coed" is done to appease male egos and to smooth the running of male facilities. As superintendent of a women's prison, she believes that coed prisons, as they are presently designed, do not meet the unique and special needs of the female offender. From Phelphs contend that ratification of the ERA should have an effect on eliminating patterns of sexual discrimination in effect on eliminating patterns of sexual discrimination in the nation's prisons.

The annotated bibliography on coed prison in Part III is offered to researchers, students, administrators, and policy makers who want to build on past coed experiences. With the bibliography they can make a quick assessment of available resources. It is provided here as a reference tool. The annotations are informative and summarize the thrust of the material.

My hope is that publication of this book will stimulate further research and interest in co-correction. At present, the practice of sexually integrating our penal facilities seems to succeed, at least qualitatively, in making our prisons a bit more humane. It can, however, be abused as a means of further control. The consequences of coed imprisonment are just now starting to surface. I hope this volume adds to that growing knowledge.

Part I

GENERAL ESSAYS ON COED PRISON

Chapter 1

THE SEXUALLY INTEGRATED PRISON
A Legal and Policy Evaluation

Barry Ruback

Until the late nineteenth century, many of the prisons in the United States were sexually integrated. Indeed, women had occupied dungeons, almshouses, and jails with men and children since the mid-1600s in the American colonies.[1] There was little segregation by age, sex, or other criteria. As a result, women and children suffered as much as men, if not more.

Not until 1870, at the National Congress on Penitentiary and Reformatory Discipline, did efforts at

Research for this paper was conducted at the Federal Correctional Institutions in Fort Worth and Seagoville, Texas, at the Federal Reformatory in El Reno, Oklahoma, and at the Kennedy Youth Center in Morgantown, West Virginia, under a grant from the Criminal Justice Project of the University of Texas School of Law. The author would like to express his appreciation to Professor George Dix of the University of Texas School of Law, Professor Walter Steele of the Southern Methodist University School of Law, and Dr. Jerome Mabli, Director of Research at the Federal Correctional Institution in Fort Worth.

reform reach a national stage. At this conference complaints were voiced about the unconscionable idleness of the prisoners, the reports of brutality, and the mixing of women and children with hard-core male offenders.

In 1873 the first separate prison for women was opened—the Indiana Women's Prison. Its founders believed that women criminals should be rehabilitated apart from men and isolated from the corruption and chaos of the outside world. Discipline and regularity were the rule; obedience and systematic religious education were expected to help the women develop orderly habits and appropriate moral values.[2] Today there are 55 correctional facilities for women in the United States.[3]

Recently, however, a few prisons in the United States have opened their doors to felons of both sexes. These sexually integrated prisons have been the subject of a few articles in popular magazines,[4] but the results of these experiments have not heretofore been discussed in a legal context. The purpose of this article is to examine the benefits and the disadvantages of the sexually integrated prison. The article will be divided into four parts: first, a discussion of which standard is appropriate to test the constitutionality, under the equal protection clause, of the current practice of sexually segregated prisons; second, a consideration of the present prison system; third, a description of the sexually integrated prison; and fourth, an evaluation of the relative merits of the two different systems.

THE APPROPRIATE STANDARD UNDER THE EQUAL PROTECTION CLAUSE OF THE FOURTEENTH AMENDMENT

Because the number of female inmates is small when compared with the number of male inmates, the present single-sex system dictates either that women be incarcerated in fewer prisons or that prisons house smaller populations.[5] These differences in size and number have inevitably led to disparities in the treatment of male and female prisoners.

For example, whereas separate institutions are generally provided for maximum and minimum security risk male prisoners, this is not feasible for the relatively small number of female inmates.[6] Even though this separation may take place within the prison itself, separate programs and activities tailored to the individual needs of each group may not be warranted by the number of inmates involved. Similarly, it is often not possible for women's prisons to offer medical and counseling services as complete as those in larger men's prisons.[7] Many of the educational and vocational programs available to men are scaled down considerably or are not offered at all to women.

Male inmates suffer as well. The smaller staff-to-inmate ratio and the harsh physical environment, built with the aim of maximizing security and minimizing space, are in keeping with stereotypical assumptions about the male's greater need for retribution and reduced need for privacy.[8] Can the present system of segregated prisons, which results in unequal treatment of both male and female inmates, withstand a challenge under the equal protection clause? A discussion of this question must await a determination of the appropriate standard of review.

The Supreme Court and the vast majority of lower courts have declined to add gender to the list of suspect classifications,[9] which have historically been subject to a strict standard of review under the equal protection clause of the fourteenth amendment.[10] As a result, the states have escaped the very heavy burden of justification which the courts have imposed under this standard:[11] to wit, that the statutory classification under scrutiny must be necessary to promote a compelling or overriding state interest.[12] Instead, the courts have tested the constitutionality of these statutes through the application of the traditional standard of review whereby, as the Supreme Court has noted, "a legislative classification must be sustained unless it is 'patently arbitrary' and bears no rational relationship to a legitimate government interest."[13] The party challenging the statute must overcome a presumption of validity,[14] and if the law can be justified under any conceivable state of facts, it will not be set aside.[15]

The application of this traditional standard of review, in concert with a policy of judicial restraint, has resulted historically in the rejection of equal protection challenges to the dissimilar treatment of men and women in the area of corrections.[16] A leading example of this approach is *State v. Heitman*.[17] In *Heitman*, the Kansas Supreme Court refused to invalidate a statute that imposed fixed sentences on males but indeterminate sentences on females, reasoning that since the two sexes differ both physically and psychologically, different correctional treatment was required.[18] In the court's view, a statute that utilized such an "obvious" classification to tailor the punishment to the offender could not be deemed arbitrary or unreasonable.[19]

This deference to the legislature is not a relic of early twentieth century judicial thinking, but is rather a characteristic of decisions in which courts apply the traditional standard of review.[20] The result has been that classifications to which this test has been applied have rarely been invalidated.[21] Thus in *Sas v. Maryland*[22] the federal district court, after finding that the sole facility for defective delinquents could not be satisfactorily run as a co-correctional institution, and further that the small number of similarly situated females did not justify a separate institution for their benefit, held that the state could properly exclude female delinquents from this correctional treatment center.[23] It was the court's opinion that there was "no reason why the state [could] not limit the program to whichever sex seems immediately to constitute the greater danger to society, provided the basis for this determination is a reasonable one."[24]

Recently, however, the Supreme Court and a number of lower courts, although nominally applying the traditional standard of review, have in fact been utilizing a more stringent standard.[25] This intermediate standard, less exacting than the strict standard of review, requires that the court examine the "[legislative] means in terms of legislative purposes that have substantial basis in actuality, not merely in conjecture."[26] In addition, the classification must actually further the objective of the statute in a substantial way.[27]

Commonwealth v. Daniel[28] appears to reflect such an approach. At issue in *Daniel* was the validity of a Pennsylvania statute which provided that a mandatory indeterminate sentence, set at the statutory maximum for the substantive crime, be assessed to female defendants only. Male offenders received both a minimum and maximum sentence. The court, purporting to apply the traditional standard of review (as applied in *State v. Heitman*[29]), invalidated the statute. It found that the disparate treatment was not justified by the sex-based differences between the two groups, and it refused (unlike *Heitman*) to entertain hypothetical legislative justifications, for example, that indeterminate sentences were better suited to the female offender.

In summary, the test by which the courts measure the constitutionality of state laws that result in dissimilar treatment of men and women in the correctional process has taken on a new vitality in recent years. The courts seem less willing to indulge legislative whim, and in fact have required the states not only to present affirmatively the central statutory purpose for review, but also to show that this purpose is furthered in a substantial way by the classification involved.[30] In the final analysis this "new" standard will be employed, in light of the character of the classification involved, to gauge the relative importance of "the individual interests affected by the classification and the governmental interests asserted in support of the classification."[31]

The remainder of this article will concern itself with the identification and discussion of these competing interests.[32] However, this inquiry will not focus on the differences between segregated male prisons and segregated female prisons. While such differences are of obvious importance in identifying the individual interests of the prisoners, they have been thoroughly investigated elsewhere.[33] Rather, this article will concentrate on the differences between the sexually segregated prison—either male or female—and the co-correctional prison. It will point out the costs and the benefits of sexual integration, in order to put in context the state's interest in preserving the status quo (or in opting for a less radical change) and the prisoner's stake in changing it.

A CONSIDERATION OF THE PRESENT SEXUALLY SEGREGATED PRISON SYSTEM

A prison is by definition a closed society, unique in its characteristics and in the adjustments it requires of the inmates. Prisoners experience their new environment most significantly in terms of the deprivations suffered in the institution. They are many: loss of liberty, deprivation of autonomy, denial of goods and services, isolation from family and friends, physical and emotional insecurity, and lack of heterosexual relationships.[34] These deprivations result from what society considers to be a perfectly rational system of corrections. But if punishment is to be the purpose of the penal system, then society must also expect certain problems to arise.

Violence infects every prison in the country, though it is less prevalent in open prisons[35] or those with other types of experimental programs. It may be partially explained by the overcrowded conditions in many prisons and the frustrations inmates inevitably feel. The inmate code,[36] indigenous to each prison, compounds the problem by establishing an inmate hierarchy based on severity of the crime committed, ability to withstand punishment, and opposition to the prison administration and its policies. This code requires each inmate to "do his own time," that is, he must forget or at least not mention anything he sees or hears that might in the slightest way hurt another inmate's chances of leaving.

Prison violence is further aggravated by homosexuality, a particularly troublesome characteristic of any prison system that punishes its inmates by denying them heterosexual relationships.[37] Of course, some observers indifferently regard prisoners as less than human and therefore consider sodomy as the prisoners' unnatural lot.[38] It seems clear that homosexuality provides at least some measure of fulfillment for the inmate who endures a single-sex prison for months or years.

For the male prisoner, homosexuality serves at least two functions. First, it offers a means of sexual release. Second, it provides a way by which the aggressive inmate can dominate another—affirming his masculinity and symbolically resisting the prison environment.[39] Although the passive partner in the relationship must submit to the aggressor as a sexual object, he receives protection and sometimes material goods and is often the object of affection.[40]

There is a difficult choice for those unwilling to accommodate their peers sexually, since a complaint will lead to confinement in protective custody. This has several disadvantages: (1) denial of services and facilities such as hot food, showers, and periodic exercise; (2) denial of the opportunity to perform labor and earn credits to reduce prison time; and (3) angering the prison administration with the inconvenience and extra work of protecting the complaining prisoner.[41] As a result of the problems and the generally unsympathetic attitude of prison officials, many inmates just give up and allow themselves to be sexually abused. For the young inmate, a forced homosexual encounter can have profoundly harmful effects that may last a lifetime.[42] If a person chooses not to complain or if the staff does not respond, his choices are either to submit, to fight, or to jump over the fence.

In the female prison, homosexuality is generally a reaction to a need for affection rather than a need for a sexual release. Whereas in the male prison the passive partner is in demand, in the female prison the aggressive inmate, often called a "butch," has "his" choice of partners. The "male" partner in the female prison is the object of competition and favors, which usually come in the form of material goods. For the female inmate,

> a homosexual love affair may be viewed as an attempted compensation for the mortification of the self suffered during imprisonment. During a period when personal worth is most severely questioned, sexual involvement implies that the inmate is worth something, because another person cares about her and pays attention to her. Homosexuality also alleviates depersonalization. In prison, the inmate is stripped of identifying and distinctive qualities, capabilities, and symbols until she comes to resemble all others around her, but through an intimate relationship she is again found personally distinctive.[43]

Another adjustment to the prison environment found only in women's prisons is the family system.[44] An elaborate kinship system will include not only a nuclear family of a father, a mother, and children, but also brothers and sisters, uncles, aunts, and cousins. These family lines are scrupulously observed, and rarely does an incestuous relationship develop.

Thus homosexuality occurs in both male and female institutions as a characteristic response to the social and sexual deprivations of the single-sex prison. The proclivity is also typical of other sexually segregated institutions such as schools and mental institutions, but it is magnified in prisons because the residents are physically and psychologically capable of sexual activity and, in addition, are sexually experienced. The inmates may choose their sexual release in nocturnal sex dreams, masturbation, or homosexuality. Most take the last alternative, the one with the most attendant problems for the weaker inmates who must submit, for the stronger inmates who must be disciplined, and for the prison administrators who must attempt to control the situation.

THE CO-CORRECTIONAL PRISON

The sexually integrated prison is a relatively new innovation in adult correctional institutions, still really an experiment. It was conceived as a solution to two problems: the pervasive homosexuality in single-sex prisons, and the difficult readjustments to society which almost all inmates experience on release from prison.

Readjustment, the second goal, is almost certainly facilitated by the more natural environment of the co-correctional institution. Although the primary problem of homosexuality is also solved by the sexually integrated prison, there is now some debate within the Bureau of Prisons about whether an open, sexually segregated prison might not offer an equally effective and less costly solution.

The first sexually integrated facility in the United States was the Federal Correctional Institution (FCI) in Fort Worth, Texas, established in late 1971 by the U.S. Bureau of Prisons. Most of the research for this article was conducted there. Many institutions for young offenders, including the Federal Youth Center (FYC) in Morgantown, West Virginia, are also sexually integrated. Since FCI Fort Worth became sexually integrated, the FCI in Lexington, Kentucky, the Massachusetts Correctional Institution in Framingham, and the FCI in Pleasanton, California, have also become co-correctional.

Prerequisites

All administrators interviewed at FCI Fort Worth and at the FCI at Morgantown agreed that a sexually integrated institution must be open. An open institution is one that allows residents to leave the prison for certain specified reasons, such as work or study release, and allows outside visitors into the prison for educational, social, or religious purposes. It is necessarily a minimum security prison. The inmates are free to interact with each other on the grounds of the institution. Separating the sexes would tantalize, frustrate, and spur attempts to break through barriers. Such a situation almost resulted in a riot at FCI Seagoville in Texas, when women prisoners from the Federal Women's Reformatory at Alderson, West Virginia, were kept there before their transfer to FCI Fort Worth. Considerable tension presently exists at Terminal Island, California, a federal facility consisting of one prison for men and another for women—separated by several fences.

The possibilities for a workable co-correctional program are limited not only to prisons of a particular nature—open and minimum security prisons—but also to prisons of a minimum size. Charles Campbell, the warden of FCI Fort Worth, believes that the number of residents at a co-correctional facility must be limited to about 500.[45] With overpopulation, discipline crumbles and hostilities grow. Although Warden Campbell believes that all prisons need larger staffs, he is convinced that the sexually integrated prison particularly needs a large staff to lend a rehabilitative rather than a warehousing atmosphere.

An Appraisal of the Effectiveness of the Sexually Integrated Prison

ADVANTAGES. The traditional measure of a prison's success is its recidivism rate. Preliminary figures seem to indicate that FCI Fort Worth, a sexually integrated prison, is one of the most successful prisons in the country according to this criterion.[46] Of those inmates out of prison from 8 to 27 months, 80.4% remain in the community. The Comprehensive Health Unit[47] boasts a very high success rate—92% still in the community—while the NARA unit,[48] traditionally the highest recidivist population in federal prisons, has 69.6% still in the community. This is 14 percentage points higher than any other NARA unit in the Federal prison system.[49]

Although these figures are very promising, some qualifications are necessary. First, not all of the inmates in the study have been out on the streets for the two years usually required in recidivism studies. Second, the preliminary study relies on FBI statistics, which suffer from a time lag in processing and from dependence on state criminal records. Even if these figures are indeed accurate, and many people at FCI Fort Worth and in the Bureau of Prisons believe they are, one may still question whether the success is due to sexual integration. Since so many programs operate simultaneously at Fort Worth, it is impossible to isolate this one aspect with test-tube precision. But it is likely that co-correction contributes to the success.

Although success is most easily measured by the number of inmates who do not return to prison, whether by commission of a new crime or by revocation of parole, there are other significant indicia. For example, most inmates in prison under the NARA program receive 10-year sentences that they pay on the "installment plan." A man might do two years on his sentence, stay out for six months on parole, then return to prison to start the same cycle again. Most NARA inmates eventually serve their entire 10-year sentences in the prison in this piecemeal fashion. With these prisoners, "success" may mean an increased period between release and return.

In addition to improving a prisoner's prospects for remaining in the community, sexual integration enriches life in the prison for inmate and employee alike by generating a more natural social environment. Many male inmates feel that the women bring a humanizing influence that significantly reduces the number of assaults, senseless beatings, and homosexual rapes. Based on their personal observations, residents at FCI Fort Worth opined that physical violence between the men was less common than in other prisons. From the women's standpoint, the favorable sexual ratio of four men to one woman, and the resulting attention, minimizes hostilities among the women. The lessened tension similarly inures to the benefit of the staff.[50]

The more natural environment of the sexually integrated prison also cushions the impact of transition for the incoming prisoner and eases adjustment to the real world for the alumnus. Lacking the peculiar isolation of other prisons, the sexually integrated institution does not foster the bitterness pervading most of them, which may fester and erupt in thoughts of revolution.

Aside from the general improvements in the prison environment, a co-correctional program causes positive developments in hygiene and social behavior. First, both sexes are motivated to care about their appearances—a good sign because it shows the individual's concern about the attitudes of others toward him. This healthy socialization prepares the inmate for the outside world. Mental hospitals have long considered concern about appearance a sign of recovery.[51]

Second, inmates learn or relearn how to act in the presence of the opposite sex. Most of the men at FCI Fort Worth who had transferred from closer custody institutions said that they were initially afraid to talk to women prisoners. After several years abstinence, they had forgotten the social graces. Some of the residents said their readjustment to the presence of women took as long as three months. It is clearly preferable for the prisoner to make this adjustment, if possible, before coping with a myriad of additional difficulties upon release.

Third, both sexes seem to develop healthy relationships at a sexually integrated prison. Many of the women in prison at Fort Worth are former prostitutes, habituated to abnormal and one-dimensional relationships with men. Many of the men are divorced and have had unhappy relationships with women. The FCI offers the atmosphere and the time for an individual to learn how to interact with the opposite sex, and once having done so, how to enjoy friendships with members of the opposite sex.

A final advantage of the sexually integrated prison is an increase in the prisoner's self-esteem. The person gains confidence from interacting with members of the opposite sex. Complementary programs for education and job training can reinforce this self-confidence and encourage the inmate to consider himself or herself as an individual rather than a member of the criminal subculture. As self-esteem increases, conformity to the convict code and the criminal-projected life-style is reduced.

The metamorphosis is admittedly idealized, because the propinquity of criminal groups both inside and outside the prison and the attraction of their members and purposes retard progress. Nevertheless, residents at FCI Fort Worth say that the institution has helped them become individuals with a sense of self-worth. Sexual integration is not the only factor involved in this change, but it is an important one.

DISADVANTAGES.   The largest and most predictable problem of sexual integration in the prisons is sexual activity. At Fort Worth, this problem consumes the major portion of the correctional officers' time,[52] and yet they are still unable to stop the illicit activity. Most of the staff oppose unfettered sexual activity, not because they feel it is wrong, but because they sense the disapproval of the general public and therefore the Bureau of Prisons.

The rules of FCI Fort Worth permit hand holding but proscribe kissing and putting one's arm around another person. Despite the rules, however, some men and women enjoy intercourse on a fairly frequent basis. They escape punishment because they can evade the guards. For example, it is widely known that the guards do not stand by the door of the Federal Prison Industries room, located in the basement of the men's building, until 7:30 AM. Before then, men and women can meet without interference. Another popular trysting place is the kitchen. The cooks are concerned with preparing food, not with supervising the inmates. As a result, they are more lenient with the inmates than are the guards. Many times the cooks will let the residents slip off and return without a word being said. A favorite spot in the kitchen is the walk-in refrigerator; it may be cold, but at least it's private.

Not all of the sex in the prison is free. In fact, most of it comes only after some sort of payment has been tendered. Initially, prostitution at a federal prison shocks the observer. But upon reflection, it seems the natural upshot of confining unredeemed prostitutes with sexually deprived males. The rumored cost of intercourse in the summer of 1974 was fairly expensive; the average price was about four cartons of cigarettes ($10 dollars at the commissary), with the best woman going for five cartons ($12.50). Women of lesser demand went for three cartons. This chain of exchange continues as most of the prostitutes hand over their takings to their husbands, boyfriends, or, in some cases, to their girl friends. The recipients in turn act as procurers for the prostitutes.

In addition to the fallout from the prostitution and pimping, illicit sexual activity can produce pregnancies. Authorities in some cases must determine whether the child was conceived before incarceration or on a furlough. If neither explanation is plausible, the woman and the man involved are shipped to other prisons. Although the problem at Fort Worth is significant, it has not reached the crisis stage experienced by the Kennedy Youth Center in Morgantown, West Virginia. Perhaps this is because several of the women at Fort Worth have had hysterectomies.[53]

To prevent pregnancies, prisons must provide birth

control pills or abortions. Information about abortions received by women inmates at a downtown Fort Worth hospital is considered confidential and is therefore unavailable, but official institutional policy about birth control pills is public knowledge: Only women with less than six months to serve on their sentences, and therefore eligible to leave on furloughs, can receive them.

The manager of the women's unit at FCI Fort Worth, when asked about the use of pills by women in the furlough category, said that when a female resident goes to the doctor, she can ask for any medication she wants.[54] Many do request birth control pills, and while the doctor-patient relationship is a cherished confidence outside the prison walls, probably nothing inside is kept secret from the inmate's treatment team. The team knows if the woman is on the pill and whether she is within six months of release. The unit manager also said that many of the women have menstrual problems that require treatment by hormones found in birth control pills. Several residents commented sarcastically on the large number of women at FCI Fort Worth with menstrual difficulties. One might object that these tax-supported measures aid and abet promiscuity; on the other hand, some women interviewed protested that they were forced to take the pill.

A second disadvantage of the sexually integrated prison is its increased cost. The FCIs at Fort Worth and Seagoville are comparable in a number of respects,[55] the primary dinstinction being the presence of women at Fort Worth. The major difference in the cost per inmate per day is directly attributable to the larger correctional staff at Fort Worth,[56] which the administration feels is necessary to prevent sexual activity. The increased cost of the staff is probably the only expense of a sexually integrated prison that is not incurred by a progressive segregated prison.

A final series of disadvantages generated by the presence of women at FCI Fort Worth can be categorized as interference with the men's rehabilitation. The greater immaturity of the women and the staff's willingness to tolerate it results in disruption of prison routines and inequitable administration of discipline. Staff and observers at FCI Fort Worth generally agree that the women inmates are more immature and less independent than the males. Their irresponsibility is reflected in their histories and present behaviors. Many either were convicted as aiders and abettors or committed their crimes at the requests of men. Thirty-three percent of the women were convicted of drug violations—offenses that indicate personal inadequacies. A total of 61% of the women have some form of drug addiction in their backgrounds.[57]

At the FCI this irresponsibility continues as large numbers of women are late for work or school or go to sick call to avoid doing their jobs. During a three-week period, the average number of women reporting to sick call was 10 per day, and one Monday the figure was 26—numbers far in excess of any in the men's units.[58]

Rather than altering the women's behaviors through firm discipline, the staff seems to positively reinforce their immaturity. Many times women will leave classes early, disrupting the class with their exit and the rest of the institution with their wandering about in unexpected places. As a general rule, women receive less punishment for the same offenses than do men. Moreover, the staff tolerates profanity from the women but not from the men. Accepting such childish behavior insures that prisoners will continue to act childishly, acting out the same immature ideas and attitudes that may have brought them to prison in the first place.

Although the women are watched more closely than the men, probably because there are only 100 women to 400 men, they receive privileges and preferential treatment from the staff under the same sort of double standard applied in disciplinary matters. For example, it is much easier for a woman to see the warden or an associate warden. Women also obtain furloughs more easily than the men. This may be because the women have less violence on their records, but inmates attribute it solely to sex. Women receive money to buy clothes when they first arrive, while the men are given government-issue khakis. (The General Services Administration has surplus uniforms for the men but not for the women.) In addition, women get toiletries such as hand lotion; the men receive nothing comparable.

A few men at the prison complained of the women's presence, alleging that involvement with them inevitably led to trouble. They objected that the proximity of the women caused some men to "go too far" sexually with the women. More often than not, the men rather than the women received "incident reports" as a result. These reports can prolong incarceration and may mean transfer to a closer custody institution. For the most part, this complaint came only from the men who did not have "walking partners," that is, constant female companions.

A second objection, raised by men who had women on the outside, concerned the distraction the women presented. These men felt they could more easily concentrate on bettering themselves through the prison's rehabilitative programs if no women were available. For many of the men, however, social contact with women is definitely therapeutic.

AN EVALUATION OF THE RELATIVE MERITS OF THE TWO DIFFERENT SYSTEMS

Most of the advantages and disadvantages of the co-correctional prison have been noted in the preceding section. This section will pose four questions about the interests of the prisoners and the state, weighing from various perspectives the differences between the segregated status quo and the co-correctional prison, as well as the differences between the segregated prison and other alternatives. This evaluation will address the need for sexual integration on both policy and legal grounds.

Does a Male Prisoner Benefit More From a Sexually Integrated Prison Than From a Sexually Segregated Open Prison?

The comparison is made with an open prison rather than with a traditional penitentiary: this paper has already stated the premise that a sexually integrated prison would not be feasible for inmates who require closer custody than that provided by an open prison. A comparison with the benefits of an open prison is not so simple a judgment, since the open segregated prison provides a number of the advantages that the co-correctional prison offers.

The problem of inadequate social contact with women could be significantly reduced if the numbers of female staff and female visitors were increased. Although the openness of a prison can reduce homosexuality, as this writer observed at FCI Seagoville, the visible presence of women is in itself an even more significant factor. The optimum number of women staff is still unknown, but the ratios of 16 women on the staff at FCI Seagoville and 17 women on the staff at the Federal Reformatory at El Reno to male populations of 450 and 950 respectively are clearly insufficient. Very few of the male prisoners at these institutions ever see the female employees, and several inmates who had resided at both FCI Fort Worth and FCI Seagoville confirmed that the incidence of homosexuality at Seagoville was higher.

Assuming that enough women did join the staff of the prison, many of the problems of the segregated male prison, which are primarily rooted in homosexuality, could be solved. Male prisoners would miss only the friendships with female peers possible in a sexually integrated prison. If women staff members and outside visitors could effect the beneficial changes in the prison environment and provide male prisoners the social interactions discussed in the preceding section, then sexually integrated prisons would not seem to justify their costs on this ground.

One remaining justification would be the more natural atmosphere created by having both sexes in the institution. No one can seriously argue that an all-male open prison is as natural as a co-correctional institution. The question then becomes whether the more natural environment and the easier readjustment to society are worth the additional costs.[59]

Does a Female Prisoner Benefit More from a Sexually Integrated Prison Than from a Female Reformatory?

The mere presence of men seems to make little difference in the sexual habits of female prisoners; denied heterosexual intercourse, the women tend to become situational homosexuals.[60] Based on the interviews conducted during the 10-week internship, at least 15 and possibly as many as 25 of the women engaged in fairly frequent homosexual activity. Assuming that this figure is about 20% of the women at FCI Fort Worth, it is hard to say that the improvement is phenomenal. By comparison, male residents at Fort Worth estimated that only about 3% of the men engaged in homosexual activities.[61] One female resident explained that the high incidence of female homosexuality is partly due to peer group pressures: Nonparticipants are considered snobs. It seems fairly clear that the co-correctional prison does not solve the problem of situational homosexuality among women.

On the other hand, the sexually integrated prison does meet the emotional needs of women better than the all-female prison. The families that develop in women's prisons are only surrogates for real families and real heterosexual relationships. Even though the women at Fort Worth were denied a full emotional life, they nevertheless felt that the men's presence made the situation more normal. Consequently, they felt happier and better adjusted emotionally than at all-women prisons.

A final consideration in this evaluation is the educational opportunities provided the women by an integrated prison. According to the Bureau of Prisons' data on the men and women at FCI Fort Worth, the women have significantly lower IQ scores than the men.[62] This disparity is probably due to the fact that the women have less schooling, although the causal sequence may run the other way. Because the women are less educated than the men, they might retard the men's educational process. On the other hand, exposing them to the more educated men might have a rehabilitative effect on the women.

Moreover, the programs offered in co-correctional prison are better than those available at prisons for women. Some of the women who had been at the Federal Reformatory for Women at Alderson said the educational programs offered at Fort Worth are better than those at Alderson, but the differences in the programs of the state prison systems are even more significant. Most states spend money on women's prisons more as an afterthought than as a planned rehabilitative program. Indeed, some states do not even have women's prisons and have to send their female felons to prisons in other states.[63]

Since most of the prison systems for women in the United States are inadequate, sexual integration would give the women a better chance to learn a marketable skill as well as to gain a basic education. Because these programs will more likely be available to all prisoners if prisons are sexually integrated than if they remain sexually segregated, bringing this benefit to the women is one justification for co-correctional prisons.

In summary, sexually integrated prisons have two

advantages over single-sex prisons for women: better emotional health and perhaps the most indentifiable advantage of all—better educational facilities. But sexual integration does not greatly improve women's behavior.

Is Any Justifiable State Interest Served by Sexually Segregating Prisons?

Whether the present correctional system can be justified by state interests depends on how one views the purpose of prisons. If one sees prison solely as a means of punishing violators and keeping them off the streets to prevent further crimes, then the penal system should be as severe as possible without shocking the sensibilities of contemporary society. Clearly, the sexually segregated prison accomplishes that end. Violators are punished not only physically by the spartan environment, but also psychologically by the absence of the opposite sex. Moreover, one-sex prisons breed homosexuality, in itself a further punishment.

Regardless of the philosophy of prisons—punishment or rehabilitation—the state can assert substantial fiscal interests in sexual segregation. The additional staff required for a co-correctional prison results in significant additional expenses. Moreover, if the prison is a minimum security institution, state interests would include the prevention of illicit sexual activity and the resulting problems. Of course, the discussion is limited to sexually segregated prisons in which integration is feasible, since co-correction and its requisite openness of interaction would probably increase the danger of violence in a maximum security prison, and thus make the state interests greater. But in the minimum security institution, the state interest in preserving the status quo would ultimately depend on the weight given rehabilitation in the penal system. The more importance attached to rehabilitation, the more difficult it is for the state to defend the present system on fiscal grounds.

For Whom?

If it is established that a prison should be sexually integrated, the next question is whom to admit. In establishing the sexual ratio, there are two alternatives: admission to the institution without regard to sex, and admission of a specified number of inmates of each sex. Ideally, there should be an equal balance, but since there are fewer female than male inmates, this would not be possible. At most, prison administrators could set target quotas based on the prison populations and facilities available.

In addition to sex, there are a number of other factors that are important in choosing inmates for the sexually integrated prison. First, security risks should be excluded, especially any inmates who would pose a danger to other prisoners,[64] since such persons would be unsuited to the minimum custody necessary for a co-correctional program.

A similar consideration is prior criminal involvement. Those with prior criminal records should generally be rejected. The multiple offender seems on the balance less suited to such a program. As a hardened criminal, he might take advantage of the prison's openness and nonviolent atmosphere. Although he too needs rehabilitation, the chances of success are realistically bleak and the resources available—that is, the dollars to pay for the program—are scarce.

A third consideration is age. The experience of FCI Morgantown would indicate that the age group should be mixed to simulate the world outside. Moreover, a population composed only of young men and women creates overwhelming tension and emphasizes sex as the only important factor in relationships.[65]

CONCLUSION

The advantages of the sexually integrated prison are

largely intangible. The disadvantages are fairly great: increased cost, pregnancies, prostitution, and pimping. Thus the decision is between intangibles and observable phenomena, that is, whether the sum of the benefits to each individual resident is greater than the collective disadvantages. From a policy standpoint, one must decide whether the individuals are worth the trouble and expense. If they are, then appropriate prisons should be sexually integrated.

Many prisoners object that co-correctional prisons are merely a frill, a sugar coating on a rotten system. They argue that if reform is really the goal, then more money should be spent to expand probation and parole programs. Their arguments make sense, but the country is not yet ready to eliminate most of its prisons. Given that premise, lawyers and administrators can only improve the prisons through amelioration behind the walls.

But while the co-correctional prison may be sound policy, it does not rise to the level of a constitutional right. The state may assert legitimate interests in efficient administration as well as in the maintenance of prison security and order, the lack of which may retard rehabilitation. Sexually integrated prisons go far toward eliminating or reducing problems that have plagued the prison system for years. Unfortunately they are also the source of new and vexing problems.

To the extent that sexually segregated prisons avoid these new correctional problems, it may be persuasively argued that legitimate state interests are substantially furthered. Absent grossly inferior facilities for either sex and a lack of alternatives except integration, the present system would undoubtably withstand a challenge under the equal protection clause. Although the prospects for constitutional support do not seem sanguine, nevertheless the sexually integrated prison offers a means to reduce some of the violence and alienation currently rampant in prison systems.

Notes

1. Burkhart, K. *Women in prison.* New Jersey: Doubleday, 1973, p. 250.
2. *Ibid,* p. 253.
3. *Ibid,* p. 254.
4. *Newsweek,* July 23, 1973, p. 23; Harrigan, E. The Big House Goes Coed. *Texas Monthly,* March 1974, 34; *Ebony,* November 1973, 191.
5. Note. The sexual segregation of American prisons. *Yale Law Journal,* 1973, *82,* 1229, 1231.
6. *Ibid,* 1234-1235.
7. *Ibid,* 1236-1237.
8. *Ibid,* 1237-1244.
9. *Stanton v. Stanton,* 421 U.S.—95 S. Ct. 1373, 1377 (1975) (invalidating Utah statute requiring child support of sons until age 21, but of daughters only until age 18).

    However, in *Frontiero v. Richardson,* 411 U.S. 677 (1973), a plurality of the Court held sex to be a suspect classification, invalidating a federal statute governing medical and housing benefits to spouses of members of the armed forces. Such benefits were allowed to female spouses without regard to actual dependency. Male spouses, however, were obliged to prove dependency on their wives for over half of their support.

    In *United States v. York,* 281 *F. Supp.* 8 (D. Conn. 1968), a federal district court invalidated a Connecticut classification based on sex under the strict standard of review. *Ibid,* 14. The statute in question permitted adult women to be imprisoned for periods in excess of the maximums applicable to men guilty of the same substantive crimes. The state failed to carry *its burden* to show this disparate treatment was *necessary* for the deterrence or rehabilitation—i.e., the purposes of the statute—of women. *Ibid,* 16.
10. E.g., *Loving v. Virginia,* 388 U.S. 1, 9 (1967) (holding unconstitutional Virginia's antimiscegenation statute); see *Graham v. Richardson,* 403 U.S. 365 (1971) (invalidating state statutes favoring citizens over aliens in distributing welfare benefits).
11. *Dunn v. Blumstein,* 405 U.S. 330, 343 (1972); cf. *San Antonio Independent School District v. Rodriquez,* 411 U.S. 1, 16 (1972).
12. E.g., *Dunn v. Blumstein,* 405 U.S. 330, 337 (1972); cf. *McLaughlin v. Florida,* 379 U.S. 184, 196 (1964).
13. *McLaughlin v. Florida,* 379 U.S. 184, 196 (1964); *Eisenstadt v. Baird,* 405 U.S. 438, 447 (1972).
14. *McGowen v. Maryland,* 366 U.S. 420, 425 (1960); see *Goeaert v. Cleary,* 335 U.S. 464, 466-467 (1948).

15. *McGowen v. Maryland*, 366 U.S. 420, 426 (1960); *Metropolitan Casualty Ins. Co. v. Brownell*, 294 U.S. 580, 584 (1935).

16. Note. *Yale Law Journal*, 1973, *82*, 1244 –1245.

17. 105 Kan. 139, 181 p. 630 (1919).

18. The Kansas court remarked: "It is a patent and deep-lying fact that ... fundamental anatomical and physiological differences affect the whole psychic organization. They create differences in personality between men and women, and personality is the predominating factor in criminal careers. ... [The] result is a feminine type radically different from the masculine type, which demands special consideration in the study and treatment of the nonconformity to law." *Ibid*, 634. Contra, *United States v. York*, 281 *F. Supp.* 8 (D. Conn. 1968).

19. *State v. Heitman*, 181 P. 2d 630, 634.

20. Note. *Yale Law Journal*, 1973, *82*, 1245.

21. Gunther, P. The Supreme Court, 1971 term—Foreword: In search of evolving doctrine on a changing court: A model for a newer equal protection. *Law Review*, 1972, *86* 18.

22. 295 F. Supp. 389 (D. Md. 1969).

23. *Ibid*, 418.

24. *Ibid*, 419.

25. Gunther, 20.

26. *Ibid*, 21.

27. *Ibid*, See *St. Mary's Law Journal*, 1975, *6*, 917.

28. 430 Pa. 642, 243 A. 2d 400 (1968).

29. 105 Kan. 139, 181 P. 630 (1919).

30. E.g., *Commonwealth v. Daniel*, 430 Pa. 642, 243 A. 2d 400 (1968); see Note, 82 *Yale Law Journal*, 1973, *82*, 1247-1248, in which it is concluded that *Daniel* and similar cases enumerate a test which "refuses to accept a legislative rationale a priori, but rather asks for substantial and empirically grounded justifications which seem reasonable and which are narrowly drawn to reflect real—and relevant—differences between men and women."

31. *Dunn v. Blumstein*, 405 U.S. 330, 334 (1972).

32. For a thorough discussion of the probable impact of the Equal Rights Amendment on the disparate treatment of men and women in the area of corrections, see Note, *Yale Law Journal*, 1973, *82*, 1253-1267; see generally Conlin. Equal protection versus equal rights amendment—Where are we now?" *Drake Law Review*, 1975, *24*, 259.

33. Note. *Yale Law Journal*, 1973, *82*, 1229.

34. Sykes, G. *The society of captives*. New Jersey: Princeton University Press, 1958, pp. 63-83. The signs pointing to the prisoner's degradation are many—the anonymity of the uniform and a number rather than a name, a shaven head, the insistence on gestures of respect

and subordination when addressing officials, and so on. The prisoner is never allowed to forget that by committing a crime, he has forgone his claim to the status of a full-fledged, *trusted* member of society.

35. While most correctional institutions are closed, that is, the inmates must always remain at the prison and visitors are severely limited in the amount of time they can spend at the prison, the open prison allows the prisoners .more freedom within the prison walls, more chances to go outside the prison on certain specified types of trips, and more opportunities to see outside visitors.

36. The inmate code is a system of group norms that are directly related to mitigating the pains of imprisonment. Sykes, G. & Messenger, S. The inmate social system. In *Theoretical studies in social organization of the prison.* New York: Social Science Research Council, 1960, p. 11. The cumulative effect of this prisonization and adherence to the 'con code' is to sponsor a united or cohesive front to outsiders." Bramwell, P. *An investigation of the influence of group pressure upon inmate leaders and nonleaders,* 1967, p. 14.

37. "The most difficult problem a warden faces is homosexuality. Homosexuality causes more quarrels, fights, knifings, and punishment in prison than any other single problem." Martin, J. *Break down the walls.* 1954, p. 177.

38. "Sex in prison was and is present, as it was in schools. The older compromise is to keep it vicious, clandestine, and homosexual—less personalizing, that is." Comfort, A. Institutions without sex. *Social Work* 1967, *12,* 107-108.

39. Gagnon, J. & Simon, W. The social meaning of prison homosexuality. 32 *Federal Probation,* 1968, *32,* 23, 27.

40. *Ibid,* 26.

41. Cape, W. Prison sex: Absence of choice. *Fortune News,* April 1974, p. 5.

42. Interview with Robert Davis and Stanley Talega. *Fortune News,* April 1974, p. 4.

43. Kassebaum, W. & Kassebaum, G. *Women's prison.* Chicago: Aldine Publishing Co., 1965, pp. 74-75.

44. One sociologist has described this system in greater detail: We may define the prison family as a set of inmates each of whom is linked up with all or some of the others of the family by ties of kinship, who act together in the service of common interests indicated by reciprocal rights and duties in events such as economic crises, protection against other inmates, acting in service roles for other families or isolated inmates. Furthermore, a prison family is a group of related kin linked by ties of allegiance and alliance who sometimes occupy a common household and are characterized by varying degrees of solidarity.

Giallombardo, R. *The seasonless world: A study of a women's prison.* Doctoral dissertation, Northwestern University, pp. 217-218, 1965.

45. Interview with Warden Charles Campbell, FCI Fort Worth, July 31, 1974.
46. Heffernan, E. *Interim report on research on the Fort Worth Federal Correctional Institution.* May 19, 1974.
47. This unit is composed of male inmates who are too ill to be housed in other prisons. It also includes some men, such as former judges and sheriffs, who would likely be killed in closer custody institutions.
48. The NARA unit at FCI Fort Worth is composed of male inmates convicted under the Narcotics Addicts Rehabilitation Act. There are similar programs in many federal prisons.
49. Interview with Warden Charles Campbell, FCI Fort Worth, May 29, 1974.
50. According to the members of the correctional staff at FCI Fort Worth, employees of the Bureau of Prisons have the highest rate of heart attacks in any federal agency. The reason is apparent.
51. Fast, J. *Body language.* New York: Pocket Books, 1973.
52. Interview with Lieutenant Clizbe, FCI Fort Worth, May 29, 1974.
53. The situation at KYC was at one time alarming—10 of the 58 women in one unit were pregnant. Evidently at KYC sex is possible without fear of apprehension because of the large grounds with plenty of cover vegetation. Moreover, KYC does not have older inmates. Without quasi-parental ties to older individuals, sex is the primary concern of all the residents.
54. Interview with Peter Vaslow, Women's Unit Manager, FCI Fort Worth, May 28, 1974.
55. First, they are both minimum security institutions. Second, their populations are similar in size: Seagoville has an ideal population of 450 while Fort Worth aims for 500 individuals—400 men and 100 women. Third, everyone at Seagoville, as at Fort Worth, has two years or less to serve, either because their original sentences are less than two years, or because, after serving their time in other prisons, less than two years remain of their federal sentences. Fourth, both Seagoville and Fort Worth have a number of experimental programs.
56. Comparison of Fort Worth and Seagoville staffs:

	Fort Worth	Seagoville
Executive staff	6	4
Unit management	6	5
Correctional operations	102	68
Case management	24	13
Safety	1	1

Education department	14	7
Community programs	3	—
Religion department	2	1
Hospital	26	5
Mental health	4	2
Personnel office	5	3
Business office	13	10
Food service	11	9
Mechanical service	21	20
Commissary	2	2
Federal prisons industries	2	5
Vocational training	2	5
Total	244	160

57. Bureau of Prisons' data for March 21, 1974. Each prison in the federal system receives a breakdown of its population quarterly in a computer printout.
58. Data collected during the period from June 3 to June 21, 1974.
59. A lower recidivism rate, if directly attributable to sexual integration, would offer a considerable benefit for prisoners and would significantly reduce the state's interest in segregated prisons. But a direct correlation between sexual integration and the highly successful recidivism rate at FCI Fort Worth remains problematical. The most that can be said is that the staff considered sexual integration as a substantial factor in the low rate of recidivism.
60. Interview with Chaplain Summers, FCI Fort Worth, May 29, 1974.
61. This figure is the mean of the responses of 20 male residents at FCI Fort Worth.
62. According to the Bureau of Prisons' data of March 21, 1974, over 27% of the women at FCI Fort Worth score below average on intelligence tests, while 22% place above average. In contrast, only 11% of the men have low average or inferior scores, and 38% are above average.
63. Note. *Yale Law Journal*, 1973, *82*, 1231–1243.
64. See *Kish v. County of Milwaukee*, 441 F. 2d 901 (7th Cir. 1971); *Gates v. Collier*, 349 F. Supp. 881 (N.D. Miss. 1972) (right to reasonable protection from assaults by fellow inmates).
65. Interview with Dr. Jerome Mabli, FCI Fort Worth, July 1, 1974.

Chapter 2

CHARACTERISTICS OF
CO-CORRECTIONAL INSTITUTIONS

James Ross
Esther Heffernan
James Sevick
Ford Johnson

Among the basic interests of decision-makers contemplating either the implementation of co-correctional programs, or the modification or termination of ongoing programs, have been questions about how others do it, how others have been affected by shifts in philosophy or changes in policy, and what changes other jurisdictions anticipate. This chapter describes certain key characteristics of the institutions we visited.

CHARACTERISTICS OF EXISTING INSTITUTIONS

When we visited the 10 selected coed institutions, a wide range of institutional characteristics was displayed. This section represents a "snap-shot" of these institutions in terms of five categories: facility, inmates, staff, programs, and policy. Each of these categories is further differentiated into other factors. Except where noted, the discussion is

Table 2-1 Characteristics of Coeducational Correctional Institutions

Characteristic	Mean	Range Low	High
Inmate population	437	131	1041
Male inmates	286	13	358
Female inmates	151	24	421
Inmate sex ratio (M/F)	5/1	3/2	20/1
		3/1	9/1
Staff size	203	55	330
Staff-to-inmate ratio	1/2	1/1	1/4
Custody staff size	100	30	195
Custody-to-inmate ratio	2/9	1/2	1/8
Budget	$3,658,900	$881,000	$7,284,200
Per capita costs	$10,676	$3,583	$14,432

confined to visited institutions. Table 2-1 summarizes the ranges and means for selected characteristics.

Facility

RATED CAPACITY. Visited institutions ranged from approximately 150 in two state institutions to over 1,000 in one federal institution. Among unvisited institutions were three rated at either under, or slightly above, 100.

SECURITY LEVEL. All the institutions were either minimum—or medium—security institutions. They varied widely, however, in the degree to which the level of physical security—locked gates, mass lighting, number of fences—corresponded to what may be associated with the nominal security level.

PHYSICAL PLANT. The 10 institutions included some of the oldest and newest prisons in the country: The oldest state institution opened in 1877 and the newest in 1965; the oldest federal institution was completed in 1934 and the newest received its first inmates in 1974. They ranged from small facilities with only a few buildings to sprawling complexes with a dozen or more buildings on hundreds or even thousands of acres. Eight of the ten facilities formerly operated farms, and two of these still function as full-scale farms.

Architectural modifications to accommodate a two-sex population were limited. Self-enclosed units or buildings were generally given over in toto to new arrivals, although in some cases partitioning was added. Buildings were modified or refurbished in at least five institutions, generally to make a building more livable or to convert a space previously used for other purposes. In at least one case, a minimum-security cottage was made more secure to accept medium-security males.

INMATE QUARTERS.   Male and female inmates lived in physically separate housing—either different buildings or in cottages—at each of the state and one of the federal institutions. In one of the federal institutions, most of the women lived on what was virtually a separate compound, and in the two other federal institutions, inmates lived in a combination of separate coed and single-sex buildings, and in a series of connected buildings facing on a common yard.

Actual inmate living space included private rooms, semi-private rooms, open dorms, several types of cubicles, and makeshift space in the halls. With a few exceptions, the two sexes received similar quarters. Women may have been more crowded than men because of recent shifts in sex ratios, but efforts to provide more privacy to women wherever possible—private or semi-private rooms, or at least cubicles—were generally evident.

BUDGETS AND PER CAPITA COSTS.   Budgets for 1976 ranged from $681,000 to $7,264,200. However, five of the 10 operated on a budget between 3 and 5.5 million dollars in 1976. Eight institutions spent from approximately $9,000 to $14,500 per year on each inmate, and four of these spent between 10 and 12 thousand dollars per capita. State institutions varied from $3,683 to $14,432 in per capita expenditure, federal institutions from $6,327 to $14,327 per capita. Only one institution had at any time received LEAA funds directly for co-corrections.

Inmates

POPULATION SIZE. The size of the 10 coed institutions ranged from 131 at a former state womens' institution to 1,041 (and rising) at a federal facility. Four state institutions held fewer than 208, one state and one federal approximately 300, one state and one federal slightly over 500, and two federal over 1,000. The federal institutions were generally regarded as over capacity, while state institutions were either at, or under capacity, even though inmates of one sex or the other might have been over capacity. State institutions were under capacity because either certain buildings had fallen into disuse, or not enough inmates of one sex were admitted to utilize the space that continued to be allocated to that sex, or the security level for one sex prevented the level of space utilization possible if it were occupied by the opposite sex.

SEX RATIOS. Sex ratios ranged from nine females to one male at a former state womens' institution, to 20 males to one female at a state institution where the co-correctional program was being phased out. However, the populations at seven of the 10 contained fewer than four of the majority sex to one of the minority. Three of the facilities—all federal— had sex ratios that approached one male to one female. Four state institutions maintained ratios of from three to four females to each male. Populations at unvisited institutions were disproportionately constituted by one sex.

SELECTION CRITERIA.   Among the selection criteria used in existing co-correctional institutions were the following: inmate choice, nature of referral, age, time-in-sentence status, clean record in previous institutions, history of non-violence and low escape potential, absence of sexual assault history, absence of gang leadership history, security level, first offender status, proximity to geographical release point, presence/absence of relatives at the institution, capability to perform special work detail, interest in further training, eligibility for special unit programs, eligibility for community programs, cognitive test performance, personal interview indications of "readiness."

It should be noted, however, that distinctions between formal and informal, or official and "casual" criteria, are often blurred. Moreover, exceptions are often made on either a case-by-case basis (such as in some protection cases), or for an entire group (such as Youth Act females, who often fall below the age cutoff intended by some institutions). Distinctions need not be made between the state and federal systems' applicability of criteria for males and females.

Because five of six state institutions housed the entire incarcerated female population in the given state, selection criteria in these institutions really applied only to males, except insofar as there were differences between institutional capabilities for handling unsentenced females. The one institution located in a jurisdiction that offered placement options for women applied essentially the same criteria to both sexes: that they be minimum security inmates who were eligible for programs and had no history of gang leadership. Volunteering was still a criterion for males but had probably been eroded as a criterion for females, who—unlike males—were given an additional interview to determine "readiness." Consideration also was given to whether males were from that region of the state.

The most frequent criteria for males at the other five state institutions were inmate choice, nature of referral, a clean record at previous institutions, a history of nonviolence, and minimum security status. Four of five stipulated that male inmates express an interest in, or volunteer for, co-corrections, that they have minimum security status, and that they be referred from other institutions. But in the case of at least one coed institution, transfers included those who had only undergone reception and diagnosis elsewhere. Three of five required a clean record at previous institutions and a demonstrated history of nonviolence and low escape potential (at least as an adult).

Other selection criteria have less widespread application, or were more difficult to identify. Two of five institutions directly restricted the age of male admissions: one to males over 50, and the other to males under 22. At least two other institutions indirectly restricted the age of male admissions: one by requiring that males be first offenders, and the other by primarily admitting males who had served several years on life sentences to serve as a special work detail. At least one institution required the absence of a sexual assault history, but one institution openly received sex offenders.

One institution required that a prospective inmate have no relative already at the institution (which really applied only to spouses), but a second institution attempted to transfer in spouses who were located elsewhere in the state system. Two institutions required eligibility for community programs, and at least two (probably more) required the capability to perform special work details. At least one institution stipulated that only inmates with less than a specified amount of time remaining on their sentences could be admitted; a second required first offender status; a third, an interest in "further training," although the institution had no identifiable training to offer; and a fourth, cognitive test performance, as the basis for admission into a special unit program. At least two institutions called for an additional interview to determine "readiness for co-corrections."

Other factors may have played into the process of inmate selection in a more subtle manner, such as proximity to geographical release point, recommendation "from friends of the superintendent" at other institutions, and the general appearance of an inmate's file. Some institutions provided for alternate criteria; for example, an inmate not qualifying for community release programs may be admitted based on capabilities in the performance of special work details.

Although the criteria above also applied to the unvisited institutions, certain criteria appear to have been more frequently used, such as inmate age and ability to perform specified work details: Two institutions restricted male admissions to an older, more tractable population capable of heavy labor; and two other institutions admitted only younger males, with one of them further specifying that they be first offenders. With two exceptions, the unvisited institutions housed the entire incarcerated female population in the jurisdiction: One housed women who were considered unsuitable for the state's minimum security coed institution discussed above, and the other gave preference to women from the region of the state in which the prison was located.

In the federal system some selection criteria differ between institutions and generally apply differently to males and females. Inmate choice appeared to be significant in at least three institutions, although choice was less applicable to women who were more frequently direct commitments from the courts. Age cutoffs were wider for females than for males: The cutoff was lower for females at three institutions, and higher at another institution that housed youthful offenders. Time-in-sentence guidelines tended to be applied more liberally to females, who either exceeded the two-year restriction nominally present in at least three of the four institutions, or were directly sentenced to the institution for periods of only a few months.

Two of the four institutions required minimum

security status and eligibility for community release programs. Two required eligibility for special unit programs, and at one institution this was an alternate admissions criterion. Three encouraged the transfer-in of spouses incarcerated at other federal institutions. Proximity to geographical release point was a general consideration for admission to all four institutions, but was applied less rigorously to females. At least two and as many as four institutions required the absence of a sexual assault history.

Staff

STAFF SIZE AND STAFF-TO-INMATE RATIOS.   Staff size, staff-to-inmate ratios, and custody-to-inmate ratios displayed wide ranges and did not consistently reflect either jurisdictional norms or scale differences. Staff size ranged from 55 employees at a state institution housing 197 inmates to 330 at a state institution that held 290 inmates. In between these extremes, there were three state institutions and one federal institution employing from 114 to 140 staff members; one state and two federal institutions employing from 230 to 289, and one federal institution that approached 330.

Staff-to-inmate ratios ranged from one-to-one to one-to-four. Four states employed approximately one staff member per inmate; one state and one federal institution employed approximately one staff member for every two inmates; and the remaining one state and three federal institutions maintained staff-to-inmate ratios higher than one-to-two but less than one-to-four.

Both the size of security staffs and custody-to-inmate ratios exhibited even wider variation. Security staffs ranged in size from 30 at a state institution with a total staff of only 55, to 195 at a state institution with a full staff of 283. Four state and two federal institutions had security staffs under 100, and two state and two federal institutions had between 130 and 195. Custody-to-inmate ratios ranged from one-to-two to one-to-eight. Five state institutions had custody-to-inmate ratios of one-to-two or one-to-three, and the other state institution had a ratio of nearly one-to-seven. Custody-to-inmate ratios at federal institutions ranged from one-to-four to one-to-eight.

STAFF INTEGRATION. Every institution visited maintained a more or less integrated staff, and when an institution had "gone coed," additional staff had been hired (especially for custody) to strike a better balance with either the introduced population or the population that was under-represented on the staff inherited from a noncorrectional facility. The sex ratio of staff generally mirrored that of the inmates. However, the composition of staffs by sex still generally reflected the traditional composition of the institution as a single-sex or predominantly of one-sex institution. At two of the three federal institutions, which had traditionally (since opening) been predominantly male but which recently have housed inmate populations approaching parity, females were under-represented on both total staff and security staff.

The integration of staffs by rank is more difficult to estimate. It appears that career opportunities for women in corrections have not been reduced, and if anything have been enhanced, by co-corrections. However, men rather than women generally hold the top administrative position in the integrated institutions, and, in at least three jurisdictions, a women's population that had been under a female administrator was placed under a male administrator.

STAFF BACKGROUND AND ATTITUDES. The attitudes of staff toward co-corrections, offenders of the opposite sex, staff members of the opposite sex, and corrections in general, were often perceived by administration, staff, and inmates as contributing to a program's success or failure. At least four institutions hired a substantial segment of staff without background in corrections. Two of these were federal institutions which "inherited" Public Health Service staffs, and at least two others strove for staff "heterogeneity" on the assumption that background in single-sex environments might impede staff functions in a coed environment.

At least five institutions hired staff transferred from the jurisdiction's maximum security institutions. At four of these, staff attitudes (presumably retained from "behind the walls") were perceived to have an adverse effect on the program. The varied attitudes among staff mirrored those in the larger society—from condoning male aggressiveness toward female inmates to supporting a woman's right to a range of options equally as wide as that offered to the men.

STAFF IN-SERVICE TRAINING.   At least one institution operated staff in-service training focussed on the co-correctional program. Two or three other institutions briefly dealt with co-corrections in institutional orientation programs. In some cases co-corrections was not viewed as the appropriate focus of training because, in the words of one training officer, "if they need special training to deal with it, they don't belong here." The administrators of several state institutions noted that, because training would necessarily occur after-hours, union stipulations for overtime payments to training program participants provided a disincentive to formulate such programs.

Programs

STRUCTURED INTERACTION.   All visited institutions claimed that all structured programs—with some qualifications— were sexually integrated. In this discussion, structured programs consist primarily of educational programs and work details. Unstructured programs are considered below, and include recreation, dining, inmate organizations, chapel, and leisure time. Several factors seemed to limit full integration of structured programs: enrollment ceilings, movement restrictions by time or place, grant stipulations, the association of some programs with single-sex units, conflicting program schedules, inmate pressures, the pre-ponderance of one sex, lack of supervision in an area, and the administrative decision that certain programs should be restricted.

The administrative decision that programs should be restricted has occasionally been spoken of as "the need to shelter" certain programs and inmates of one sex (who were in a minority or might be pressured out of programs), or as "a special program focus" (women's consciousness raising). Or it has been ascribed to an attempt to achieve "more effective results," or blamed on "insufficient resources."

Program participation is often curtailed by movement restrictions at certain times or in certain places, or by lack of supervision in an area. In one institution, for example, males were not permitted to work in the kitchen because kitchen workers had to start work before dawn, when movement over the grounds was prohibited, and only those residing in the building that contained the kitchen—the women—could reach this work detail without going out-of-doors. Other examples were lack of supervision in an area such as warehouses, and restricted integration of work details to a degree in *all* institutions. And women were generally the ones excluded, except where they were in a clear majority.

At least one state institution had an enrollment ceiling for the minority sex. In two state institutions, LEAA-funded educational grants restricted the participation of males: One stipulated that funds could be used only for females, and the other required 85% female participation. An HEW-funded child visitation program at a third institution excluded prospective male participants.

In nearly all institutions, some unit-based programs were restricted, by the unit, to a single sex. In at least one institution, where ostensibly "inmates are treated as inmates, and not as male and female," males were precluded from nearly all educational programs and work details— except for one specialized work detail—by conflicts between their work schedules and the times when other programs were available.

In several institutions inmate pressures restricted sexual integration, either because one sex "expelled" the other from a program (for example, in one AA group that had long been all-female, and at two other institutions where the minority population of women seemed generally pressured out of programs), or because older inmates—most of them male—were internally pressured against participation in "useless" programs, or because program offerings tended to be unappealing to one sex or the other. Generally, the participation of males and females together in structured programs, perhaps as peers, seemed to be at a high level.

UNSTRUCTURED INTERACTION. Restrictions on unstructured interaction between male and female inmates were more pervasive. As noted above, unstructured interaction includes recreation, dining, inmate organizations, chapel, and leisure time. The factors seemingly most related to the level of integration in these areas were defined adequacy of supervision, association of activities with units, restrictions on movement, and administrative decisions.

Restrictions on integration of recreational activities were evident at all institutions, and stemmed from each of these factors. At several institutions, for example, women were restricted from jogging either because supervision was unavailable, or because the activity was regarded as too difficult to supervise. At several institutions, movement restrictions at certain times or in certain places limited integration; for example, men and women swam in different parts of a lake.

Five of the 10 institutions provided for sexually

integrated dining; the other five institutions cited a lack of supervision, administrative decisions against expansion of dining facilities, and unit-based dining, as factors inhibiting the integration of dining, although two of these institutions were planning to integrate the minority sex—in one case male, and in the other female—into the main mess hall. Three of four federal and no more than six state institutions provided fully integrated dining. In the fourth federal institution and in an additional state institution, one women's unit was permitted to dine with men. At three other state facilities, meals were served in units, at least to the minority population.

Primarily because of differences in supervision, at least one federal and three state institutions restricted integration of at least some inmate organizations, particularly inmate offices. But in at least one state institution, such restrictions were made only after earlier experiments with an open-door policy. Chapel was off bounds at nearly all institutions, except during services and other structured events, because of its rumored use as a major assignation post.

The level of integration in leisure time activities—true unstructured time—is difficult to specify, because it involves an estimate of not only the quantity, but also the quality of interaction. By implication, the level of integration in unstructured activities involves the places, times, and circumstances under which interaction is permitted. At one extreme were at least two federal and one state institution that encouraged interaction under minimally intrusive supervision, and offered a wide range of settings in which interaction was permitted, including late evening activities such as daily coffee houses, and even coed swimming in warm weather.

At the other extreme were several state and at least one federal institution which generally restricted free-time interaction to a physically controlled space, such as the yard, or to evening "coed hours" held in a visitors-type room, or to special occasions such as dances. In at least two state institutions at the latter extreme, inmates not attending programs occupied a sex-specific domain. This circumstance was also found to some extent at one federal institution, where only one of the three women's units was located within the men's domain. This domain was demarcated at one institution by an invisible line passing over the grounds. Males often congregated by a low railing along the end of a path terminating at the dividing line. Several institutions specifically required that at coed activities, such as movies and athletic events, males and females sit in separate parts of the room or field.

Although it is difficult to quantify quickly the levels of unstructured interaction at a given institution, one gains a general impression of the degree to which opposite sex couples are told to "move on," and in general it seems fair to conclude that only when the male-female interaction was perceived as possessing a programmatic value in itself, was a high level of true unstructured interaction permitted and apparent.

COMMUNITY LINKS.   Links with the community took two basic forms: programs in which the community provides support to inmates, and public relations efforts emanating from the institution to the outside community. Community programs included education release and work release, furloughs and day trips, inmate volunteers in the community, and volunteers from the outside community and institutional staff as co-participants within the institution. Public relations efforts included selectively publicized programs, performances, newsletters, public appearances, and other activities geared to gain or maintain community acceptance for continued political and programmatic viability.

The purposes for community programs included the maintenance or development of family ties, primarily through furloughs; learning how to work in the community; a means of increasing the sexual integration of the institution, either within the institution through contact with volunteers of the opposite sex, or outside in the community; and an alternative to sexual activity within the institution. Public relations programs existed not only to maintain political viability, but also to provide access for the institution to programs available in the community, and to maintain contact with families.

Only two federal and one or two state institutions could be said to operate "thriving" community programs. Other institutions were struggling either to gain or to regain access to the community, or to determine what direction the institution would take in the absence of community programs. Most institutions still involved the community in institutional life by receiving volunteers to the institution, especially in education and religious programs. At least half the institutions poured energies into public relations activities to increase the inmates' access to the community, to build resources, or simply to stay afloat. In most institutions it was evident that a significant aspect of public relations was providing the "outside world" with assurances about "what's going on in there." Changes in links with the community are detailed below.

MEDICAL SERVICES.   The level of medical services available at the visited institutions seemed comparable to that at noncoed facilities, but it is difficult to comment on. It was argued in a few institutions that medical budgets were strained because they were based on long-term projections for a different type of population. Subjects of particular import in coed institutions were birth control, pregnancy, abortion, and prenatal care.

Women in nearly all the institutions had access to birth control. Only at one institution did inmates strongly complain that birth control was difficult to come by, saying that "they turn you inside out and upside down." In most institutions, only birth control pills were generally available, but IUDs were also provided occasionally in some federal and state institutions. The official rationale for the availability of birth control involved some notion of "protection of the women's health," and provision of the right to contraception to those on furlough. However, the function of birth control in "regulating the menses" was often not so much to protect a woman's health as it was to provide contraception, or as some expressed it, "keeping the menses regular *and recurring*." Many staff members at the visited institutions felt that the official purposes for birth control were a "subterfuge" and that the "real reason" was that "we can't be everywhere," and that "every woman has a right to protection." The frequency with which women were prodded to "go on the pill" seemed to vary, but nothing conclusive can be stated about it.

Pregnancy rates, which were distinguished on the basis of institutional and noninstitutional sources, were readily available at federal institutions—perhaps only because they were to be developed for the recent co-corrections conference held by the Bureau. But these rates were frequently unavailable in state institutions. State institutions seemed less willing to discuss issues of pregnancy, and careful guidelines on and protections during abortions seemed to be lacking in some institutions. Abortions appeared to be available to women at most if not all 10 institutions, although the openness with which they were performed, the amount and nature of prior counseling provided, the sources of financial payment, and the services available afterwards varied widely.

Prenatal care was available at all institutions—indeed, most of the institutions had learned to deal with pregnancies before there were any co-corrections. But the quality of prenatal care seemed to vary not only in respect to the importance with which staff regarded these services, but also in terms of the emotional support provided.

As a policy, no institutions regularly allowed babies to remain too long at the institutions with their mothers, although until recently several had permitted it, and certain state institutions had in an earlier generation operated major "mother developmental" programs. One state institution operated a Title XX Child Visitation Program, but, as mentioned above, funding stipulations allowed children to visit only mothers, and not fathers. However, institutions with furlough policies have arranged for home furloughs to allow for the mother's placement of the child after birth.

Policy

PHYSICAL CONTACT. The definition of a policy on physical contact was widely regarded as a crucial element in the operation of a co-correctional institution. As in most other categories, the 10 institutions exhibited a wide range of options in determination of this policy—from not penalizing any contact short of sexual intercourse, to a prohibition of all physical contact. Two state institutions allowed any behavior "appropriate to public places," and at these institutions physical contact between inmate couples was evident. The four federal institutions were affected by the recent efforts to standardize the articulation and implementation of contact policy throughout the Bureau, and only hand holding and walking arm-in-arm were permitted by policy.

The four other state institutions permitted absolutely no physical contact, one such policy specifying that, "any physical contact such as having one's hand on the shoulders of another, legs intertwined or touching, one person resting or leaning on the body of another, etc., will be considered physical contact and subject to a disciplinary charge." However, three of these four no-contact facilities spelled out certain times during which the rules against contact would be suspended: One allowed walking arm-in-arm after church on Sundays and permitted dances at which inmates perceived that physical contact was encouraged. A second institution permitted occasional dances at which kissing and body contact were condoned. A third institution permitted hand holding and "accidental" body contact during roller skating. The fourth institution had only recently "tightened up" its contact policy, and indicated no immediate intention to relax its new policies. Inmates and staff alike at these four institutions commented on their difficulties in adjusting to no-contact rules. All ten institutions stated, with some qualification, that contact policy would be enforced equally with same-sex and opposite-sex contact.

The articulation of contact policy and the implementation of that policy are often two different matters. Each institution had its rumors and legends about often used rendezvous points, times when a room was left empty, couples who had "set up house," and guards who would "look the other way." The implementation of policy was obviously affected by the attitudes among inmates, custody, and other parts of the staff, that "sexual relationships will occur in prison, it is merely a matter of what kind," and that "sexual relationships between men and women are normal and inevitable." These stances were reflected in statements such as "when you put women and men together they're *going* to get down, no matter what you do to stop them." Implementation of policy seemed to depend on attitudes as well as on the physical environment: expansiveness, hidden closets, dark corners, and so on.

Among the federal institutions, where both articulation and implementation of policy have historically varied, the current level of implementation was still becoming "coordinated," and inmate evidence of the levels of implementation ranged from the commonly expressed conviction that "if you get caught, you're going to pay," to inmate claims that guards cooperated in planning times and places.

At the two relatively "liberal" state institutions, it appeared that sexual contact between a man and a woman, if "discreet," was condoned. Staff at one of these two state institutions suggested that their policies toward heterosexual contact were an extension of the institution's tolerance of homosexual contact. Although several administrators were adamant in stating that homosexual and heterosexual contact received equal sanctions, a few administrators candidly admitted that "public priorities" demanded focusing on control of heterosexual activity. With only one strong exception, it was nearly universally maintained that homosexual contact was, in fact, regarded more lightly, even if not as the inmate's "unnatural lot."

SANCTIONS FOR PHYSICAL CONTACT.   Sanctions for contact policy violations included placement in administrative or disciplinary segregation, exclusion from coeducational activities and interaction with the opposite sex, withdrawal of privileges such as furloughs and release programs, and transfer to single-sex institutions. Distinctions were ordinarily made between major and minor violations, and correspondingly differentiated sanctions commonly applied.

All 10 institutions used transfer as the most extreme sanction for contact violations, but there were variations in the uniformity with which this was used. Males at almost all state institutions were ostensibly to be "sent back" for sexual activity or even lesser contact, and the federal system recently coordinated co-correctional policy to require "sure and swift transfer" for contact violations. Females in coed institutions have been less subject historically to transfer as a disciplinary action for several reasons: Five of the six state institutions were the sole facility for incarcerated females in the jurisdiction, and the most extreme sanction available was placement of women in segregation or a higher security status; in the federal system, women may have represented a "scarce resource" necessary to sustain a co-correctional program; co-corrections could less palpably be presented as a "privilege" to women, who had fewer or no alternatives to co-corrections; and, finally, many women were regarded as having problems "in the sexual area."

Indeed, although each federal and state institution had transferred at least one male (and in some cases no more than one) for sexual contact, it was evident that in neither federal nor state systems have contact policies been rigidly applied even to males, for whom co-corrections could more realistically be presented as a "privilege." Only recently has "sure and swift transfer" echoed throughout the Bureau of Prisons, and its implementation has significantly affected at least one institution where the policy had been not to transfer. Because of its location and security level, this prison had been used as a transfer point, and the options for transfer *from* the institution were limited.

The federal system has also emphasized the importance of applying equal sanctions to male and female inmates, transferring both for sexual contact, and allowing a second chance to both after a successful term of at least six months has been served at single-sex institutions. State institutions also endorsed the concept that a policy of transferring only males can lead to exploitative situations in which a male can be "blackmailed" or subject to potential physical violence to which he would not respond. At least two states offered transferred males the opportunity to request a "second chance." However, state systems generally did not have the resources to implement a policy that would provide "fairer," more equal sanctions—just as, in the Federal system, the range of options for women is more restricted.

Whether sanctions should be uniformly applied for same-sex and opposite-sex contact was an issue at most institutions. In several institutions decisions had been openly reached in particular cases not to transfer inmates involved in same-sex contact—even when there were alternative placements—for two reasons: such behavior, although potentially threatening the heterosexual atmosphere, did not constitute a violation of "the rule" of co-corrections; and, second, "shipping them out" to a single-sex institution would probably only engender "more of the same." As a result, there appeared to be a tendency to respond to homosexual contact—regardless of the sex of the participants—with the same sanctions applied to women in state systems.

MOVEMENT AND SPACE RESTRICTIONS.   As indicated above in the discussion of structured and unstructured interaction, all institutions subjected inmates to certain types of movement restrictions applicable to one or both sexes, either by time or place. The most common were imaginary or actual perimeter lines around cottages and dorms, to be crossed only by cottage or dorm residents, or by persons of the same sex as residents; restrictions on movement outside of dorms at certain times of the day; restrictions against movement into, or near, certain places, or movement only while under close surveillance; nonoverlapping traffic patterns; and the separation of inmates, by sex, into two domains, to be left only by inmates participating in specified programs. Nearly all institutions prohibited movement around dorms for the opposite sex, and three or four had sex-locked domains. Recent changes in movement restrictions are discussed below.

DATING BEHAVIOR.   Federal institutions were more articulate in discouraging "serious" relationships between inmates, at least "long-term serious relationships," and "relationships beyond the confines of the institution." However, only one institution was found to restrict program participation by "serious" couples, and to require program managers accordingly to screen applicants to their programs. Most institutions stipulated that inmates could marry only if they had met before their incarceration.

However, at least one state institution had witnessed several inmate marriages that had been much supported by the institution's administration, and had occasioned nearly institution-wide furloughs for wedding attendance.

Chapter 3

CO-CORRECTIONS

FCI Fort Worth after Three Years

Charles F. Campbell

Although FCI Fort Worth is frequently referred to in press stories as an "experimental" prison and seen as something of a demonstration project within the Bureau of Prisons, *its assigned mission at the outset was in fact based on the pragmatic needs of the service.* But it was rushed into use after acquisition of the facilities from HEW in October of 1971, and may have set some kind of record in reaching its optimum population.

A task force set up by the Director early in 1971 identified the needs upon which the mission of the institution was based and roughed out ideas for a program model developed around five or six functional units.[1] Otherwise, the task force had its hands full dealing with all sorts of administrative and logistical complexities. Virtually all of the detailed planning of FCI Fort Worth programs was done in something of an improvisatory manner after the institution opened.

There was a philosophy at the outset, but no clear plan

of action about how to implement the philosophy. As the venture progressed, a commitment to three or four basic concepts evolved. I would call those that can be identified *mutuality, heterogeneity,* and *engagement with the free world.* These concepts are inextricably related. As I describe our programs there will be references to these concepts and, I trust, some light shed on why we subscribe to them.

In identifying the best use for the new FCI at Fort Worth, the task force determined (1) that we should include a strong drug abuse component, (2) that the time had arrived to do something about a program for alcoholic offenders, (3) that we needed to provide for some of the many older men with chronic health problems wasting away behind the high walls, and (4) that we needed to include space for women offenders to relieve Terminal Island and Alderson, since both were jammed full despite the goodly number of women farmed out to Colorado and elsewhere.

The five functional units at FCI are based on these categories of offenders. There are two drug abuse units, and although they are called the DAPS and the NARA Units, we no longer place offenders committed under the NARA legislation[2] exclusively in the NARA Unit. Both these units have space for about 115 offenders who have had drug abuse problems, without regard to the nature of their sentences.

The STAR (Steps Toward Alcoholic Rehabilitation) Unit consists of about 100 residents who are alcoholic or have otherwise demonstrated problems with alcohol such as spree drinking or exceptional irresponsibility while under the influence of alcohol.

The Comprehensive Health Unit, a title we came up with largely because of our liking for the catchy acronym CHU provides space for about 85 older residents, most of whom have health problems, ranging from arthritis to serious heart disease.

We rather dislike having to say "and then we have the Women's Unit," as if being a woman is what we want to change about the 100 residents in this unit. Half of these women have had some sort of drug abuse problem. About 25 have been heroin addicts. The women residents at FCI Fort Worth represent a reasonably good cross section of women in prisons elsewhere, except that we do not have women who have no hope of release in the foreseeable future.

There is a commonplace assumption that women in prison are generally tougher and more confirmed in criminality than men. The theory is that the courts are reluctant to send women to prison and do so only after exhausting other alternatives. This is a sensible supposition, but its validity could not be proved by our experience. Without question, some of our women are extremely unstable and difficult to work with, but many are stable and relatively nondelinquent.

It's probably true that our Women's Unit has a higher proportion of difficult, emotionally volatile residents than any of the other units. But an important reason for this is that there are very few facilities in the Federal Prison Service for the dispersal of such women. Difficult to manage male offenders can be housed at the maximum security institutions or scattered among two dozen other institutions. Until Lexington opened in early 1974, there were only four federal facilities for women, and before 1971, there were only two.

It isn't true that female first offenders are invariably placed on probation, especially now that different sentences for codefendants when one is a woman and one a man could be viewed as sexually discriminatory. Our women's population has consistently included some relatively genteel income tax evaders and bank embezzlers. Also, we usually have a few young women who were involved in cocaine and marijuana smuggling, some of them with college backgrounds, as well as a significant number of previously nondelinquent women serving stiff sentences for drug offenses. Typically, the women in this latter group were manipulated into involvement with drug trafficking by more sophisticated male offenders looking for ways to reduce risks to themselves.

It took us a while at FCI Fort Worth to get our views toward the women's population into perspective. We believe we have now reached a good beginning point, at least, in learning what needs to be learned about women in a co-correctional setting.

During the months preceding activation of the facility in the fall of 1971, we engaged in long hours of cogitation about the problem of how to manage men and women in the same institution. There was no body of knowledge to rely on. Thus we knew we would need to proceed cautiously and learn from trial and error. We made certain assumptions about the type of behavior we should be prepared to deal with, but I can think of only a few of the assumptions that haven't proved to be wrong.

The assumption that a viable institutional program could be developed for such a varied mix of offenders, including men and women, was one that has proved to be right. This was an assumption the Director of the Bureau of Prisons and his task force had before I came on the scene in March of 1971. We engaged in no systematic theorizing about what might be encountered in a co-correctional experience. Instead, all we had was a shared conviction that different kinds of things had to be tried. We had certain pragmatic needs; we had the prospect of a new facility at our disposal; and we had some good experience with innovations like the unit system, the correctional counseling program, and work and study release. Thus it was logical to view Fort Worth as an opportunity to be seized.

The most dramatic departure was co-corrections. I will take credit for coining the term, but not for first having the notion that co-corrections might be viable. It must have been in 1969 when Roy Gerard, then Director of the Robert

Kennedy Memorial Youth Center at Morgantown, West Virginia, told me in a private conversation that he was dead serious about having a women's cottage at the Kennedy Youth Center some day. Two years later and four months before FCI Fort Worth opened, the first contingent of young women arrived at the Kennedy Youth Center. By that time, Roy Gerard had moved to the Central Office as Deputy Assistant Director, and thus Jay Flamm had the distinction of becoming head of the Bureau of Prisons' first co-correctional facility.

The advent of the coeds at Kennedy created little public stir, perhaps because for many years there had been state training schools for boys and girls. Kennedy's program was erroneously seen as similar to these. The fact is that 18-, 19-, and 20-year-olds are men and women, most especially where their sexuality is concerned. Moreover, during the past two years the age level of the Kennedy population has gone up significantly. At present it is a co-correctional facility for young adult offenders.

Whether the country's first "coed prison" was the Kennedy Youth Center at Morgantown, West Virginia, the Federal Correctional Institution at Fort Worth, Texas, or someplace else, let it be said that the decision to launch co-corrections in the federal system was independently made by Norman Carlson, the Director of the Federal Bureau of Prisons. He has given full support to the experiment and has subsequently activated co-correctional programs at Lexington, Kentucky, and Pleasanton, California. I am compelled to state these historical facts because I believe co-corrections will prove to be of considerable significance to corrections in years to come, and it is important that the record be kept straight.

One of the assumptions we felt rather comfortable with during the weeks preceding our getting underway in 1971, was that the women we would start with would be carefully selected, stable, tractable women chosen on the basis of their predictability to tolerate the stress of living with rigid restraints in close proximity with male offenders. We were wrong. What happened is that our first group of female residents were the 45 believed to have been most seriously involved in a disturbance that occurred at Alderson in September of 1971, in the wake of the Attica tragedy. This group included the primary leaders and the more vociferous participants in the disturbance, as well as a number of women who had no significant role in the disturbance but had previously acquired bad reputations with the staff. Also in the group were some rather passive women who appear to have been in the wrong place at the wrong time. Reports I have gotten say that some jumped on the bus out of Alderson just to be with their friends or to get away from Alderson for other reasons. Others were rounded up and placed aboard the bus because of past derelictions rather than because of involvement in the disturbance. While it would not be accurate to say our initial group of women residents consisted exclusively of women who had been serious management problems at Alderson, it was hardly a group we would have selected.

In any case, beginning our venture at Fort Worth with this group of women had great significance. It was a compelling learning experience for all of us. It provided a dramatic illustration of how much people are inclined to respond according to the way they are treated, as well as a compelling demonstration of the powerful influence of expectations. We had no reasonable choice but to tell these women we needed their help, that a large share of responsibility for the co-correctional experiment would be resting on their shoulders. Apprehensive though we were, we behaved toward them as if we couldn't have been more delighted to have them. Forty-five rowdy, foulmouthed women responded to this treatment magnificently. We had some tense and difficult times then and during the months thereafter, but to observe the growth of these women in dignity and self-respect was a tremendously gratifying experience.

I am aware that among people in corrections, including many of my Bureau of Prisons colleagues who have had no opportunity to see for themselves or to get reliable first-hand reports, there is a great deal of curiosity about what really goes on with the men and women inmates at FCI Fort Worth. To begin with, I can report that the fears that there would be great preoccupation with sex, that the women would be constantly seeking ways to make themselves available to the men, that the men would display persistent sexual aggressiveness, have proved to have been unjustified.

Most certainly there are violations of the rigid rule against sexual contact, but the best evidence suggests a low incidence of this kind of behavior. It is logical to believe that such behavior occurs far less frequently than does homosexual behavior in all-male and all-female institutions. Of 1800 incident reports from November 1971 until July 1974, only 26 have been for inappropriate sexual behavior between men and women residents. Although substantially more misconduct than this goes unobserved, we can be sure that if such conduct were a prime preoccupation among our residents it would be encountered more frequently.

Another factor that gives us this impression about the level of sexual activity is the incidence of pregnancy. FCI Fort Worth's policy on contraception is the same as those at Alderson and the Terminal Island Women's Division: If a woman is in furlough status or scheduled for imminent release she can expect the physician, at her request, to prescribe an appropriate contraception program for her. While discretion in implementing this policy is left to the physician, a recent check revealed that 25 of 110 women residents were on "the pill." Substantially more than this have furlough status and thus could have contraceptives if they chose.

Since the institution opened in October 1971, nine pregnancies have occurred as a result of co-corrections. Only one confirmed pregnancy has resulted from co-corrections during the past 18 months. This reflects more chance taking during the first year and a half. We also hope this pattern in the incidence of pregnancy reflects the improved procedures and improved supervision skills, as well as a growing positive impact of FCI Fort Worth's approach to the conduct of residents.

Three hundred and fifty women residents have been part of the FCI program since the institution opened. To assess accurately the significance of the nine pregnancies during this period, one must consider how many undesirable pregnancies there would have been had these women remained in the community, and what quality of help and support would have been available under such circumstances.

I am not sure, but it seems to me our problem with pregnancies began to abate at about the same time Sister Esther Heffernan[3] told us that we seemed to be as concerned about pregnancies about as much as other prisons are concerned about riots.

Lastly, the impression we have about sexual behavior among the residents of FCI Fort Worth is influenced by what residents tell us during informal closeout interviews and at other times when they would seem to have nothing to gain by deliberately distorting their impressions. My assessment of information from this source leads me to believe that at any one time we have a few women, possibly as many as 10 or 15, willing to jump at any opportunity to make themselves sexually available to the male residents, that at least this many are unavailable sexually under any circumstances, and that the remaining women are disinclined to become sexually involved with men residents, given the high risks involved and the minimal satisfaction likely to be realized. I furthermore believe there is validity to the apparent resident consensus that the administration's very strict policy toward violations of the "no sex" rule plays a major role in the low incidence of such behavior. Men and women residents who get caught having sex run a high risk of being transferred to other institutions. Such transfers are not viewed as punitive, and unless there is some other kind of accompanying misconduct, we state for the record that the transfer is being effected only because of the resident's demonstrated unsuitability for a co-correctional setting. This does not reduce the chagrin our residents have over the prospect of getting "shipped."

In attempting to understand the reasons for the limited extent of sexual activity at the institution, another factor must be considered. For most of our women, sex is hardly new. Many have been prostitutes, and thus we can be sure that many have never developed a wholesome sexual adjustment. The FCI Fort Worth setting provides few opportunities for them to use their sexuality in the overt and exploitive ways they have been accustomed to in the past. At the same time, the setting affords them substantial protection from overt sexual exploitation by the men. Being able to say "Get away from me, man—you're gonna get me shipped," is probably a necessary option for women residents if co-corrections is to work effectively. This should not be taken to mean that there is an absence of exploitative behavior, but that sexual exploitation appears to be minimal.

I am not yet willing to offer any theory to explain the astonishing passivity of the male residents. It is a phenomenon to be observed with interest. Up to now we have not been able to understand the parameters of the men's sexual interest in the women. Overtly restrained as they are, they have been the source of much pressure from the women to become "walk partners." Since there are four men to every woman, this provides the male resident with some status satisfaction, but apparently it usually doesn't pay off in sexual benefits. This may be one of the reasons for the remarkable lack of aggressiveness on the part of the men and could also be a reason why many of the more self-assured, physically attractive male residents elect not to seek "walk partner" relationships with the women. The competitiveness that does exist appears to be extremely low key. We know of only about a half dozen fights in these three years attributable to jealousy of the women residents.

We can say nothing definitive about the incidence of homosexual behavior at FCI Fort Worth, but we can report that in three years no incident of predatory homosexuality has come to our attention. We have never had a complaint, direct or indirect, about homosexual intimidation or abuse. Male role playing by the women residents, described by Rose Giallombardo[4] and others and observable in many women's prisons, does not exist at Fort Worth. And several women believed (by staff, fellow residents, and apparently by themselves) to have been lesbians, have returned to a feminine orientation. Several overt male and female homosexuals and two male transexuals have spent time in the FCI Fort Worth population with no significant adjustment problems.

The FCI experiment has undoubtedly alleviated some of the concern over what might happen in a "coed prison," but is it fair for us to be asked what are the advantages? What anticipated benefits justified such a controversial departure in the first place? I have already referred to the pragmatic aspects of FCI Fort Worth's beginning. If there was a definitive rationale for co-corrections before our being involved in it here, it was never told to me. A conviction on the part of the Director and some of his colleagues, including me, that this and other innovations needed to be tried, was what we were going on.

Especially at that time, early 1971, there seemed to be a lot of evidence around that what we were doing wasn't working very well. We were acutely aware that the confinement of offenders under conventional circumstances had an inescapably dehumanizing effect on people, despite strong, well-trained staff and a heavy emphasis on helping programs. We were convinced that isolation from the community was a major contributor to the deleterious effects of confinement, and we had been talking determinedly about the "normalization" of our institutions.

For several years we had moved not only toward developing better ties with the community, but also toward normalizing prison settings by bringing in volunteers and—even before this—by using employees in men's institutions. We had lived fretfully for many years with the knowledge that situational and predatory homosexuality was prevalent. These factors, together with a pressing need for more space for women offenders, went into the making of the decisions to have women and men at Fort Worth.

I have come to feel strongly that men need women and women need men, quite aside from their sexual needs and desires. It has become obvious that some of our women residents, who had never before had a relationship with a man other than on the basis of sexual exploitation, are now finding out what it means to have a friend who also happens to be a man. And men residents are making similar discoveries about women. Deprivation of this kind of relationship may be one of the more destructive things about confinement. Inability to have this kind of relationship may contribute to the kind of behavior that leads to confinement. But before we got underway at FCI Fort Worth, I don't think any of us could have articulated this notion. In all candor, we weren't sure what we were getting into, but we could hardly visualize its being worse than some things we were already tolerating.

It seemed to me at times during those early days that the special opportunity we had at FCI Fort Worth to break away from the old structures was a thing of destiny. It happened that two women's facilities were seriously overcrowded; it happened that the facility we were inheriting from HEW was within the city of Fort Worth, a singularly fine community as far as resources for correctional programming are concerned; and it happened that we inherited the facilities under circumstances that made it necessary for us to staff the institution primarily with former employees of HEW's defunct Clinical Research Center. This last factor may have been more significant than anything else in enabling us to implement so many dramatic innovations. Though not unanimously progressive, this group of employees had no hardened preconceptions about how a correctional institution should function. Some of them were not strong, but most have proved to be excellent employees. Not only has there been virtually no effective staff resistance to innovation, but we have enjoyed staff support of our programs in a way that may be unprecedented.

Additionally, it happened that the special offender groups, identified by the Director's task force as needing most to be served by FCI Fort Worth, provided what now appears to be a thoroughly workable mix for a co-correctional institution. Without knowing quite when it happened, we found ourselves strongly subscribing to the notion that heterogeneity was an essential concept for us, and moreover, that co-correction was an essential ingredient of this heterogeneity and at the same time dependent on it.

Mutuality is a related notion, one with which we have tried to permeate the FCI scene. We believe with missionary zeal that all of us are in this together—men and women, young and old, black, white, and brown, staff, residents, and free world friends. We are fellow human beings with common interests that transcend the differences and conflicts between us. This is a notion that challenges the traditional barrier that has stood implacably between inmates and prison staff for as long as there have been prisons.

A commitment to the idea of mutuality in a heterogeneous setting, catalyzed by a strong engagement with the free world, has breached the barrier at FCI Fort Worth. The barrier has not crumbled, but it has been breached in a manner that could not have occurred without an infusion of healthy free world influence. If heterogeneity is good, it follows that an enriched, broad-ranging heterogeneity is better. Mutuality, which draws its virtue from inclusiveness, needs a healthy divergence in the parts and pieces it includes.

Mixing first offenders and recidivists in the same institution flies in the face of progressive ideas about corrections. We are advocating it here, but only under circumstances that include the presence of club women, college students, church people ranging from Pentecostals to Unitarians, off-duty policemen, Rotarians, and nuns (some of whom look like fashion models), and there must be opportunities for them to be friends with the residents and to be actively involved in constructive activities with them. We have 250 volunteers. They are essential to the FCI effort.

The formula must also include opportunities for residents to go into the community with these friends and for other reasons, on work release, field trips, and family furloughs. Last year FCI Fort Worth residents made approximately 25,000 separate trips into the community with overwhelmingly positive results.

Parenthetically it should be stated here that the criteria for imprisonment at FCI Fort Worth require that residents be within two years of a probable release date. This results in our having a mix of people committed directly from the courts with relatively short sentences and transfers from other institutions including some who are in the last years of extremely long sentences. We do not avoid taking "management problems." On the contrary, the Fort Worth setup has frequently proved to be a good solution for persons who have had extreme adjustment problems at other institutions. However, we have ruled out offenders whose backgrounds reflect a pattern of seriously assaultive behavior. But we rarely encounter a referral whose history of violence is bad enough to be turned down on this account.

First priority at Fort Worth was given to the creation of a special kind of setting. We had no interest in the usual notions about having a good "institutional climate." My attitude about this is that an "institutional climate" is by its nature not good for people. We wanted instead a dramatically different feeling, one characterized by warmth, excitement, and a strong sense of purpose shared by residents and staff alike. Mutuality was the key. Our plan was to be casual about nonessentials like haircuts, manner of dress, and use of the staff's first name by residents, but very stringent about important matters such as responsible behavior with regard to drugs and sex, considerate conduct toward others, and hard work toward achievement of established goals.

An almost palpable mystique evolved from this emphasis. This mystique, which all who visit for a while will attest to, may or may not be here to stay, because it is fragile and temperamental. It pulses strongly at times. At other times it seems almost to abandon us, but it has not and it must not, because if the FCI Fort Worth idea is to work, this psychic factor must be functioning at all times in some form and at a reasonable level of strength.

Recently I referred to this special FCI Fort Worth feeling as the "unprogram." My colleagues and I agreed that we have a great "unprogram," but some questions were raised about how the program was coming.

It's very hard to be tough minded and systematic while at the same time maintaining a high level of spontaneity and spirit. Initial enthusiasms wane and people want to know what's been done for them lately. At the end of summer in 1973, I came back to Fort Worth after an absence of two and a half weeks and noticed a decided heaviness about the place. I learned there had been several escapes. Also, we had been boasting about not having had a reportable assault since the institution opened two years before, and thus my spirits were hardly raised when we had three assaults in 10 days during September of 1973. None of the assaults were serious, but I began to have some real concerns over whether we might be losing the unique spirit that had characterized FCI Fort Worth.

The honeymoon was obviously over. Would we be able to sustain the mystique or would we lapse into an institutionalized pattern that would bring to us the passive hostility that permeates so many institutional settings, and with it all the other pathology? By the experience of the months that followed, I became more convinced than ever that the concepts we relied on were sound. We were able to get it together. It was hard, and it continues to be hard, but when the components of what we are trying to preserve are understood and the need is recognized, the hard work is tremendously rewarding.

Two factors seemed to have contributed to the flagging spirits and the accompanying uncharacteristic tension among the residents. I am enough of a Skinnerian to realize that feelings between people come about and are sustained by the way they behave. We, the staff, were not behaving the same. We had grown weary during the long, hot second summer of our life. We weren't keeping the faith. We weren't applying the concepts with the same determination. We were coming up with new ideas but not moving with them. We weren't communicating with residents and line staff with the same level of energy and enthusiasm. And some of us were absent, on trips and vacations, while some of us had been reassigned to other institutions.

Aggravating the situation was our population's increase to almost 550 residents. At that time and at other times we have noticed something like a critical mass effect which besets us every time the count goes over 535. From our experience it seems that 536 is one too many people for the concept to work.

In addition to having an excellent Central Office and Regional Office Support, FCI Fort Worth has been aided greatly by its colleagues at Texarkana, Leavenworth, La Tuna, and elsewhere. They have suffered chronic overcrowding in their own institutions, while deferring transfers to Fort Worth whenever asked to do so. This has permitted us to keep the population under 535 most of the time during the past 12 months. The significance of the Fort Worth experiment seems to be recognized by key Bureau of Prisons staff throughout the system. It furthermore appears to be understood that if FCI Fort Worth should go sour, it could go very sour. What I've said here is that we have to work very hard and that we also "need a little help from our friends."

During the first two years at FCI Fort Worth, programs tumbled into existence on top of each other. Some of them expired all but unnoticed. Others have thrived and acquired something akin to traditional status. In subsequent months there has been less spontaneity in the development of program ideas, but those coming on now may prove to be the strongest. When ideas are proposed which will need a share of our resources, we are asking that the proposal be put in written form with an evaluation component included. This is a serious deficiency in much that we are doing now.

During this less spontaneous but more systematic phase, the functional units have made great improvements in program development. To describe the work of the functional units, even in outline form, would require far more space than is available here. Three of the units have some form of level system which ties preferred housing and other privileges to goal achievement and responsible behavior. Undue ardor in subscribing to one particular treatment modality is discouraged at FCI Fort Worth. We have not objected, however, to primary reliance on a given approach such as the emphasis on reality therapy in the NARA Unit or the plans now under way to institute a counseling program based on the "functional helping" idea in the women's program. It seems clear, however, that the units are most comfortable with an eclectic approach in the development of programs. We have encouraged constructive competition between the units in program development. This competition is at times rather vigorous, but it appears to contribute to rather than detract from esprit de corps among all unit personnel.

In addition to the unit manager, caseworkers, and education specialists, each unit has four correctional counselors. These employees, most of whom were previously correctional officers, play an extremely important role in setting the tone of the unit. They have the greatest exposure to the residents and perform a wide variety of duties ranging from routine problem solving to crisis intervention. Most of them also are involved in some formal group and individual counseling.

One of the unfortunate by-products of our heavy involvement in community programs, especially with respect to furloughs, has been an escalation of the paper work demands on unit personnel. Data gathering requirements add to this load. This factor, together with the responsibilities unit staff have for making the tough yes-and-no decisions affecting the residents, results in a certain amount of strain between residents and unit staff. Unhappily, caseworkers and counselors, who are on the front line, frequently must wear the black hat. On the balance, however, relationships between residents and unit staff are excellent.

Not previously mentioned is FCI Fort Worth's therapeutic community, which stands independent of the other units. Some 25 to 30 men residents are members of the community. The staff consists of a caseworker and a unit manager who also serves as mental health coordinator for the institution. About 10 women residents participate in this program on a live-out basis. The name the community chose for itself, *The Alternative,* refuses to catch on and thus it is generally referred to as 4-4 (because of its fourth floor location in 4 building).

Modeled after Dr. Marty Groder's Asklepieion Community at the Federal Penitentiary at Marion, the 4-4 Community utilizes transactional analysis (TA) and the Synanon game in combination with other approaches. Significant roles, in the form of training and leadership, have been filled by ex-Marion inmates who were products of the Asklepieion Community there. One of these residents attained his Provisional Teaching Membership in the International Transactional Analysis Association while serving as Training Coordinator for the 4-4 Community. About 30 men and women from the Fort Worth-Dallas area come into the institution on Monday evenings for training in TA and for participation in 4-4 groups.

The 4-4 Community is an impressive program. Unfortunately, since its residents start out in one of the other units, releasees from the community were "lost" in the Bureau's information system and thus have not been identified as a separate group in the follow-up data that has been accumulated. Our hope is to back up and get the necessary data. I believe it will confirm the impression we have that 4-4 releasees are doing very well.

All unit personnel are urged to stay familiar with the great variety of activities and opportunities available and to encourage residents to find the right combination for themselves. Needs must be identified and goals established, but except for objective goals requiring specific study and training, the means of achieving the goals should depend on the inclinations of the individual. But since the inclination of some residents would be to do as little as possible, it is good to build in some short-term payoffs. We have not objected to reasonably devised operant motivation, but when there is a wide choice of options there is greater likelihood that the resident will find constructive activities which of themselves bring satisfaction.

But we should not insist that everything be done for a specific purpose. While we believe in correctional programming based on the establishment of goals, there is also something to be said for being able to do things because you want to. The other evening I went to see a play that set off a deep reaction within me, lifted my spirits, and I think made me a better person. And I am better for having had the choice of going to that play or spending the evening in some other way.

I will comment on some of the activities available to FCI Fort Worth residents.

The Nurture Group Program, a chapel-related activity, takes 20 to 30 residents out of the institution every week to participate in structured small group discussion and socializing in the homes of local church members. The spectrum of religious groups involved ranges from Seventh Day Adventists to Black Muslims.

The Volunteers to the Community Program sponsors a cadre of residents who work without pay from eight to 20 hours a week for nearby social agencies and charitable organizations. Those who belong to this activity have a weekly rap session, and new members must acquire the endorsement of the group before being approved for a volunteer assignment in the community.

Seven Steps, an organization that has been viewed with suspicion by correctional people, has been a good program here. The outside leadership is provided largely by ex-offenders. FCI Fort Worth Seven Steppers work actively in the community with the Dallas County Juvenile Courts and with the Sheriff's Department in supplying drug abuse information and participating in rap sessions with the clientele of those agencies.

FCI residents, primarily those in the STAR Unit, have their own *Alcoholics Anonymous Chapter,* assisted by AA members from local communities. The residents also make regular trips to AA meetings in town, and periodically some of them attend out-of-town AA retreats. Residents participate similarly in *Toastmaster Club* activities at the institution and in the community.

The Fish House is another in a whole array of chapel-related activities. Operated jointly by residents and volunteers from local churches, it runs a coffee house every Friday evening featuring music, poetry, and drama.

Virtually no staff direction is provided, but there has been much staff and staff family participation. From 150 to 200 residents show up at the Fish House on Friday evenings.

The Gospel Choir has become an institution in itself at FCI Fort Worth. In addition to singing regularly at protestant services, the choir makes at least one guest appearance in the community each month and is able to select from many invitations. The membership of the choir is predominantly black but has never been totally black. The choir not only makes wonderful music, it also provides a valuable structured group activity for its members.

The Hen House had its beginning when staff wives met with women residents before Christmas in 1972 and again last year to bake cookies. Mailing homemade cookies home from prison at Christmastime seemed to us like a good departure from the usual. On other occasions women residents have gone by ones and twos into the kitchens of staff wives and worked with them in preparing their favorite recipes for special occasions at the institution. The Hen House meets once a month, giving women residents a regular opportunity to be with their friends among the staff wives. They spend the evening sewing, knitting, and talking together.

The Change Agent Course is typical of the activities that sprang up spontaneously during the first year and a half and later evolved into a structured part of a formal program. It consists of resident-led instructional sessions on the basics of the more popular approaches to counseling and personality development: functional helping, reality therapy, and transactional analysis. This activity has had a remarkably positive impact on the population. It is now one of the Education Department's regular social education offerings.

A former resident instructor was recently engaged to come back into the institution two evenings a week to run advanced Change Agent sessions. Emphasis in this program is on learning to help oneself by helping others. Another ex-resident is employed 20 hours a week as instructor in an *Achievement Motivation Program,* designed to point new residents in the right direction in their use of the opportunities available to them at FCI Fort Worth.

Other Education Department courses in the social education area range from Hatha and Kundalini yoga to *Career Survival,* a training package aimed toward turning residents on to academic and vocational training opportunities. Basic academics and vocational needs have not been neglected. FCI Fort Worth has a 50-carrel training center, a 12-carrel learning laboratory, and a resource library that includes more than 5,000 tapes and program instruction sets. A major part of the instructional work is done by contract teachers who are employed for 20 to 30 hours per week.

We do not offer very much in-house vocational training. Residents go out on work/study placements to the Fort Worth Skill Center, Elkins Institute, business colleges, and the Tarrant County Junior College, which is adjacent to the FCI. The Texas Vocational Rehabilitation Commission helps finance much of this training. Tarrant County Junior College has an excellent variety of vocational training courses, in addition to its two-year academic track. The energy crisis inspired us to obtain about a dozen bicycles, and this is the usual mode of transportation for our residents who are students at the TCJC campus. TCJC also offers college courses at FCI for those not eligible to attend classes on campus.

During the first year FCI established a relationship with organized labor which has developed into a significant program. The director of the AFL-CIO's Human Resources Development Institute (HRDI) Office in Fort Worth indicated an interest in working with our Education Department in developing construction trades training for

FCI residents, leading to union membership. During the first year the Construction Trades Council of Fort Worth, through HRDI, provided instructors for courses in carpentry and ironworking. We were able to enlist the help of Texas Vocational Rehabilitation in paying instructors' salaries. FCI provided the facilities, materials, and clientele. HRDI coordinated the program, in conjunction with FCI Education Department Staff.

At present this program offers training in three trade areas with plans to expand to a fourth. All costs are paid by a Labor Department grant obtained through the Texas Criminal Justice Council by HRDI. This funding allowed HRDI to employ a full-time coordinator, clerical support, and a monthly stipend for trainees. The funding is not likely to be renewed for a second year, but we expect to continue the program in some manner. It is significant because it represents a breakthrough in our relationship with organized labor. The absence of a working agreement between corrections and organized labor has greatly reduced the value of many excellent training programs in correctional settings throughout the country.

Those of us who have toiled for the Federal Bureau of Prisons for a long time were encouraged by the results of a study done by BOP research staff and published in April of 1974. It shows that over 67% of federal offenders released in 1970 did not become recidivists for two years following their release. While differences in methodology prevent exact comparison, it should be noted the success rate reported in this study is extremely close to the 65% success rate that Dr. Glaser reported for federal prison releasees in 1956.[5]

FCI Fort Worth has some follow-up data of its own on residents released since the opening of the institution. While the current success rate is substantially higher than the 67% figure reported by the recent Bureau of Prisons recidivism study, it is not a comparable figure. Our sample is relatively small and included residents who had been in the community from seven months to 28 months. There are other factors related to the population characteristics of Fort Worth that prevent valid comparisons between our follow-up figures and the Bureau of Prisons' 67% success rate. For example, FCI Fort Worth has about 100 alcoholic offenders and an even greater number of heroin addicts, both high risk groups. On the other hand, women and older offenders tend to be low risks.

To get a good picture, we obviously need a great deal more in the way of follow-up, as well as analysis and evaluation of the follow-up data on hand. We do, however, have cohorts parallel to one group of offenders at FCI Fort Worth and similar offenders elsewhere in the Bureau of Prisons institutions. I refer to those offenders committed under Title II of the Narcotic Addict Rehabilitation Act of 1966. With these offenders more data is required to be submitted from the beginning of their imprisonment. This enabled us to make a direct comparison. The data show that NARA offenders released from FCI Fort Worth, all of them heroin addicts, were remaining in the community at a 24% better rate than like offenders coming out of other Bureau of Prisons NARA Programs. The FCI Fort Worth sample is very small. Also there may be cultural factors related to our predominantly Mexican-American group as opposed to the Puerto Ricans and blacks who predominate in other programs.

Taking these possibly modifying factors into account and conceding the likelihood of other unanticipated factors, it appears to me that the difference reflected by these factors is worthy of attention. It could be reduced by half and still be considerable. To understand the possible implications of these data, however, it is necessary to consider the fact that during the time span covered by our follow-up survey the Fort Worth NARA program was decidely less sophisticated and less well developed than other NARA programs located in Federal Bureau of Prisons institutions elsewhere. My belief is that we may be looking at an important piece of evidence that *the setting in which a program functions is more important than the program itself.*

With or without empirical evidence I believe this to be true. I believe the total sum of the experience that confined offenders have during all their waking hours must, on the balance, be positive if a prison sentence is to be anything but destructive.

We cannot afford to accept as inevitable the pathological influences that characterize prisons. Radical innovations are needed to eliminate them. Beyond this, strong and pervasive programs are needed to offer opportunities and meet special needs. And we should provide a range of choices that takes into account the infinite variety of differences between people, including those we casually label sociopaths and persons with character disorders.

It would be too much to ask the person in charge of an undertaking like FCI Fort Worth—one that wasn't given much of a chance for survival by some—to do other than emphasize the positive in an article like this. But it must be said that we do not view co-corrections or the accompanying concepts that characterize the Fort Worth program as a panacea. We have had all kinds of problems not discussed in detail here. Some of our critics remain unconvinced that we can have such a program and not have serious problems with escape, rampant sexual misconduct, and contraband drug use. While we have had some difficulties in these areas, we consider other problems to be more important. Four Bureau of Prisons institutions had higher escape rates than we did during the first half of this year, and the escape rate at Fort Worth was down 20% in Fiscal Year 1974 over the previous year. Evidence of inordinate contraband drug use is conspicuous by its absence and, as discussed, the sexual conduct of the residents at Fort Worth is by and large commendable.

My view is that our main problem is related to the way we work with women residents. I don't think it can be seriously questioned that our women are in a much healthier situation here than in conventional all-women's facilities. But despite some rather glowing instances of self-discovery, my fear is that the women at FCI Fort Worth, as a group, are not gaining benefits commensurate with what their presence contributes to the setting. The women are highly visible, and either because of the severity of their problems, their winsomeness, or sometimes their sheer energy, they are being helped, in some cases dramatically.

But many of the more passive women aren't being reached. The women's group has persistently lacked cohesiveness. It has been suggested that a strong "consciousness raising" effort is sorely needed, but this is a notion that has remarkably little appeal to our women. I am not all sure that doctrinaire "women's lib" ideas are compatible with the FCI Fort Worth philosophy, but we need to find a formula that enable our women residents to receive all the dimensions of help they need. I am sure that one negative factor is the 4-to-1 ratio of men to women. This is a likely cause of our tendency to indulge the women on the one hand and to deny them equal opportunities on the other. A 3-to-2 ratio would be better.

Maintenance of the long-neglected physical plant we inherited is another problem made more difficult by the heavy involvement of our residents in programs and by the fact that we have an entire unit of male offenders who have physical limitations. In addition to this we have problems with poor communications, excessive paperwork, and other staff burdens resulting in less responsiveness to the needs of our residents than we should have. We also have problems in monitoring the utilization of resident time and in managing a work and study release program that puts 15% of the population all over the Fort Worth/Dallas Metroplex every day of the week. And we have the problem of developing the trust and support we need from some of our colleagues in the Federal Criminal Justice family, some of whom have misgivings about our approach to working with confined offenders. We think we see improvements, but we must confess our performance in these areas has been mediocre at best.

We are nonetheless encouraged by the FCI Fort Worth venture at this juncture. More time is needed before its significance can be fully assessed, but my belief is that some things important to corrections have been demonstrated. I do not suggest that FCI Fort Worth ideas are widely applicable in all correctional settings, but it has been shown that dramatic changes can be made in the way we run institutions, without loss of control.

A major deterrent to progress is the fear that innovations will result in a loss of control or in some way compromise security. Typically, innovative efforts in institutional corrections are tolerated, sometimes encouraged and supported, if they are kept on a small to moderate scale and are not allowed to have too great an impact on the operation of the prison. My suspicion is that this is one of the reasons that innovative corrections haven't been able to demonstrate much success.

I submit that we need innovations that have an enormous impact on the operation of prisons. We are concerned about upsetting the staff, but what we sometimes need most is to upset the staff, to get them excited, and to let them begin to see that the work they do may not be so futile after all. But it is at the same time necessary to be extremely cautious about the way we install innovations. Radicalism should be implemented conservatively. The innovator cannot afford the luxury of foolishness, but this kind of caution doesn't retard success. If we examine some of the old shibboleths we have sworn by for years, we will see how foolish some of them are. Logic is on the side of change, and if the correctional process is to serve its purpose, surely we must know that change is imperative.

Notes

1. Levinson, R. G., & Gerard, R. E. Functional units: A different correctional approach. *Federal Probation*, December 1973.

2. Narcotic Addict Rehabilitation Act of 1966, Title II.

3. Sister Esther Heffernan, Ph.D., the author of *Making it in prison*, has been involved in a comprehensive research effort at FCI since March 1973. Her report was completed in November 1974.

4. Giallombardo, R. *Society of women: A study of a women's prison.* New York: Wiley, 1966.

5. Glaser, D. *The effectiveness of a prison and parole system.* New York: Bobbs-Merrill, 1964.

Chapter 4

A COED PRISON
Esther Heffernan
Elizabeth Krippel

The basic criteria for admission to Federal Correctional Institution (FCI), Fort Worth, are that a man or woman be within two years of a probable release date, qualify for participation in one of the functional Unit Programs, have no record of violent behavior, and be from the South-Central region of the United States. Exceptions have been made, however, in regard to each of these criteria, most notably the last. Within these guidelines, the roads to FCI Fort Worth are many and varied.

In the summer of 1973, approximately 60% of the residents were "transfers" from other institutions in the federal system. Most had applied for admission to Fort Worth to take part in one of the treatment programs or simply to be closer to home. For a few, these officially "acceptable" reasons masked the hope of "doing easy time." In other cases transfers were initiated by the staff at the other institutions, primarily for reasons of health and age. The other 40% of the resident population was committed to Fort

Worth directly from federal courts. For many of these it was their first commitment to a correctional facility.

Few residents arriving at Fort Worth are totally unaware of the fact that the institution is unique in many respects. Widely reputed along the grapevine as "the best place to do time—if you have to do time," FCI's coed setting, its opportunities for passes, furloughs, and work or study release, and sometimes the treatment orientation of its programs are discussed with prospective residents in county jails and federal prisons across the country. Nothing, however, seems to prepare them fully for the reality that greets them.

In terms of physical layout and security measures, FCI Fort Worth seems typical of institutions officially listed by the Federal Bureau of Prisons as "intermediate term facilities for adults." Located on the fringes of the city's southwest side, its yellow stone buildings with their red tile roofs are easily visible from Interstate 820 to the south or Seminary Drive which borders it on the north. An eight-foot fence rims the property and encloses within its protective shield not only the main institution but two groups of staff housing and the remnants of the dairy farm that once gave the facility its still more widely known name, "the narcotics farm." The five main buildings cluster around a pleasant yard with a healthy and surprisingly undisturbed flower garden in the center and colorful park benches located at various points in the yard.

A 12-foot fence surrounds these buildings and is topped with electrical wiring that allows for surveillance from a large panel in the control room. Just outside the fence at intervals of about 50 yards there are powerful perimeter lights for use in guarding the institution at night. To almost no one's displeasure, these have never been fully utilized because of the energy crisis which surfaced just as the installation was completed. Standard security measures also include closed-circuit television cameras which keep a watchful eye on all who pass into or out of the administration building. Residents expressed some initial dismay and fear that "this is going to be just like any other joint" when these were installed. Now they have forgotten that such security measures are present.

SOCIAL RELATIONSHIPS

Social relationships, especially with one's fellow residents, play a significant role in the life of almost every resident. Eighty-five percent of those interviewed maintain that "going it alone" is just not possible at FCI: "a lot of people come here with the idea that that's how they'll do their time but they change. Only those who are real loners on the outside stick with it." "You can't go it alone here—at least not for very long. The atmosphere is such that you really can't keep to yourself."

While acknowledging the need for people in their lives, most residents are very cautious in picking their associates. Many, in fact, state that they prefer to use the term "acquaintances" rather than "friends" to describe their relationships. In some instances, this is simply one of the realities of prison existence. "It's pretty hard to make real friends in prison. People are never the kind of people inside that they are outside." For others, having "acquaintances only" is a protective device.

> There are people I talk to, but I don't tell anyone my business and I *certainly* don't want to know anyone else's. That will get you into trouble every time. Suppose a guy tells you that he's messing with drugs and then he gets caught—he'll accuse *you* of being the snitch.

It is also seen as a way of protecting oneself from another "danger":

> I wouldn't say I have friends here, but there are a couple of people I can talk to. I think one of the big reasons why so many people leave and come right back is that they miss their

old friends. That's one reason I don't want to get too close to
anyone here.

Even in the case of "acquaintanceships," however,
there is some degree of involvement, and the question which
needs to be answered is "What is it about Fort Worth that
makes "going it alone" almost impossible even for people
who came with the intention of doing so?" Undoubtedly,
the answer is found in the multiplicity of relationships
available in an environment which not only allows for but
encourages their development. Unlike other institutional
settings in which relationships tend to be structured by
adaptive patterns to the deprivation of "normal" affective
relationships, Fort Worth provides normal opportunities
for relationships because of its heterogeneous population,
its co-correctional environment, and its extensive contact
with the outside community.

CO-CORRECTIONS

This quality is most clearly reflected in the comments of
some residents who see the presence of members of the
opposite sex as a definite plus: "It makes it more like the
outside world to talk with the men and see them around all
the time." "It makes time go faster and easier because you
don't think about the streets and home so much." "It's good
to see all the pretty ladies around—it helps morale!"

Not only does it contribute to a generally pleasant and
normal atmosphere, the coed setting is also seen as a key
factor in reducing the number of problematic relationships
traditionally associated with prison life: "Anyone who has
done time in a real joint will tell you that homosexuality is
the biggest source of trouble. Here that seems to be almost
completely eliminated." "Having women around just
makes the place alive. You don't see the dudes dragging
along, not caring how they look, always on edge or looking

for a fight over some little thing." Seventy percent of the residents think the co-correctional setting is clearly a positive factor.

Although not actually negative in their reactions, 19% of the residents indicate that they have mixed feelings about the coed setting.

> For some it's a very good thing; for others it simply opens up a whole new set of problems. People like ——— can gain a great deal. Women have always been the source of his problems, and here he has had to learn new patterns of behavior and new types of relationships with women. I'm sure there are women who need the same kind of help in their relationships with men.

When strongly negative feelings are expressed, the reasons are almost invariably related to the difficulties of adhering to the rules on physical contact; in effect, these "normal relationships" are not "normal" enough! "Its a bad scene, man! The women are like the flowers out in the yard—for decorative purposes only! It's one of the things that beats you for your brains around here." A woman expresses much the same feeling: "I like being around the men but it's just too hard. The rules on physical contact are unreal, and they change from one policeman to another."

There are a few, of course, who maintain that the limitations on association are not strict enough.

> Eating with them [the women] is OK, I guess, and things like that, but that should be ALL.

> There'd be a lot less drugs and alcohol around here if this wasn't coed. The women are always egging the men on to get stuff for them.

If the co-correctional setting provides an atmosphere of normalcy, it does so because it multiplies the number of affective relational opportunities usually available within a prison environment; acquaintanceships, friendships, or group affiliation may be either single-sex or heterosexual relationships.

Single-sex relationships, whether among men or among women, tend to develop between those who are of the same race, approximately the same age, and who share a similar background in criminal history, previous commitment, and social status.

A resident's approval of the co-correctional environment at Fort Worth does not necessarily mean that he or she is involved in any of the various forms heterosexual relationships may take. Nor, on the other hand, does a resident's disapproval of the coed setting imply noninvolvement in such relationships. Only 11% of the residents, all of them men, state that they have "steered clear" of any contact with the opposite sex. Another 21%, one of whom is a woman, indicate that their communication is generally limited to "passing the time of day" with those they happen to meet on their jobs, in class, or waiting on line in the mess hall. For 68%, however, the relationships between men and women play an integral role in their lives at Fort Worth.

FORMS OF RELATIONSHIPS

In general, there are six forms of heterosexual relationship at Fort Worth. The first is friendship. Interestingly enough, it appears that there are two major sources of friendship between a man or woman in a group situation. For men and women with intact marriages, co-corrections provide a more real atmosphere where they can enjoy the supportive companionship of the other sex while the control structures provide a normative support that protects the marital status of the participants. For women who have had a history of prostitution, and for men who have served long stretches without contact with women or in the role of pimp, the friendship provides a comfortable means of exploring non-exploitive ways of relating to the other sex.

The second set of rules might be described as "protective uncle" or "mothering aunt" relationships. When a young woman arrives at Fort Worth she frequently is rather overwhelmed with the advances made, and will accept the support of an older man in an uncle role. The support is mutual, because like the friendship role, the uncle role provides an older man with an opportunity to move into relationships with women in a noncompetitive and non-demanding way, while for the younger woman it allows breathing space and a time to determine if there are younger men with whom she would like to associate, or with whom she would prefer to remain merely a companion.

The "mothering role" was described by one of the women as follows: "There are some very lonely people here, especially older men. I have all the romance I need outside, so I spend quite a lot of my time with the older fellows." Again, it provides mutual support without any obligations.

The third form of relationship is direct dating, and like its counterpart on the outside, it is entered into by both partners with a variety of intentions. In some cases friendships develop into dating relationships, and rather casual companionships become very intense without either partner originally intending it so.

However, among the residents there are a set of cautionary norms about becoming too emotionally involved, since "prison romances never work." Persons are warned that when "the other" goes out first the relationship ceases, because "they want to forget what went on inside" or "they have so many other choices on the street." One of the women who was in the original Alderson transfer mentioned that "most guys are married, the chance of meeting and marrying is slim, and the 'getting down' here is just humiliating and degrading, and women are just being used."

From several of the interviews it appears that as the

balance shifts from the predominance of women who transferred from other institutions to those who come directly from the courts, there is an increase in the amount and intensity of sexual involvement. This is another area of "messing around" in which the presence of older transfer residents plays a critical role: It is their pressure on new residents not to jeopardize the "good things going at Fort Worth," rather than external controls, that are the most effective in controlling sexual behavior.

The fourth form of relationship involves the residents at Fort Worth who are married. In an attempt to keep marital bonds intact, a real effort is made to affect the transfer of the other partner to the institution. In some cases the transfer has had the desired outcome, but in others the presence of intervening relationships may set the stage for another transfer, or a very strained situation. This is an area in which the adaptive norms to control heterosexual behavior within the institution are not clear-cut:

> Here there is a direct normative conflict between the institutional regulations (which have been developed with the legal and community moral standards in mind regarding both pre-marital and extra-marital relations) and the whole questions of marital rights. This is a critical question which has not been resolved in single-sex institutions either, and state legislatures vary in their willingness to allow visitation privileges and furloughs. Are marital rights forfeited with the commission of an offense? Can institutions for internal regulatory reasons have the right to restrict family contacts? There have not been any precise answers to these questions within either the State or Federal systems, and they pose an even greater problem at Fort Worth. The staff, the couples involved and the other residents are normatively ambivalent. General conjugal relations are seen as a violation of regulations—and therefore serious—but at the same time as not "wrong"—and therefore not subject to the same formal and informal sanctions which cover other violations. As a result an informal "double standard" seems to have evolved which does not appear to be destructive of the normative

structures, but which will remain a point of tension until there is some resolution of this conflict of rights.

The fifth and sixth relational roles are exploitive and appear to be played by relatively few residents. The first is a "commissary companionship" in which older men are willing to "pay for" a companion to sit with in the dining room and chat with in the yard. In reality it may not be as exploitive as some observers assume, since in time it may move to a form of "uncle" relationship. For women who have lived by prostitution it represents a very nondemanding trick, and for the men it provides enough practice in talking to women to establish a confidence to move to a relationship with a noneconomic basis.

And finally, there is a very limited amount of prostitution at Fort Worth. In most cases it appears to be a part of the reaction of women committed directly from the courts with a background of prostitution who respond initially to a ready market, and only later are able to shift to one of the alternative life-styles available.

In addition to the heterosexual relationships arising in a co-correctional situation, some of the men and women who have been involved for a relatively long time in prison homosexuality continue their relationships at Fort Worth, but without the coercive physical or psychological pressures that typify the single-sex institution. However, one of the women noted that "there are very few lesbians, the ones that are here have men who are helping them turn around."

That final comment, however, on "men helping them turn around," leads to a more critical aspect of the effect of co-corrections on the women at Fort Worth. While to some extent the situation at Fort Worth is simply an extension of the larger question of the role of women in society, there are certain ways in which prison intensifies these issues. As a result of the sex ratio, there is pressure for each woman to become a walk partner. Women who do not wish to participate tend to withdraw to the unit, but there are not enough of them to develop any cooperative or cohesive programs within the women's unit itself. As the women move into the walk partner relationship, they also tend to enter programs that reflect the interests of the men with whom they are involved. While the programs themselves may be valuable, the women's histories of criminal involvement are often related to the activities of their husbands or lovers, and this dependency relationship is simply continued in the prison.

Although one of the values of co-corrections in an institution like Fort Worth is that men and women can relate to each other in diverse settings, its unintentional result is that the women have no "program" of their own in which they can develop leadership roles and cohesive structures that would provide them with alternate life-styles.

Chapter 5

A STUDY OF A COEDUCATIONAL CORRECTIONAL FACILITY

The Massachusetts Correctional Institution at Framingham

Linda Almy, Vikki Bravo, Leslie Burd, Patricia Chin, Linda Cohan, Frank Gallo, Anthony Giorgianni, Jeffrey Gold, Mark Jose, John Noyes

The exploratory results of our study of the Massachusetts Correctional Institution at Framingham will be discussed in three general categories: perceptions of social climate, perceptions of programs, and perceptions of the coed nature of Framingham.

PERCEPTIONS OF SOCIAL CLIMATE

The results of the communication and information flow section seem to substantiate what McCleery (1961) had to say about communication systems in an authoritarian system: that any endeavor to maintain both an authoritarian system and conditions of equality among inmates involves inherent contradictions. The men at Framingham feel that there was better communication between themselves and staff at their former all-male institutions, and this indicates something of a breakdown of communication in the less structured setting at Framingham. This conclusion is borne out also in their response that rules are more explicit in the more structured setting.

McCleery talks about information being valued in a structured setting in such a way that an informal hierarchy is formed among the inmates in which "information" is equated with "power." So in essence there are actually two systems operating at the same time. At Framingham this does not seem to be as evident, as McCleery has suggested. With the easing of structure, inmates at Framingham feel more able to share in decisions about how the institution is run.

On the subject of punishment and reward, inmates of both sexes, whether at Framingham or elsewhere, seem to agree that the staff will punish them if they mess up in some way. Likewise, there seems to be little difference between men and women at Framingham in their reluctance to take punitive action against other inmates if they feel he or she has done something wrong. The responses to these two statements seem to be more of a reflection of inmates' perceptions of authority and how they relate to it, rather than a reflection of how they view and relate to each other as members of an oppressed group.

Although males and females at Framingham agree that there is little chance of other inmates punishing them for infractions, the fact that nearly four times as many males feel this would happen in their former institutions tends to be consistent with the literature review. For example, Studt (1968) talks about inmates using their own patterns to maintain order in the C-unit system, while Grusky (1959) talks about the differences in prison structure being related to differences in the informal inmate structure. Again this tends to point out the differences between the inmate subculture at Framingham and that of the male institution from which the Framingham inmate came.

Generally, inmates believed that neither staff nor other inmates rewarded them for good behavior, although the women responded positively to this statement twice as often as the men. To understand why this is so, perhaps it would help to have a clearer definition of the word *reward* as it pertains to the men and women. Men "rewarding" other men is apt to take on a negative connotation compared with women "rewarding" women.

Twice as many women as men also tend to agree that inmates tell other inmates when they think he or she has done well. The sharp rise in positive responses to the staff telling inmates that they've done well seems to indicate that praise from an authority figure is more acceptable to both men and women. The fact that more than twice as many men agreed with the statement when applied to Framingham tends to indicate that there is less suspicion about staff/inmate relationships at Framingham than there is at the all-male sending institutions.

Whether at Framingham or elsewhere, men almost unanimously agree that staff is concerned with keeping them under control, while slightly more than one-half of the women felt that way. This finding is consistent with the perception that men are dealt with more harshly than women when it comes to disciplinary matters at Framingham. This discrepancy may reflect the stereotyped male drive for independence, while the women may be more accepting of the stereotyped submissive role relegated to them.

More than twice as many men at Framingham than those at former institutions believe the staff is concerned with helping them with their problems. This feeling may reflect their reluctance to associate themselves with staff at all-male maximum security prisons, where this type of behavior is considered as "selling out." Grosser (1960), Clemmer (1958), and Korn and McCorkle (1954) all refer to the need for inmates to dissociate themselves from staff in order to survive in a maximum security prison. Men tend to differentiate themselves from staff to a greater extent in the all-male maximum security prisons.

In the maximum security prison, inmates are much more apt to push other inmates around, consistent with the various roles in the system described by Sykes (1958). It is interesting to note that on the question of "inmates pushing other inmates around," the large discrepancy between male responses about Framingham compared with those about their former institutions tends to verify the different nature of the inmate subculture at Framingham. Although it is generally agreed by both sexes that inmates are just interested in doing their time, the women did not feel quite as strongly about this as the men did.

Inmates' relationships with the outside community appear to be contingent upon their frame of reference. Men tend to view their relationship with the outside community in more positive terms. Two out of three women at Framingham felt that the outside community looks down on them, as did nearly three out of four of the men when they were in their former all-male institutions. However, only little more than one-third of the men at Framingham felt this way. Since men are sent to Framingham mainly for prerelease programs, they tend to spend more time out in the community, are more comfortable there, and apparently enjoy a better rapport with the people. This notion is borne out somewhat by the Framingham men's tendency to view the people on the outside as more helpful in securing jobs and getting into community groups and educational programs. This aspect of the Framingham program seems to be consistent with the view of Carter et al. (1972) that correctional institutions should extend outside the traditional institutions and into the community. Studt et al.

(1968) also suggested that prisons should be transitional so that a "continuum" can be formed with the greater community.

Along with the lessening of structure and more community involvement, the men at Framingham almost unanimously feel that they have some control over planning their future in the community. While approximately one-third of the inmates at Framingham feel the community will punish them if they screw up, two-thirds of the women feel that the community will also tell them if they do well. The men at Framingham are split 50-50 on this statement, a fact indicating that the women see the community as slightly more responsive to their efforts than the men.

Women tend to think people in the community are more concerned with keeping them under control than with helping them with their problems. The men at Framingham do not share this view—perhaps a reflection of their positive experience as part of the prerelease program. However, the men shared the womens' perception when applied to the sending male institution. This same reasoning prevails in that approximately 20% of women feel hassled by the outside community, while none of the men there feel hassled. Almost all of those interviewed agreed that it's hard to tell inmates apart from other people when they are out in the community, thereby confirming that inmates feel that they are seen as ordinary people while in community programs, not as freaks with two heads or any other distinguishing abnormalities to set them apart from the rest of society.

The remaining 17 items of the social climate scale will now be discussed. As above, interpretation of the data will refer to the literature review of one-sex prisons. Conclusions will first be drawn about individual items, and then about this section as a whole.

In general, a large majority of respondents reported that inmates help new inmates get adjusted to the institution. This concern of "inmates helping inmates" was thought to be much more prevalent at Framingham than at the sending institutions. Studt (1968) described an inmate code to which new inmates are oriented in the original C-unit system. Apparently this practice of acclimating new inmates is also true of a co-education prison.

Evidence suggests that although almost all of the inmates are friendly, real friends are difficult to find, more so for women than for men. In this matter, men usually preferred Framingham to their former all-male institutions, where feelings about friendship were in all probability more negative. Clemmer's study (1958) of a male institution showed that at least 70% of his sample felt that friendships are brief and pragmatic, and that familiarity in prison breeds contempt. In a more relaxed environment such as Framingham, this is still true, but not to such a great extent. However, the women at Framingham may see this issue of friendship from a different perspective. Since most of them cannot compare Framingham to another prison, they are basing their opinion only on experiences on the outside.

According to the results of our questionnaire, the staff at Framingham was not judged to be dealing fairly with everyone; nor was the staff at the all-male sending institutions. Our results also indicate that, when asked to compare Framingham to their former institutions, many more men felt that some inmates get away with a lot while others can't get away with anything. This attitude could be attributed to the perception that men were treated more strictly than women at Framingham, whereas the rules were thought to be applied more uniformly to all inmates at the institutions from which they were transferred.

From the literature review, it seems that unequal treatment of inmates is quite common. Cloward (1960) states that the inmate elite are sometimes allowed certain infractions by the staff as a reward for helping the staff maintain control over other inmates. At any rate, it is clear that the staff's treatment of men and women is perceived as unequal by most inmates.

Inmates generally do not think of Framingham as

peaceful and orderly, but many more men than women agree that it is. It is likely that, by comparison, men experienced much more tension at their former all-male institutions, especially at Walpole. Every inmate in our sample who transferred from Walpole felt strongly about this. There could be many reasons for the inmates' failure to find peace and order in prison, especially in the all-male sending institutions. For example, Sykes and Messinger (1960) list six major deprivations of prison life. Grosser (1960) describes an inmate culture with social controls independent of official controls. Furthermore, Korn and McCorkle (1954) suggest that an inmate needs to be in conflict with the staff for psychological reasons. These factors may all contribute to feelings of tension and unrest in inmates at the sending institutions, and to some extent at Framingham.

Although only a minority of respondents felt that many inmates think they are too good for you, many more women than men felt this way. The evidence suggests that women are more likely than men to perceive a caste system and a certain amount of snobbery.

A minority of inmates, but more women than men, felt that inmates try to take advantage of you or fight you to get what they want. Our results indicate that more women may be on the defensive in their interaction with fellow inmates and that women are less supportive of one another. In women's prisons the literature indicates that much competition can result from the creation of social roles based on the homosexual subculture. Butches and femmes exploit each other to get what they want. As for men, there seems to be more exploitation of one another and fighting at their sending institutions. According to Sykes (1958), the inmate subculture of the maximum security male institution places a premium on the use of force, and stronger inmates often take advantage of weaker inmates. One major reason why less tension of this type is perceived by the men at

Framingham may be their frame of reference, that is, their sending institutions. Also, women may be reacting to one another's competition for men, which would result in less support for each other.

To the question of whether inmates show good judgment, there were mixed reactions. Most of the inmates answered negatively, while a significant part of the sample said that they were unsure or didn't know. There seems to be some uncertainty over exactly what constitutes good judgment. This whole question could be seen as vague in that good judgment would probably not have caused an inmate to do something resulted in his or her incarceration.

In contradiction to the previous items indicating a perceived lack of solidarity among women at Framingham, more men than women believe that inmates won't work together to get things done for the institution. Men were seen as more willing to get together at their previous institutions. If they were to spend a lot of time there, they cared enough to get things done for the institution. For women, Framingham is more "their" institution—men are like guests who can always be shipped back.

Connected with the issue of working together is the one of leadership among inmates. According to the results of the questionnaire, women are split nearly 50-50 on whether there are any leaders among inmates or whether there are a few inmates who run everything, while men seem to be more biased toward lack of leadership at Framingham. The opposite is true for men when asked about the institution they were transferred from. Evidence suggests that there is an element of leadership or elitism at the male institution which was not seen to the same degree by men at Framingham. This perception is not as clear-cut among females. It is very likely that men at Framingham perceive a different subculture at Framingham compared to their previous all-male institutions.

Further results to support this inference lie in the

question of peer pressure among inmates at Framingham. More women than men agreed that an inmate who insists on being different is given a bad name. On the other hand, most males said this was true of the institution they were transferred from. Findings suggest that there is more peer pressure among women at Framingham and men at other institutions, but that men are more individualistic at Framingham. This is further indication that there may not be a very distinct male subculture at Framingham, perhaps because they perceive themselves as being at the end of a long period of incarceration. In his study, Garabedian (1963) observed that cohesiveness among inmates diminished as they approached release.

In the remaining two items there is more evidence that men may feel more at ease at Framingham than they did at their sending institutions, and that women feel more hassled at Framingham. It is significant that half of the men in our sample felt that inmates mind their own business, and none felt that inmates get on your back for no reason. About one-third of the women agreed with both opinions.

The social climate at Framingham is seen by men as more relaxed than at one-sex prisons. There seems to be a much less rigid subculture for men than for women, who still seem to adhere to some of the roles described by Ward and Kassebaum (1965) and Giallombardo (1966). Generally, men perceive less peer pressure and less exploitation at Framingham than the women do, and less peer pressure and exploitation than at their former institutions. Friction among women seems to lie in the area of emotional interpersonal relationships.

In general, then, the men tend to have a much more positive perception of their fellow inmates as well as of the relationships among inmates. Again this may have been because the men used their former institutions as the frame of reference in responding to questions on the social climate scale. It is unlikely that the women had a comparable frame of reference. They may have responded to these items with a noninstitutional setting as their frame of reference.

PERCEPTIONS OF PROGRAMS

The inmates' perceptions of programs focused on four program areas—furloughs, work/education release, counseling, and cadre. In some cases it was possible to compare inmates' perceptions of programs with those of the staff, since the staff frequently expressed their views on programs in the course of the interviews that were conducted to elicit information for the descriptive section of the study.

FURLOUGH PROGRAM

The vast majority of the inmates viewed the furlough program as a positive one. This feeling was consistent with the staff's views on furloughs.

The goals that were stated by the administration for the furlough program were very much the same as the benefits that the inmates felt they derived from the program. The most positive goal expressed by both administration and inmates was that inmates could retain contact with the outside for a variety of reasons, such as maintaining bonds with family and friends and adjusting to the continuously changing outside world. Perhaps more men than women responded positively to the furlough program because a number of the women were new arrivals and had not yet qualified to participate in the program.

It appears there were no major complaints about the furlough program, other than that some of the minor rules appear too strict. This feeling could be due to the fact that at a less structured prison such as Framingham, greater demands for inner control are placed on the individual and that at maximum security prisons, inmates are not given as much responsibility for their own actions. Because Framingham offers more freedom, inmates are more responsible for upholding the rules that are laid down.

It is interesting that 70% of the inmates interviewed saw the furlough program as a privilege, while only 46% of the inmates saw the work and education release program as a privilege. This difference might be due to the inmates' feeling that a furlough is a "vacation," an enjoyable but infrequent privilege which they have to earn through positive behavior. On the other hand, work and education release might be seen as somewhat of an everyday chore and, therefore, less of a privilege.

Work/Education Release Program

The goals of the administration seem to coincide with the inmates' views on the positive value of the work/education release program. For example, both administration and inmates viewed the program's main benefit as reintegration with society. Approximately one-third of the inmates in the sample had been on work/education release, which is representative of the total population on work/education release.

The reason more men might have felt the work/education release program was administered fairly could be that the main purpose for which most men are sent to Framingham is to participate in this program. One of the benefits of the program stated by the inmates and seconded by the administration was that the institution gave them the support they needed to enable them to go out and find work.

Some of the concerns that the inmates felt about the program were also some of the concerns that the staff felt— for example, a shortage of jobs as a result of the unsound economy, inadequate transportation, and the 15% charge that the inmates are required to contribute to the state.

Counseling Program

Perhaps the reason that the counseling program evoked such strong emotional responses is that the counseling experience itself tends to be a strongly emotional one. Even those inmates not involved in counseling responded with strong affect to this question, seemingly reflecting the outside society's fears of being "mentally ill."

Because so many of the inmates (64%) said they have been in counseling, it is possible that inmates confused social service with DLM (Division of Legal Medicine Counseling Service). This could have been the result of imprecision in the questionnaire's definition of counseling. It is also possible that the inmates do not perceive a distinction between the functions of social service and counseling staff in the institution, and/or that there is so much overlap in the roles of social service and counseling staff that the distinction is, in fact, not clear.

Our question on inmates' perceptions of how the staff viewed counseling met with varying responses. Perhaps the inmates had no idea of how the staff really view it. However, their subjective responses provided some interesting data on the perceived relationship between correctional staff and counseling staff.

The various responses regarding the benefits of counseling could be compared to the general population's view, since those that are more motivated, in general, find counseling more helpful.

Cadre Program

One of the administration's reasons for bringing the cadre, a nucleus of older male inmates serving long prison terms, to Framingham was to add stability to the institution, whose inmates were sentences for 18 months on the average. This goal coincides with the inmates' nearly unanimous opinion that the cadre is more mature and more involved, that it adds a great deal to the institution, and that it is a good example for all. Therefore, it seems that the cadre program is providing some stability for the institution, while at the same time offering a positive correctional experience for those who participate in it.

Most Important Programs

The programs most frequently mentioned by inmates as the most important programs at Framingham were the computer program, work release, furloughs, and institutional education. Men were more likely to include the computer program among the most important programs, while women were more likely to include institutional education. This difference probably reflects the facts that the computer program tends to be more oriented toward men, while institutional education tends to be more oriented toward women. Work release was mentioned by an equal number of men and women, and the numbers mentioning furloughs were very similar.

In summary, on the four program areas that provided a focus for this section, the inmates' perception of furloughs and work/education release were very positive; their perceptions of the cadre program were positive; and their perceptions of counseling were mixed. Where comparisons were possible, the goals of the programs stated by the staff were generally consistent with the benefits derived from the programs and expressed by inmates.

Perceptions of the Coeducational Correctional Experiences

Our results leave little doubt that the inmates' perceptions of attitudes about the coeducational aspect of MCI Framingham were positive. Although there were, indeed, some strong negative opinions, the overall results showed an overwhelming preference for coed incarceration over one-sex institutionalization.

The first five questions in this part of the questionnaire dealt with general attitudes about a coed prison experience: what the goals might be; how successful the institution was at meeting the goals; and what the advantages and disadvantages of a coed correctional facility are. For interpretive purposes, the results of these questions can be grouped together. The themes that seem to dominate the responses are that for a prison this seems to be the best approach; that the experience at Framingham will be more helpful than harmful; that the coed program has its problems but is generally successful; and that the major difficulty with the coed program, as perceived by both sexes, is that there is a double standard of treatment for men and women.

One point to keep in mind when examining the high positive response of the inmates (86%) in describing their general experience at Framingham, is that although the question does not specifically ask for a comparison to other institutions, a comparison is implied. Thus it is assumed that the superlative descriptions do not mean that Framingham is superior to not being in prison, but is superior to being in other prisons. This does not deny the significance of the 86% positive response, because it is extremely rare that inmates will ever speak positively about the prison in which they are incarcerated.

What also proved interesting about this first question is that more than half of the cadre interviewed expressed some ambivalence in their responses. Some reported difficulties in adjusting to the coed aspect and the unusually "free" atmosphere. It is believed that this difficulty is due to the longer periods of institutionalization that the cadre has had and to the socialization that goes along with it. All of the cadre men had been incarcerated for at least four years on their present sentence. After these men learned how to function well enough to be selected as a member of the cadre, and then to be placed in a much less structured environment where different personality skills are required for social acceptance, it should not be surprising that problems in adjustment were reported.

We consider it extremely significant that 43 of 50 inmates perceive the coed program as successful. When asked to name disadvantages, 36% saw none at all. What is interesting about these views on advantages and disadvantages is that what some inmates perceived as advantages were listed by others as disadvantages. For example, some men listed the presence of women as a distinct advantage, whereas a few said it was a definite disadvantage.

The final question, which had several parts, attempted to probe for a description of the quality of the relationships between men and women. The general theme was that there is no difference between relationships inside Framingham and those on the outside. This response was almost unanimous. What puzzles us is that the sexual restrictions placed on the inmates must lead to some differences with the outside. This response may well reflect the frame of reference; in other words, relative to relationships in other prisons, relationships at Framingham are seen as more similar to those on the outside.

As we probed for specifics on relationships, our results became very interesting. There was virtually unanimous agreement that men and women are not treated equally, especially regarding disciplinary matters. This perceived inequality was related to the fact that men could be shipped back to their sending institutions, while no such sanction exists for women. In addition, there was a feeling that staff, in general, dealt less harshly with women than with men. men.

The results of the question on the ways that relationships in Framingham differ from those at one-sex institutions seem to be self-explanatory. Perhaps these are the reasons that people see Framingham as such a positive experience. One response from a number of inmates was that some staff were more willing to overlook female homosexuality than heterosexual behavior. This leads us to some speculation. We know from our literature review that homosexuality in all-female institutions is common. Since we know that institutions are generally systems that resist change, we can speculate that some staff from the old system felt threatened by the new male inmates and may have found it easier to cope in the old way. These responses came from both male and female inmates.

Our questions about a sexual code were incomplete because, although they ask if there is a code, they do not probe far enough into the nature of the code. We asked the question because of evidence in the literature that forms of sexual codes exist in one-sex institutions. There was some evidence that a code does exist at Framingham. The code seems to be that inmates "do their own thing" as long as it does not intrude on others. If one gets caught breaking a rule, one takes the penalty. Correction officers' attitudes on the enforcement of sexual rules were perceived as ranging from laissez-faire to very strict and rigid.

This attitude is in line with the prevalent jailhouse codes in the literature: "Break as many rules as you can without getting caught." Since this stance was evident only in regard to sexual matters at MCI Framingham, it appears that when people are treated like adults, as they are in the various programs, they act like adults. When people are treated like prisoners, as they are by the sexual rules of the facility, they act like prisoners. To think that men and women can be confined in a limited space for many hours a day and not pursue each other sexually seems unrealistic.

We found traditional stereotypic views in the inmates' attitudes about sexual roles. In fact, the only inmates expressing other than traditional sexual roles were the female homosexuals. It appears that inmates reflect the sex role stereotypes usually found in the community from which they come.

The final questions were about the long-term effects of

the relationships at Framingham. Most inmates did not expect these relationships to last after release. Perhaps because inmates are released at different times and return to different communities, they don't expect long-term relationships.

In summary, then, inmates generally regarded the co-educational correctional experience as a very positive one. Although some difficulties were reported, they viewed the Framingham experience as an important step in the process of reintegration into the community.

DISCUSSION OF RESULTS ON RECIDIVISM FOLLOW-UP

Although the difference between the expected versus the actual recidivism rates was not statistically significant, it seems clear that the Framingham program is having some effect in reducing recidivism rates (one criterion for success). Since our sample is small and the follow-up period short, differences as great as those we found indicate a real need for a more extensive study of this type.

While both the expected and actual recidivism rates for men are somewhat less than those for women, it is important to note that the reduction is greater for women (6.8 versus 3.2 percentage points). This suggests the program may have a somewhat greater impact on women, and this is noteworthy in that the entire state female prison population is being exposed to the program; they are not prescreened as the men are.

The difference in the recidivism rates (RR) of the commitment institutions of Concord (14%) and Walpole (0%) may be due to the fact that Concord inmates are generally less serious offenders, serving shorter sentences than those committed to Walpole. Therefore, Walpole inmates probably undergo more rigorous screening by the Classification Board before transfer to Framingham. Also, a previous study (Massachusetts Department of Correction, 1974, a one year follow-up of all releasees from state facilities in 1971 compiled by Daniel P. LeClair) showed a noticeably lower RR for Walpole commitments.

The somewhat lower RR in the few releasees going through prerelease centers (8 versus 12%) suggests that they serve as one more step to a smoother reintegration into society.

Usually, the younger the age at release, the higher the RR (Massachusetts Department of Corrections, 1974). The lower RR for young releasees in our sample is interesting but not easily explained. It may only be due to chance, but it may also indicate that the Framingham program is effective for young inmates.

The high RR for those incarcerated on property offenses is consistent with usual findings (LeClair, 1974). However, the low RR for drug offenses is unusual. We might speculate that the unique Framingham program is especially effective in helping drug offenders make an adjustment before returning to "the street."

The higher RR for those on indefinite sentences is consistent with LeClair's findings. This is also consistent with the finding of the lower Walpole RR. The large number of female indefinites is also consistent.

In the LeClair study, the RR for white releasees was almost identical to that for blacks, although white women had a somewhat higher RR than black women. There is no clear explanation for the RR difference we found in our sample, although it does seem that the Framingham program is more effective in reducing recidivism for blacks (8%) than for whites (15%).

The lower RR for single releasees contrasts with the results of LeClair's study, in which singles had a higher RR than those who had ever been married. This difference may be due to chance, or it may be that the coed program itself could produce some additional stress for married inmates.

For example, the recidivism rate of the 17 women who were married or separated was 29%.

The high RR for men with other than honorable discharges is consistent with previous data and suggests there may be a history of adjustment difficulties in some of these men.

The large number of inmates from Boston may reflect the higher crime rates there. The somewhat lower RR for Boston residents, and the slightly higher rate for female releasees from Boston, are also reflected in the LeClair report.

The large number of releasees on the lower end of the socioeconomic and occupational scales reflects the fact that the criminal justice system has always dealt primarily with persons from the lower classes. This may also be why the lower ends of the scales are where one finds the highest RRs.

The large number of inmates with short time on any job is consistent with previous data, but the relatively equal RRs across the board are not. Usually those with shorter times on one job have higher RRs. The Framingham experience, especially a consistent job through work release, may work to reverse this tendency.

The low RR for those with a grade school education and for those with more than a high school education is again consistent with previous data. However, the relatively high RR for high school grads is not consistent with previous data, and this discrepancy comes from the men in the sample. Again it may be due to the relatively small sample size.

The number of inmates indicating former drug use (52%) is more than twice as high as those released from Framingham in 1971 (25%). The same is true for heroin use. This may indicate that more drug-related offenders are being sentenced to Framingham or that more inmates are willing to acknowledge their involvement with drugs. What is striking is, again, the lack of a high RR for users, especially heroin users. This finding is inconsistent with former studies and may indicate again a greater impact of the program on drug users.

The tendency for men to be younger at first arrest suggests either that women get involved in crime at a later age or that the criminal justice system treats men and women differently. The lower RR for younger inmates arrested at younger ages again contradicts previous studies.

The large number of releasees with prior offenses against the person is again consistent with LeClair's findings. The large number of men reflects their incarceration for more violent crimes. On the other hand, LeClair found no difference between the RRs of those with no offenses against the person and those with one or more offense.

The positive relationship we found between number of property offenses and RR is consistent with LeClair's findings.

Again, the high number of releasees having previous narcotic offenses (45%) is higher than in 1971 (26%). And, again, the lack of difference between the RRs of those with and those without narcotic offenses contradicts LeClair's findings and suggests that the program had a great impact on drug offenders.

The high number of releasees charged with drunkenness is consistent with previous data. There seems to be a slight positive relationship between drunkenness charges and RR which is what LeClair found. The high RR for those with escape charges again follows that LeClair findings.

The high number of releasees with previous incarcerations suggests the magnitude of recidivism. Except for incarceration in juvenile facilities, the finding that those with previous incarcerations have a higher RR is in line with other findings. Former recidivists are higher recidivism risks.

The finding that one-half the sample served one year or less on their present incarceration indicates that the length of time served by those released from Framingham was relatively short. The positive relationship between time served and RR, at least for women, suggests that those serving longer sentences are more prone to recidivism.

Eighty-five percent of released prisoners are let out on parole. Previous studies have consistently shown that parolees have higher RRs than discharges (because they are more closely supervised and they can be returned to prison for behavior that is not necessarily criminal—that is, for a technical infraction of parole rules). The recidivism rates were virtually the same for the Framingham parolees and dischargees. This suggests that the Framingham program provides for a smoother reintegration into the community, and, accordingly, better prepares a person for parole.

Summary and Conclusions

This study of MCI Framingham had three general goals: (1) to provide a general description of the facility and its programs; (2) to generate some exploratory data on inmates' perceptions of the social climate, of the coeducational aspects, and of selected programs at MCI Framingham; and (3) to examine the impact of the MCI Framingham coeducational program on recidivism.

REVIEW OF THE LITERATURE. The first step was to review the correctional literature. This literature review focused on five areas in all-male and all-female institutions related to social climate: communications and information flow, punishment and reward, inmate subculture, sexual relationships, and relationships with the outside community. Because we found no material in the literature on adult coeducational institutions, we analyzed our data from Framingham according to these five areas. When possible, we indicated where and how coeducation has had an effect on the social climate at Framingham, compared to the effects reported in the literature and to the inmates' previous experience in one-sex institutions.

DESCRIPTION OF MCI FRAMINGHAM. The first part of the study describes the Framingham facility—its history and physical layout, its staffing patterns, and its correctional programs.

EXPLORATORY DATA. The second part of the study was exploratory in nature. Fifty inmates were interviewed. The interview schedule included a Likert-type social climate scale and a number of open-ended questions concerning the coeducational aspects and the programs.

SOCIAL CLIMATE. The men seemed to feel that there was less communication between themselves and staff than there was at their former, more structured institutions where rules were more explicit. However, in a less structured institution like Framingham, inmates felt more able to participate in decisions concerning institutional policy.

Compared to the all-male sending institutions, there seemed to be a different subculture at Framingham with regard to punishment and reward. Although both men and women felt that the staff will punish them for an infraction, it is improbable that they would be punished by a fellow inmate. On the other hand, according to men, one was more likely to be punished by peers at their former institutions. At Framingham the staff was also more likely to praise positive behavior.

In general, more men than women felt that the staff was concerned with keeping inmates under control. This seems to be related to the perceived inequality in disciplinary measures for men and women in Framingham. Inmates at Framingham are more likely to feel that the staff is concerned with helping them with problems, compared to the opposite feeling of men concerning their former institutions. On the whole, there seems to be less suspicion of interaction between the staff and inmates in a less structured institution such as Framingham.

Men generally tend to view their relationship with the outside community as more positive than do women. Except for the cadre, men are primarily sent to Framingham as a prerelease center. Therefore they seem to view the time spent there as a termination of a longer period of incarceration and a gradual return to society.

Men experience less tension than the women at Framingham. Among men there seems to be a much less rigid subculture than among women, who are still somewhat involved in social systems similar to those found in all-female institutions. Men also seem to be less involved with each other, and this results in less peer pressure and more individuality, which is not as apparent among the women.

COEDUCATIONAL ASPECTS.   The overall results of the questionnaire showed an overwhelming preference among inmates for coed incarceration over one-sex incarceration. The major drawback of this coed program was that there is a perceived double standard of treatment for male and female inmates. Furthermore, a majority of the cadre interviewed expressed some ambivalence about coed incarceration. They were accustomed to the more structured environment of a one-sex institution, and as a result of their long incarceration, they reported some difficulties in adjusting to the less structured coed atmosphere at Framingham.

When asked about the quality of relationships between men and women at Framingham, the inmates' general response was that there was no difference between relationships at Framingham and those on the outside. A major specific issue in this area was the perceived unequal disciplinary treatment of men and women. It seemed that the men sent to Framingham were considered to be privileged, so standards for their behavior were seen as being much higher. On the other hand, the coed experience is now standard for women who are incarcerated by the state, since Framingham is the only state facility for women. Therefore the disciplinary sanction of being "shipped out" does not hang as heavily over the women as it does over the men.

When asked whether or not there is a code for sexual behavior, the response from inmates seemed to be that it is all right "to do your own thing as long as it doesn't interfere with the rights of others," or "as long as you don't get caught." Inmates' perceptions of officers' attitudes concerning this matter range from laissez-faire to very strict.

Inmates' attitudes on sexual roles tend to be rather traditional and stereotyped, except among the female homosexuals. In general, inmates seem to reflect the sexual stereotypes in the communities from which they came.

Although inmates reported that relationships inside Framingham did not differ from those on the outside, there was some evidence to the contrary. Married inmates, to be sure, had some difficulties not experienced by married persons on the outside, and most inmates did not expect relationships formed in prison to last after release.

PROGRAM.   The next section of the interview focused on four program areas: furloughs, work/education release, Division of Legal Medicine (DLM) counseling, and cadre.

Both the administration and the inmates believed that the furlough program is a positive experience. Although there are some minor complaints from inmates about some rules being too strict, most inmates see the program as highly beneficial in maintaining contact with the outside.

Inmates and administration also seem to agree on the positive value of the work/education release in promoting reintegration. The main benefit of this program was that it enabled and supported an inmate in his or her efforts to secure employment. More men believed that this program was administered fairly, perhaps because they used the sending institutions as their frame of reference. Inmates and staff had similar concerns about this program: lack of jobs due to the state of the economy; inadequate transportation; and the 15% that inmates are required to pay the state from their salaries.

It is unclear how many inmates have actually participated in the DLM counseling service, because there was some confusion between this program and the social service program. There were very mixed and very emotional responses to the questions on the counseling program.

Inmates generally responded positively to the cadre program and its members. Some did not know very much about this aspect of the institution, because this group of men seems to be set apart from other inmates.

In summary, inmates' perceptions of the furlough program and of the work and education release program were very positive, and their perceptions of the counseling program were mixed. Also, it was clear that their general view of the coeducational correctional experience was an extremely positive one.

RECIDIVISM FOLLOW-UP. The comparison between the expected recidivism rate (17.3%) and the actual recidivism rate (11.6%) revealed a substantial reduction in recidivism for the first 121 persons released from Framingham since it became a coeducational facility. The impact of the Framingham program on recidivism tended to be somewhat greater for women—from 19.6% (expected rate) to 12.8% (actual rate)—than it was for men—from 11.8% (expected rate) to 8.6% (actual rate).

An analysis of the relationship between background characteristics and recidivism was also carried out for the men and women, as well as for the total sample. On some factors, such as institution committed to, offense, race, and drug usage, some interesting findings emerged. For example, none of the 14 men originally committed to Walpole were recidivists. This finding may reflect a more careful screening of the Walpole commitments. The recidivism rate of property offenders (26%) was significantly higher than that of all other offenders (7%). Although this pattern is consistent with previous studies, the unusually large difference is noteworthy here. Black inmates, both female and male, had a considerably lower recidivism rate (8%) than did whites (15%). Finally, unlike the findings of previous studies, the recidivism rate of those with histories of drug use was no higher than that of individuals with no drug history.

In conclusion, there seems to be a clear convergence of the data supporting the coeducational correctional program at MCI Framingham. Although some negative issues were raised in the course of this study, the overall findings of this research lead to the conclusion that the Framingham program is an effective and worthwhile correctional enterprise.

It is hoped that this research has contributed to a better understanding of the coeducational experience, and that it will stimulate further study of this important area.

BIBLIOGRAPHY

Caldwell, M. Types of informal prison groups. In C. B. Vedder & B. A. Kay (Eds.), *Penology: A realistic approach.* Springfield, IL: Charles C Thomas, 1964.

Carney, F. J. Predicting recidivism in a medium security correctional institution. *The Journal of Criminal Law, Criminology, and Police Science,* 1967, *58,* 338–348.

Carney, F. J. Evaluation of psychotherapy in a maximum security prison. *Seminars in Psychiatry,* 1971, *3,* 363–374.

Carter, M., Glaser, D., and Wilkins, T. (Eds.), *Correctional Institutions.* Philadelphia: Lippincott, 1972.

Chaiklin, H., *Final report: The community reintegration project.* Baltimore: University of Maryland School of Social Work, Division of Corrections, 1973.

Chandler, E. W., *Women in prison.* New York: Bobbs Merrill, 1973.

Clemmer, D., *The prison community* (rev. ed.). New York: Holt, Rinehart and Winston, 1958.

Cloward, R. A., Social control in the prison, in *Theoretical studies in social organization of the prison.* New York: Social Science Research Council, 1960.

Coates, R. B., Miller, A. D., & Ohlin, L. E., *Preliminary analysis of initial data in a longitudinal study of youth in the community based system of the Massachusetts department of youth services.* Cambridge, MA: Center for Criminal Justice, Law School of Harvard University, 1973.

Cohn, A. W., The failure of correctional management. *Probation and Parole,* 1973, *5,* 8-17.

Cressey, D. R., Adult felons in prison. In L. E. Ohlin (Ed.), *Prisoners in America.* Englewood Cliffs, NJ: Prentice-Hall, 1973.

Day, S. R., Craddick, R. A., & Matheny, K. B. Inmate change following human relations training for non-professional correctional personnel. *Georgia Journal of Corrections,* 1973, *2,* 36-40.

deRahm, E. *How could she do that?,* New York: Clarkson N. Potter, 1969.

Dillon, V., Inside the prison clique. In R. Milton, Jr. (Ed.), *Inside prison, American style.* New York: Random House, 1971.

Fox, V., Analysis of prison disciplinary problems. In C. B. Vedder & B. A. Kay (Eds.), *Penology: A realistic approach.* Springfield, IL: Charles C Thomas, 1964.

Fox, V., *Introduction to corrections.* Englewood Cliffs, NJ: Prentice-Hall, 1972.

Garabedian, P. G. Social roles and processes of socialization in the prison community. *Social Problems,* 1963, *11.*

Giallombardo, R. Social roles in a prison for women. *Social Problems,* 1966, *13,* 268-288.

Giallombardo, R., *Society of women: A study of a women's prison.* New York: John Wiley & Sons, 1966.

Glaser, D., *The effectiveness of a prison and parole system.* New York: Bobbs-Merrill, 1964.

Goffman, E. *Asylums.* Garden City, NY: Doubleday, 1961.

Griggs, B. S., & McCune, G. R. Community based correctional programs: A survey and analysis. *Federal Probation,* 1972, *36.*

Grosser, G. H. External setting and internal relations of the prison. In *Theoretical studies in social organization of the prison.* New York: Social Science Research Council, 1960.

Grusky, O. Organizational goals and the behavior of informal leaders. *American Journal of Sociology*, 1959, *65*, 59–67.

Halleck, S. L. *Psychiatry and the dilemmas of crime.* Los Angeles: University of California Press, 1967.

Harris, S. *Hellhole.* New York: E. P. Dutton, 1967.

Heffernan, E. *Making it in prison: The square, the cool and the life,* New York: Wiley-Interscience, 1972.

Hopper, C. B. *Sex in prison.* Baton Rouge: Louisiana State University Press, 1969.

Hopper, C.: Sexual adjustment in prisons. *Police,* 1971, *15,* 75–76.

Informatics, Inc. *Pennsylvania community treatment services: An evaluation and proposed evaluation information system,* Rockville, MD, 1972.

Irwin, J. The prison experience: The convict world. In R. M. Carter, D. Glaser, & L. G. Wilkins (Eds.), *Correctional institutions.* Philadelphia: J.B. Lippincott, 1972.

Irwin, J., & Cressey, D.: Thieves, convicts and the inmate culture. In D. Arnold (Ed.), *The sociology of subcultures.* Berkeley, CA: Glendessary Press, 1970.

Jeffrey, R. & Woolpert, S. Work furlough as an alternative to incarceration: An assessment of its effects on recidivism and social cost. *Journal of Criminal Law and Criminology,* 1974, *65,* 405–415.

Keith, C. R., & Stamm, R. A. The use of the prison code as a defense. *Bulletin of the Menninger Clinic,* 1964, *28,* 251–259.

Korn, R. R., & McCorkle, L. W. *Criminology* and *penology.* New York: Holt, Rinehart and Winston, 1959.

Korn, R. & McCorkle, L. W. Resocialization within walls. *The Annals,* 1954, *293.*

Markley, C. W. Furlough programs and conjugal visiting in adult correctional institutions. *Federal Probation,* 1973, *37.*

Massachusetts Department of Correction. Department of correction philosophy. Dept. Order No. 1000.1, September 12, 1973 (mimeo).

Massachusetts Department of Correction. Monthly statistical report of the furlough program. January 1975 (mimeo).

Massachusetts Department of Correction. Monthly statistical report of the work and education release program. January 1975 (mimeo).

Massachusetts Department of Correction. Statistical tables describing the characteristics and recidivism rates of 1971 releasees from Massachusetts MCIs. Compiled by D. P. LeClair, August 1974 (mimeo).

McCleery, R. H. Communication patterns as bases of systems of authority and power. In R. Cloward (Ed.), *Theoretical studies in social organization of the prison.* New York: Social Science Research Council, 1960.

McCleery, R. The governing process and informal social control. In *The Prison: Studies in institutional organization and change.* New York: Holt, Rinehart and Winston, 1961.

Miller, M. B. At hard labor: Rediscovering the 19th century prison. *Issues in Criminology,* 1974, *9,* 91–114.

Minton, R., Jr. (Ed.). *Inside prison, American style.* New York: Random House, 1971.

Ohlin, L. E. (Ed.). *Prisoners in America.* Englewood Cliffs, NJ: Prentice-Hall, 1973.

Ohlin, L., *Sociology and the field of corrections.* New York: Russell Sage Foundation, 1956.

Powers, E., *The basic structure of the administration of criminal justice in Massachusetts* (6th ed.). Boston: Massachusetts Correctional Association, 1973.

Raymond, F. B. To punish or to treat? *Social Work,* 1974, *19,* 305–312.

Rudolf, A., & Esselstyn, R. Evaluating work furlough: A follow-up. *Federal Probation,* 1973, *37,* 48–52.

Schrag, C., Some foundations for a theory of corrections. In D. R. Cressey (Ed.), *The prison: Studies in institutional organization and change.* New York: Holt, Rinehart and Winston, 1961.

Schwartz, B. Peer vs. authority effects in a correctional community. *Criminology,* 1973, *11,* 233–257.

Scott, J. C. The use of discretion in determining the severity of punishment for incarcerated offenders. *Journal of Criminal Law and Criminology,* 1974, *65,* 214–224.

Studt, E., Messinger, S. L., & Wilson, T. P. *C-Unit: Search for community in prison.* New York: Russell Sage Foundation, 1968.

Swanson, R. M. *Work release: Toward an understanding of the law, policy, and operation of community-based state corrections* (vol. 2). Carbondale, IL: Southern Illinois University, Center for Study of Crime, no date.

Sykes, G. M. Corruption of authority and rehabilitation. *Social Forces,* 1956, *34,* 257–262.

Sykes, G. *Society of captives.* Princeton, NJ: Princeton University Press, 1958.

Sykes, G., & Messinger, S. L. The inmate social system. In R. Cloward (Ed.), *Theoretical studies in social organization of the prison.* New York: Social Science Research Council, 1960.

Thomas, C. W. Toward a more inclusive model of the inmate contraculture. *Criminology,* 1973, *8,* 251–262.

Title, C. Inmate organization: Sex differentiation and the influence of criminal subcultures. *American Sociological Review,* 1969, *34,* 492–505.

Waldo, G., Chiricos, T., & Dobin, L. *Community contact and inmate attitudes: An experimental assessment of work release.* Tallahassee, FL: Florida State University, Southeastern Correctional Criminological Research Center, 1973.

Ward, D. A., & Kassebaum, G. G. *Women's prison: Sex and social structure.* Chicago: Aldine Publishing, 1965.

Wenk, E. A., Frank, C. Some progress in the evaluation of institutional programs. *Federal Probation*, 1973, *37*, 30-37.

Wheeler, S. Role conflict in the correctional community. In D. R. Cressey (Ed.), *The prison: studies in institutional organization and change.* New York: Holt, Rinehart and Winston, 1951.

Whelan, C. S., & Gross, M. L. *Work release: The N.Y.C. program, a preliminary public policy paper.* New York: Community Service Society and Youth and Corrections Committee, 1974.

Chapter 6

STYLES OF DOING TIME IN A COED PRISON
Masculine and Feminine Alternatives
Nanci Koser Wilson

The burgeoning literature on female emancipation and sex role differences has given impetus to the study of differences in male and female criminality (which has a body of literature that is still quite small, but is beginning to grow). At the same time the recent phenomenon of co-corrections (housing male and female offenders together in prisons where they often interact with each other) gives us a unique opportunity to study differences in masculine and feminine reactions to imprisonment.

Previous studies of this topic have been limited to comparisons of data from studies of all-male and all-female prisons. Because the two types of facilities differ so radically (in population count, programming, degree of security, etc.), the comparisons made between Frontera or Alderson and male prisons are difficult to evaluate. This chapter presents preliminary findings from the study of a minimum security correctional center, which in the last year has moved from an all-male facility to co-correctional status. It is one of only a handful of prisons in the country to make this change.

Related Literature

Data on the feminine response to imprisonment have come from three important studies of female prisons—Ward and Kassebaum's (1965) study of Frontera, Giallombardo's (1966a) study of Alderson,[1] and Heffernan's (1972) work on Occoquan. The authors compare their findings to those from previous studies of male prisons. In addition, Tittle (1969) has compared male and female responses to incarceration in a federal drug treatment hospital. These studies have emphasized basic differences between masculine and feminine reaction to incarceration in terms of two import variables—solidarity and homosexuality.

The authors seem to be in general agreement[2] that the rate of female homosexuality during confinement is greater than the male rate. Table 6-1 depicts these reported differences. The more important sex-linked difference, however, lies in the meaning of homosexuality. Most authors think that males feel a need to validate their masculinity. The corollary is not true, however, for women. Giallombardo, for instance, indicates that the need to assert or defend one's feminity in the same way that the male inmate must prove his masculinity in the group if his manhood is called into question "clearly does not arise for the female offender" (Giallombardo, 1966b, p. 447). Gagnon and Simon's (1968) and Ward and Kassebaum's (1965) works both maintain that women have fewer problems managing sexual deprivation, and that their greatest deprivation is that of emotionally satisfying relationships. They believe that female prison homosexuality fulfills primarily physical needs.

A second theme in the literature is that inmate solidarity is lower among women than among men. Table 6-2 presents these reported data.

Giallombardo attributes the differences to general features of the American culture (which socializes women to be less aggressive and more emotionally dependent, and de-

Table 6-1   Reported Differences in Male and Female Homosexuality

Researcher	Type of institution	Male rate*	Female rate*	Basis of estimate
Clemmer (1940)	Maximum-security male prison	40%	—	Overt homosexuality
Giallombardo (1966a)	Maximum-security female prison	—	85%	Participation in pseudo-families "Playing"
Heffernan (1972)	Maximum-security female prison	—	48% cool[+] 58% life 31% square	
Sykes (1958)	Maximum-security male prison	35%	—	Overt homosexuality
Tittle (1969)	Coed drug hospital	23%	24%	Self-reports and patient estimates of "homosexual activity"
Ward and Kassebaum (1965)	Maximum-security female prison	—	50%	Overt homosexuality

*Expressed as a percentage of the inmate population.
[+]Heffernan provides different estimates for each type of inmate.

Table 6-2 Reported Differences in Male and Female "Inmate Solidarity"

Researcher	Type of institution	Male rate	Female rate	Basis of estimate
Giallombardo (1966a)	Maximum-security female prison	—	"Almost all"	Snitching
Heffernan (1972)	Maximum-security male prison	—	50%	Stated there was "no inmate loyalty"
			22% cool 61% life 9% square	Received tickets for fighting
			69% cool 60% life 5% square	Adherence to inmate code
Sykes (1958)	Maximum-security male prison	41%	—	"Were informers"
Tittle (1969)	Coed drug hospital	40%	21%	Attitude scale of cohesion (high score)
		34%	36%	Sharing
		42%	34%	Awareness of normative system
		55%	48%	Believed "snitching" would entail risk
Ward and Kassebaum (1965)	Maximum-security female prison	—	50–90%	Snitching

picts women as competitors rather than friends). But Gagnon and Simon and Ward and Kassebaum point to differences in offense history—suggesting that women prisoners are less likely to have extensive criminal histories or long histories of penal confinement, both of which are "relevant to the development of criminal maturity and a conwise prison orientation" (Ward and Kassebaum, 1965, p. 67).

The two themes of homosexuality and solidarity are not unrelated: Many authors point to the "play families" that women create in prisons as a functional alternative to the solidaristic inmate culture created and maintained by adherence to an inmate code. Tittle aptly summarizes this position, for which he found some support in his study of a coed drug hospital. He maintains that the previous evidence suggests that male inmates "tend to organize into an overall symbiotic structure characterized by a shared normative system epitomized in a prison code, but that within that community considerable individualism and personal isolation prevail." In contradistinction, "female inmates are characterized neither by overall cohesion nor by individual isolation. Instead they tend to organize into relatively enduring primary relationships often involving dyadic homosexual attachments and extensive 'family' relationships" (Tittle, 1969, p. 492).

In summary, then, the existing literature seems to suggest that there are clear masculine and feminine alternatives for "doing time." While men cope with the pains of imprisonment by forming a solidaristic inmate culture supported by adherence to the "inmate code," women form "play families" to provide emotional support. This basic difference is reflected in the lower rates of solidarity and the higher rates of homosexuality in women's prisons. It also reflects the important differences between men and women as their roles are defined in the outside world.

RESEARCH SITE

The co-correctional prison gives us a unique opportunity to address the issues of sex-role differences in confinement. It allows us to measure with the same instruments,
differences between men and women exposed to roughly the
same prison environment, rather than forcing us to compare
work done on men by one set of authors with research on
women done by another set of authors.

The findings presented here represent preliminary and
tentative conclusions from the study of a minimum-security
facility. The findings are applicable only to this unique type
of co-correctional facility and should not be generalized to
larger, more secure, one-sex prisons.

"Correctional Center" is a minimum-security facility
which is part of one of the largest state correctional systems
in America. Within the system are several large maximum-
security adult male prisons, a medium-security farm for
males, a maximum-security female facility, numerous work-
release centers, and various juvenile reformatories and
camps. Rarely is an individual sent directly from the
reception and diagnostic center to the minimum-security
correctional center. Rather, most inmates serve from two to
10 years in one or more of the maximum-security facilities
before being transferred to the correctional center. This
transfer is based partially on their behavior in the larger
prison and partially on their proximity to a "board date."[3]

Correctional Center is a modern, treatment-oriented
prison. Terminology changes include the use of the term
"correctional center" rather than prison, while guards are
"correctional officers," inmates are "residents," and the yard
is called "town square."

But the differences between this correctional center and
other prisons in the same state go deeper than mere label

changes. Physically, the correctional center has no wall or fence of any kind. Its facilities consist of numerous small buildings, including dormitories, a dining hall, chapel, and a gym. The effect is that of a small college campus. Each resident has his or her own room and wears his or her own clothes. Although the men and women eat and are housed in separate buildings, they interact frequently on their work assignments, in classes (a complex college and vocational program is maintained), and in certain recreational areas. Residents have a great deal of freedom in moving from one area of the institution to another, in controlling their own rooms (from decorating them to having their own keys to them), and in many other areas of institutional life.

As a consequence of all this, the resident at Correctional Center has fewer "pains of imprisonment" with which to cope. The relative freedom of movement, the private rooms with keys, the personal clothing and so on all significantly reduce feelings of loss of autonomy, liberty, and goods and services which may be felt in the other prisons in the system. Because almost all of the residents have a very short "time to the board,"[4] there is also much more of a "street orientation" among the residents. Also, as a concomitant of the availability of goods and services, there are few if any jobs in the prison that can be thought of as "power jobs" (such as kitchen worker, clerk, etc.). In fact, power plays in the form of fighting, gang warfare, and generally disruptive behavior are practically nonexistent for the simple reason that the threat of transfer back to one of the more maximum-security prisons is a potent social control mechanism.[5]

It is within this setting, then, that this chapter attempts to compare the way that men and women "do time." So far, because the study is still in progress, we have only impressionistic data on the issues of homosexuality and solidarity (which the earlier comparisons focused on). Most of the data relied on for this paper focus on agreements on programs made by the residents, and on disciplinary ticket information. However, even in the absence of hard data, a few comments on solidarity and homosexuality may be in order.

SOME OBSERVATIONS ON SOLIDARITY AND HOMOSEXUALITY

From observation and from scattered interviews with residents it is my impression that the level of solidarity is not less for women than for men in this co-correctional setting.

First of all, in general, solidarity appears to be a function of (1) the size of a prison, (2) the security level of the prison, (3) the amount of time the average inmate has to do (and concomitantly the turnover rate), and (4) the presence or absence of a "treatment" orientation.

Because Correctional Center has a relatively small population (some 400 to 450 residents), is a minimum-security facility, and has a definite treatment orientation, and because the residents generally have a short time left to serve on their sentences (which results in a high turnover of residents), we can expect that the traditional phenomenon of a solidaristic inmate culture will not apply.

While we have no information on the different degrees of solidarity between the maximum-security female prison, and the maximum-security male prisons within this same system, this much seems clear—both men and women say that they experience less solidarity when they arrive at Correctional Center.

In commenting on the lower degree of inmate solidarity at Correctional Center, one resident noted that there are "so many snitches here that you can't estimate the number." Female residents also report less solidarity at Correctional Center than at the female maximum-security prison in the system. Male and female residents alike noted that "you cannot take care of a snitch" at Correctional Center, for fear of being transferred back to a maximum-security prison.

We have no hard data yet on the types of sexual involvements among the residents. There is some reason to believe that the play families that women are reported to create in all-female prisons still exist, and so does homosexual involvement. The extent of both the homosexuality and the play families is unknown, but there is some reason to believe that the rate of homosexuality for both men and women is lower at Correctional Center.

A male resident who was asked whether he felt that the rate of male homosexuality was different at Correctional Center commented that "At [a maximum-security prison in the system] all the young guys are girls. Now they're coming out of their man bag . . . they're playing big man with the women."

On the differences between male and female homosexual involvement while in prison, a resident drew the following distinction: While both men and women seek advice and emotional fulfillment from such a relationship, the methods by which the more aggressive partner introduces a "square" to homosexuality vary. "A bulldagger's main desire is to mentally destroy a girl [by telling her] she is ugly, piggy, etc." She convinces herself that she can't get any other friends. The bulldagger can then dominate her by taking care of her. "You can cop a boy more easily," he continued, "because of his relationship to fear, cowardice, and laziness. You can cop a girl through openness, tenderness, and a strong relationship." The young girl is looking for "an all and all mighty adviser—a mother," while the young boy "finds a father." From this inmate's perspective, at least, the meaning of male and female prison homosexuality is not very different.

Although so far we have only impressionistic data on homosexuality from this study, we do know that it is still a pattern. The administration has rather strictly controlled heterosexual involvement, with a definite and stringently enforced rule against physical contact of any sort between the male and female residents. (Physical contact tickets have been written for such minor amounts of contact as holding hands).

Homosexual contact is much more difficult to control, and we still see tickets being written for a resident "being in bed" with another resident during the night. Because the homosexual activity is so much more difficult to control, some residents have concluded that the administration does not discourage it. "Down here they would rather see a woman with a woman and a man with a man," one resident commented. Other residents feel that the presence of the opposite sex actually stimulates homosexuality: "They sit down with a man and get a horny. They sit with a man all day and go take care of their needs [with a woman] at night."

Heterosexual involvement in the co-correctional prison is, of course, the topic that most catches the imagination of the general public and therefore is the issue that makes the co-correctional prison administrator walk on eggs most of the time. To the researcher, however, the *meaning* of heterosexual involvement is much more important than the extent of the physical relationship.

Residents indicate that heterosexual involvement within the prison, is "a way to do time." One couple, who had had a stable romantic relationship for a number of months, was asked whether they thought most residents wanted to "get involved" or to "stay away from it." The woman responded in the following words:

> I think most of it's just like for conversation. Maybe to help 'em—for each other to do time. Now you can get involved, you know, within time, like we did. I don't think anyone comes here with the idea 'I'm gonna fall in love,' and I'm gonna do all this. They just come here and find someone they can relate to, someone of the opposite sex, and they just sit and talk or whatever. You know, they relate to them.

The man made this observation about male residents:

> [They] don't come here lookin' for no love affair—nothin'

like that. If a man finds a woman—they're doing their time,
maybe they're sharing things together—to them if you will
look at it it's therapeutic, you know, because they're sharin'
things back and forth and that helps do time.

A larger percentage of the women get involved in
heterosexual relationships simply because of the
imbalanced sex ratio. (The sex ratio at Correctional Center is
almost 1 to 8, or approximately 50 women and 400 men).
There are some women who do remain heterosexual
isolates, however, and some men who appear to choose to
remain uninvolved. We hope this research project will eventually be able to identify what type of resident is most likely
to seek a heterosexual relationship as a method for doing
time.

STYLES OF DOING TIME

There are now two kinds of data that will give us some
clues on how men and women respond differently to the
prison environment. We have data on the number and kinds
of disciplinary tickets received by women and men, and we
also have the program agreements made by the men and
women.

The formal record of disciplinary procedures includes
the offense for which the individual is cited and the disposi-
tion of the "ticket." Program agreements are made by each
new resident with his counselor upon entrance to the prison.
Each resident is asked to specify his or her goals while in
Correctional Center. The counselor then notes the method
for achieving these goals, and the resident is finally asked to
specify his or her long-range goals.

We have these data on all women who have been incarcerated at the Center. The large number of men makes it
impossible to collect data on the entire population. For this
reason, two units that usually have about the same number

of men as the female unit were selected at random for the male sample. This sample was chosen rather than a random sample of all male residents to facilitate sociometric data gathering. It does mean that certain types of comparisons between men and women are difficult to make, however, as we shall see.

SEX DIFFERENCES

The first thing we discover is that the women seem to get more disciplinary tickets than do men in our sample.[6] The men had an average of 1.477 tickets each, while the women had an average of 2.846 tickets. This average is misleading, however, since the men in our sample tended to have served more time than the women (10.3 months for the men versus 6.4 months for the women). Controlling for this by computing the average number of tickets per month served gives us the following figures: 0.143 tickets per month served for the men and 0.446 per month served for the women.

The program agreements specify what kinds of institutional programs the men and women intend to get involved in. Some residents, however, fail to enroll in or complete programs which they request. Hence we cannot infer that all requested programs are actually fulfilled. With this caution in mind, we can look at the prison programs that men and women request. Table 6-3 below presents these differences.

More women than men appear to be involved in academic programs (66.7% versus 57.7%). Of the various types of academic programs, we find a much larger percentage of women in the GED (General Equivalency Diploma) program (48.7% versus 11.5%). Approximately the same percentage of men and women are involved in the learning lab and in taking some college courses. However, a larger percentage of the men (21.2% versus 1.3%) set a goal of

Table 6-3   Prison Programs Requested by Men and
Women

Type of program	Male residents (N = 52)	Female residents (N = 78)
Academic (total)	57.7%*(30)	67.7%*(52)
GED	11.5% (6)	48.7% (38)
AA or AS	21.2% (11)	1.3% (1)
College courses	17.3% (9)	16.7% (13)
Learning lab	7.7% (4)	6.4% (5)
Vocational	73.1% (38)	74.4% (58)
Counseling	9.6% (5)	35.9% (28)

*Percentage of the male or female residents who requested this program.
Percentages do not total 100 because residents may request more than one program.

gaining an Associate of Arts or Associate of Science degree in the college program.

Although the data indicate that a much higher percentage of women want to engage in counseling while in prison, these data cannot be interpreted to represent the overall male-female differences at Correctional Center. When the male units were selected to form the sample, all units that would contain an extremely atypical sample of the male inmate population were deliberately excluded from choice. These units were a unit composed of older men, a unit devoted to men with drug problems, and a special unit devoted to transactional analysis (TA). Because of this composition, it is highly likely that men who wish to engage in counseling will take advantage of the therapeutic community offered in either the drug or the TA unit. These two units comprise about 12% of the male population. With this in mind, we can see that male-female differences in desire for counseling probably are not great.

The institution has an extensive vocational education program, and many residents take advantage of it. The percentage of men and women requesting vocational education is nearly equal (73.1% versus 74.4%). In terms of the type of vocational education, we do see some sex differences. Most of the vocational programs are oriented toward traditionally male vocations, since the institution only recently became co-correctional. Hence there is not a wide variety of choice in terms of sex-linked occupational training.

However, the sex differences that do appear can be predicted from a knowledge of the general cultural attitudes toward "masculine" and "feminine" jobs. No women requested training in meatcutting, air conditioning repair, or water-waste management, and few women were interested in welding or office machine repair. Concomitantly, no men requested the sewing program, although one enrolled in the upholstery course. More women than men requested cosmetology training (16.7% versus 7.8%). The most popular program at the institution is training as an emergency medical technician (EMT). It appears to be equally appealing to men and women; 17 of the 66 female requests and 22 of the 51 male requests were for the EMT program.

It is in the prisoners' long-range goals that we see the greatest sex differences. As Table 6-4 shows, when asked to specify a long-range goal, 34.3% of the women and 42% of the men were unable to do so. Only two men mentioned their personal life (marriage, children, home ownership, etc.) as part of their long-range goal, but 12.9% of the women did so. Eleven percent of the men confidently predicted that they would own their own business, while only 5.7% of the women set such a goal for themselves. Some inmates were

Table 6-4   Long Range Goals of Men and Women

Type of goal	Men (N = 45)	Women (N = 70)
No long-range goal specified	42.2% (19)	34.3% (24)
Personal life was mentioned	4.4% (2)	12.9% (9)
Owning business	11.1% (5)	5.7% (4)
Prison-oriented	4.4% (2)	15.7% (11)
Job-oriented	38.8% (17)	38.6% (27)

Percentages do not total 100 because a resident could appear in more than one category.

able to think only in terms of the prison life itself. When asked to specify a long-range goal, they mentioned further programs they would like to be involved in. This was true for 15.7% of the women, but for only 4% of the men. Approximately the same percentage of men and women were job-oriented (38.8% versus 38.6%), that is, they mentioned a specific job they intended to have as a long-range goal.

We find, then, that in coping with imprisonment, the women are more apt to "get in trouble" as evidenced by their higher number of disciplinary tickets. This may, however, be a function of their higher visibility in the institution rather than their actual behavior. There are not many differences in the data on how residents "fill their time" during institutionalization. We estimate that about the same amount of men and women engage in counseling and in vocational programming. Only a slightly higher percentage of women engage in academic programming.

When we move from a consideration of how men and women do their time to a consideration of their plans for the future, however, we begin to see traditional sex differences emerge. Women are much more likely to think of the future in terms of marriage and babies, and when it comes to work, men are more likely to think of themselves as business owners and women as workers.

DIFFERENCES IN "FELONIOUS IDENTITY"

We felt that the technique of looking only at the gross differences between men and women was likely to be misleading. Those who have studied women's prisons have noted that the female prison population is much different from the male in many important respects other than sex. (See, for example, Ward and Kassebaum, 1965, p. 67).

Further, the work of Irwin (1970), Irwin and Cressey

(1962), and Heffernan (1972) strongly suggests that there are differences in the reaction to imprisonment based on the type of identity the convict brings with him to prison. Heffernan in particular found strong differences between her three categories of prisoners—the square, the cool, and the life.

Therefore it was felt that the differences between the sexes might be more accurately assessed by making comparisons within various categories of prisoners, and that the categories should be based on preprison identities.

Irwin (1970) developed a method for classifying inmates' preprison identities (or felonious identities, as he calls them) by taking into account such factors as offense, offense history, race, occupation, age, previous prison experience, drug use, and a number of other indicators. He devised eight different categories. In applying this typology to the residents at Correctional Center, we found that although Irwin devised the scheme for use with men, it worked equally well with women. That is, a high percentage of residents clearly fell into one of the Irwin categories when his scoring technique was used.

As we would expect from previous studies of the female inmate population, it differs rather markedly from the male prison population (Table 6-5). The literature suggests that women are less likely to be professional criminals, and this is

Table 6-5   Felonious Identities of Men and Women

Felonious identity	Men	Women
Thieves	28.4% (19)	8.8% (6)
Squares	22.4% (15)	16.2% (11)
Dope fiends	14.9% (10)	17.6% (12)
Lower-class persons	20.9% (14)	19.1% (13)
Hustlers	1.5% (1)	5.9% (4)
State-raised	6.0% (4)	5.9% (4)
Disorganized criminal	4.5% (3)	17.6% (12)
Heads	1.5% (1)	8.8% (6)

evidenced by the much larger percentage of male (28.4%) versus female (8.8%) thieves. A larger percentage of women than men shows up in the hustler category, although the numbers are extremely small. The same is true of the "head" category. A major difference appears in the percentage of women (17.6%) compared to men (4.5%) who are "disorganized criminals."

In comparing men to women within each of these categories, we are limited to comparisons between men and women thieves, squares, dope fiends, and lower-class persons. (The numbers in the other categories are too small to allow comparison of data.) In the following analysis,[7] however, the reader will note that the differences between the four types of felonious identities appear to be much more striking than the overall differences between men and women.

Thieves in our sample were very unlikely to experience trouble with the administration (Table 6-6). They received on the average 0.115 tickets per month served. The literature suggests that this is a category of felon who "pulls time" easily, and this can explain the finding of a low number of tickets. Eighteen percent of the men and women thieves expressed a desire for counseling in their program agreements. This is consistent with the notion that thieves may be prison-wise enough to engage in counseling to please the parole board, but are not generally oriented to counseling. Fifty-nine percent of the thieves expressed no long-range goal, and 29% of them expressed long-range goals that were job-oriented.

A clear contrast to the thieves is found in the category of squares. These individuals also received a low average amount of tickets (0.172 per month), consistent with the theory that squares attempt to please the administration, although they are perhaps not as adept at avoiding trouble as are the prison-wise thieves. A larger percentage (25%) of the squares desire counseling, and their long-range goals are much different from the thieves' goals. Only 31% of the

Table 6-6   Differences in Program Agreements and
Disciplinary Tickets Among Felonious Identity Types

	Thieves	Squares	Dope fiends	Lower-class persons
Average number of tickets per month	0.115	0.172	0.511	0.252
Percentage desiring counseling	18%	25%	39%	9%
Long-range goal				
None	59%	31%	38%	32%
Job-oriented	29%	63%	56%	36%
Prison-oriented	5.9%	6.3%	6.3%	27%

squares failed to specify a long-range goal, whereas 63% of them expressed long-range goals oriented toward jobs or education.

Dope fiends are most likely to do time poorly, at least as far as avoiding trouble with the administration is concerned. They received an average of 0.511 tickets per months served. Thirty-nine percent of them expressed an intention to engage in counseling, which is the highest percentage of any of the four categories. Two possible interpretations are (1) that dope fiends know they have to engage in some form of therapy related to their drug problem if they have any hope of favorably impressing the parole board, and/or (2) that dope fiends recognize their own need for counseling to deal with this problem. Approximately 38% of dope fiends failed to specify a long-range goal, and 56% of them expressed a goal oriented toward getting a job.

Lower-class persons received a fairly high number of tickets (0.252 per month served), indicating that they attempted neither to please the administration as squares do, nor to stay out of trouble as a general policy for doing time well, as we would expect of the thieves. Consistent with findings from the "outside world" as well as within the prison, we find that lower-class persons do not find themselves comfortable with counseling. Only 9% of them expressed an intention to receive counseling as part of their program. Thirty-two percent had no long-range goal, and 27% had long-range goals that were oriented to prison life. Only 36% had job-oriented goals, which is slightly higher than the percentage of thieves who had these goals, and much lower than the percentages for dope fiends and squares.

Comparisons between men and women within the four categories show us some interesting differences (Table 6-7). The overall counseling pattern is repeated for both the men and the women, except that male thieves are more likely to engage in counseling than are the square Johns. The finding that more women than men engage in counseling in this sample is repeated within each felonious identity type. (However, the reader is again cautioned that these probably do not represent true differences because of the way in which the male sample was selected).

The pattern of "trouble with the administration" as evidenced by average number of tickets is somewhat different for men and women. For both sexes, it is the dope fiends who are most likely to receive tickets. But lower-class women rank second in average number of tickets while

Table 6-7   **Differences in Program Agreements and Disciplinary Tickets Among Felonious Identity Types, by Sex**

	Thieves		Squares		Dope fiends		Lower-class persons	
	M	F	M	F	M	F	M	F
Average no. of tickets per month	0.063	0.316	0.151	0.212	0.595	0.456	0.127	0.450
Percentage desiring counseling	12.5%	33.3%	9.1%	44.4%	14.3%	54.5%	0%	16.7%

lower-class men rank third. Male thieves are the least likely of all men to receive tickets, while female thieves rank third in number of tickets. Square Janes are the least likely to receive tickets, while square Johns rank second in this regard. It will be noted not only that the ticketing pattern is different for men and women, but that in every category except "dope fiend" the women receive more tickets than the men, reflecting that general finding for all men versus all women.

Comparisons of the long-range goals of men and women within each category would not be meaningful because the samples are too small.

CONCLUSIONS

These data are limited because they are based on a relatively small sample of men and women. Further, they speak to only a small portion of the question of whether there are differences in the ways that men and women do time. However, one thing does seem clear. While we find some differences in reaction to incarceration when we compare men to women, we see more striking differences when we compare different types of felons to each other.

It is a general finding that women are more likely to attract the attention of the administration through disciplinary tickets, but dope fiends, be they male or female, are the most likely of any of the four categories of felons to receive tickets. Dope fiends, whether male or female, are also the types most likely to engage in counseling, and lower-class men and women are the least likely.

The differences between felon-types is also clearly evident in their long-range goals. While we see very few if any differences between men's and women's inclination to be job-oriented, we see strong differences between the various types of felons in this regard. For example, while

63% of square Johns and Janes are job-oriented, only 29% of thieves are so oriented.

This chapter, then, supports the theory that the way in which felons "do time" is a function of their preprison identities. Further, a felon's sexual identity appears to be less important than his "felonious identity." Square Janes are more similar to square Johns than they are to dope fiends or thieves. Lower-class women are more similar to lower-class men than they are to other women, and so forth.

The differences between male and female inmate cultures reported in the literature may hold true for one-sex prisons. And this research project may yet discover striking differences between men and women at Correctional Center. But the evidence available thus far suggests that when men and women do time in a similar environment, the differences in their styles of doing time are not great. Instead, the types of preprison identities that they bring to the prison dictate the ways in which they will do their time. In short, there may be masculine and feminine styles of doing time, but the clearest differences in styles of doing time are between thieves and squares (or dope fiends and lower-class persons) rather than between men and women.

NOTES

1. Giallombardo (1974) had also researched juvenile facilities for females, but since this paper focuses on adults we will not consider these findings.
2. With the exception of Tittle.
3. The first time that the inmate's case is heard by the parole board, for possible parole release.
4. The first time a resident's case is heard by the parole board.
5. See Wilson (1975) for a further discussion.
6. Disciplinary ticket data are available for 44 men and 52 women, and computations are based on these totals.
7. See Tables 6-6 and 6-7.

REFERENCES

Clemmer, D. *The prison community.* New York: Holt, Rinehart and Winston, 1940.

Gagnon, J., & Simon, W. The social meaning of prison homosexuality. *Federal Probation,* 1968, *32,* 23–29.

Giallombardo, *Society of women: A study of a woman's prison.* New York: John Wiley, 1966a.

Giallombardo, R. Social roles in a prison for women. *Social Problems,* 1966b, *13,* 268–88, reprinted as "The female inmate social system" in Guenther, *Criminal behavior and social systems.* Chicago, Rand McNally.

Giallombardo, R. *The social world of imprisoned girls: A comparative study of institutions for juvenile delinquents.* New York: John Wiley, 1974.

Heffernan, E. *Making it in prison: The square, the cool and the life.* New York: Wiley Interscience, 1972.

Irwin, J. *The felon.* Englewood Cliffs, NJ: Prentice Hall, 1970.

Irwin, J., & Cressey, D. Thieves, convicts and the inmate culture. *Social Problems,* 1962, 142–155.

Sykes, G. M. *The society of captives.* Princeton, NJ: Princeton University Press, 1958.

Tittle, C. Inmate organization: Sex differentiate and the influence of criminal subcultures. *American Sociological Review,* 1969, *34.*

Ward, D. A., & Kassebaum, G. *Women's prison: Sex and social structure.* Chicago: Aldine, 1965.

Wilson, N. Speak softly and carry a big stick: Social control in a minimum-security prison. Paper presented at meeting of the Southern Sociological Society, Washington, DC, 1975.

Chapter 7

PROBLEMS WITH RESEARCH IN CO-CORRECTIONS

John Ortiz Smykla

Over the past seven years, research into coed prisons (co-corrections) has been exclusively or substantively descriptive and/or generally qualitative, and has generally viewed co-corrections as one variable in the institutional environment (Karacki et al., 1972; Almy et al., 1975; Heffernan & Krippel, 1975; Ruback, 1975; Lambiotte, 1977; Patrick, 1976; Ross & Heffernan, 1977; and Smykla, 1978a).

Evaluation research into co-corrections, on the other hand, is quite limited. In general, evaluation research is concerned with questions of program effectiveness. In this respect, it is goal-oriented, focusing on output rather than input. In a Phase I LEAA-funded national assessment of co-corrections in the United States, Koba (1977) found that several evaluative designs do indeed exist, but they either remain at the proposal stage, were partially implemented, or are currently being implemented, including those of Cavior (no date), Flynn (no date), Heffernan (1973), Jackson (1973), and a coordinated federal effort by Burkhead, Cavior, and Mabli (1977).

The early design by Cavior (no date) was not implemented because of an absence of adequate momentum in the
Bureau of Prisons to justify a major effort. Designs by Heffernan (1973) and Jackson (1973) focusing on the Federal
Correctional Institution at Fort Worth, Texas, were only
partially implemented because of difficulty in establishing
an adequate data base within the institution and in
gathering compatible comparative data from other single-
sex institutions. An extensive evaluation of the Massachusetts Correctional Institution at Framingham was
projected by Flynn (no date), but administrative changes
within the institution interfered with implementation. The
coordinated federal effort by Burkhead, Cavior, and Mabli
(1977) was seriously hindered when two coed institutions reverted to one-sex status and a serious fire damaged a one-
sex comparison facility. Evaluation research in progress by
Cavior (1978) and Smykla (1978b) involves longitudinal
analysis on the transition back to one-sex institutions in
three federal facilities and questionnaire data on inmates'
responses to the changing social climate.

The most common measurements used in these evalua-
tions include program participation rates, disciplinary infractions, recidivism rates, and social climate scales. Certain
other kinds of data have been tabulated for institutional
purposes, such as pregnancy levels and data on assaults and
staff turnover, but such data have not been published. Koba
(1977, p. 59) contends that these circumstances reflect the
early state of the art in co-corrections research and not the
actual data collection and research per se.

From the descriptions of difficulties encountered in
developing or implementing research designs in this field
discussed, several substantive research issues emerge. These
issues or problems have in the past hindered attempts at
gathering valid data. In planning future research in co-
corrections, these exigencies must be considered. These
problems are the subject of the remainder of this chapter.

DISPERSION OF COED PRISONS

As of this writing, there is one adult coed prison in each of the following states: Texas (federal facility), Kentucky (federal facility), Massachusetts, New Jersey, Wisconsin, Missouri, Vermont, Maine, Indiana, and Pennsylvania. This dispersion of facilities over half a continent hinders access by researchers, contributes to the problem of providing comparative data, and results in a wide range of implementational and operational issues that were discussed in Chapter 2.

ISOLATING THE PHENOMENON

Sexual integration of inmates is only one characteristic of a prison environment. The degree to which sexual integration can be isolated, explained, and evaluated apart from the total institutional setting is problematic. Where we find sexual integration of inmates we also find other reintegrative interventions such as unit management, high community involvement, inmate participation in decision making, availability of contraceptives, work and study release, and furloughs.

The problem facing administrators, decision makers, and researchers is the extent to which additional data about institutional programs must be gathered to provide meaningful evaluation of the effects of sexual integration apart from other dimensions. An experimentally designed and controlled project would provide this much needed insight.

SHIFTING PRIORITIES AND OPERATIONS

Several researchers have faced the problem of shifting programs. There have been modifications of what we speculate are critical variables for the success of co-corrections: sex ratios, age distributions, program content, policy on physical contact, security level, and the degree of community involvement. Arbitrary administrative changes in these independent dimensions impede ability of our research to isolate the phenomenon and determine measures of success.

Co-correction has not developed a program philosophy of its own. Without a goal structure questions about what we did (effect evaluation), whether it achieved its results (effect), why it worked (process), how large were the results (impact), and which is the best between alternative programs (efficiency) can never be properly asked or answered.

COMPETING HYPOTHESES

There are instances of confounding variables in co-corrections. From a research perspective it is necessary to consider them conceptually even if they cannot be empirically separated. For instance, several authors have noted that inmate pressure groups in coed prison are rare. Is this because such pressure groups are circumvented by the resumption of heterosexual contact, or because pressure groups are more common to institutions housing inmates with longer terms? Without attention to these confounding variables, evaluative questions and answers about the sexual integration of inmates will be restricted to an oversimplified relationship between the independent and dependent measures.

TIME FRAMES

Measurement requires the passage of time. Because most coed prisons came into being in 1974 and 1975, there has not been enough time to allow use of recidivism rates for valid and generalizable interpretation. The National Advisory Commission on Criminal Justice Standards and Goals has suggested a three-year recidivism measure. What we find instead is a range of recidivism measures from as little as six months of baseline data to 20 months.

Time also raises another issue related to the initial subjects of any intervention like coed prison: The presumed effects of the independent variable are less likely to be seen with persons who have been only minimally exposed to the co-correctional setting. The fact that nine institutions began as coed facilities and then reverted to one-sex status is evidence of the need for better timing and caution against the myth of overnight success.

INSUFFICIENT DATA COLLECTION ABILITY

No coed adult state institution reported in Koba's Phase I national assessment of coeducational correctional institutions had a research office or staff member whose primary function was research or data collection. They did find, however, that the research ability in the Federal Bureau of Prisons was quite extensive.

Our short history in coed incarceration has shown us that without a goal structure coed facilities revert to one-sex prisons. State administrators should not expect a complex program like co-corrections to be easily understood within a short period of time. Our desire to understand the coed concept will require our willingness to provide the resources necessary to collect data now and in the future.

LACK OF A RESEARCH ORIENTATION

Interest in systematically documenting the outcomes of co-correctional policy has been conspicuously absent. The

chronicle of evaluation efforts has demonstrated that. Koba
and associates cite one instance in their survey of the gap
between research concerns and institutional demands: "The
research director in one state corrections department
complained that he could not obtain valid data on pregnancies, because such incidents were covered up: 'They spirit
them out, give them an abortion, and then put them on
furlough status as a reward for keeping their mouths shut' "
(1977, p. 67). Unless we commit ourselves and our resources
to the long-range goal of understanding co-corrections, program structure and staff support for research will never be
realized.

NONCOMPARABILITY OF DATA

Without planning and a research perspective, data
collection will happen in ways that make comparisons
across jurisdictions impossible. Together with arbitrary
shifts in priorities and operations in a given jurisdiction or
in the institution over short periods of time, the difficulty in
making comparisons across jurisdictions increases.

It is probably true that we now need a national conference on co-corrections. The Federal Bureau of Prisons has
already sponsored a co-corrections conference for its own
staff and has discussed co-corrections at a recent conference
on women. Unfortunately these conferences, which can be
most useful in gaining an understanding of the dynamics of
co-corrections, are limited to Bureau staff and exclude rep-
resentatives from state agencies, universities, and private
organizations. We should expect that as professionals we are
all committed to the pursuit of knowledge about co-
corrections. Veils of secrecy should be removed and the
public brought into participation in the system. Otherwise,

we contribute to the lack of a planning and research perspective in this field.

SENSITIVITY TOWARD SUBSTANTIVE MATTERS

One of the major issues affecting implementation of co-correctional policy is the degree of real or perceived public criticism. This is especially true with co-corrections since for centuries one-sex prisons have been the prisoner's natural lot. Sensitivity toward issues like physical contact, pregnancies, abortions, marriages, rapes, and conflicts between married persons all impede the receptiveness to data collection.

If we aggressively seek ways to enlist the support of the public we will probably find that a sizable amount of untapped public support does exist. Universities and colleges, exoffender groups, business groups, interest groups, civic groups, volunteer groups, VISTA, and law enforcement agencies and courts wooed through improved relations are "publics" that can assist in public education for the future of coed prison.

LACK OF INSTRUMENTATION

There is a distinct lack of measurement instruments designed for research in co-corrections. Cavior and Cohen (1979) have developed a scale to assess inmate and staff attitudes toward the coed setting. But the scale needs further application at other institutions before it can be said to hold wide promise.

Our coed institutions, state and federal corrections administrators, and university researchers will need to work closer on evaluative research. None of these groups possesses all the skill or resources necessary to evaluate co-corrections. Only by merging different research orientations will we ever understand the important political, social, economic, and humanitarian consequences involved in coed incarceration.

References

Almy, L., Bravo, V., Burd, L., Chin, P., Cohan, L., Gallo, F., Giorgianni, A., Gold, J., Jose, M., & Noyes, J. *Study of a coeducational correctional facility.* Unpublished Masters Thesis, School of Social Work, Boston University, 1975.

Burkhead, J., Cavior, H., & Mabli, J. *A comparison of two approaches to incarceration: Cocorrectional and single sex institutions.* Unpublished research proposal, U.S. Bureau of Prisons, 1977.

Cavior, H. Details of U.S. Bureau of Prisons evaluation efforts in cocorrections in a letter to John Ortiz Smykla, March 20, 1978.

Cavior, H. *Evaluation of cocorrections in the Federal Bureau of Prisons: A research proposal.* Unpublished research proposal, U.S. Bureau of Prisons, no date.

Cavior, H., & Cohen, S. The development of a scale to assess inmate and staff attitudes toward cocorrections. *Human Organization,* 1979, *38*:12-19.

Flynn, E. *Fort Worth and Framingham: Report for the Harvard Center for Criminal Justice.* Unpublished manuscript, no date.

Heffernan, E. *Research design for Fort Worth FCI study.* Unpublished research proposal, U.S. Bureau of Prisons, 1973.

Heffernan, E., & Krippel, E. *Final report on research: Fort Worth FCI.* Unpublished report, U.S. Bureau of Prisons, 1975.

Jackson, D. *Resident socialization and interpersonal relationships in the Fort Worth Correctional Institution.* Unpublished research proposal, U.S. Bureau of Prisons, 1973.

Karacki, L., Minor, J., Cavior, H., & Kennedy, B. *Going coed: A case study of the establishment of a coed program at a previously all male institution.* Unpublished report, U.S. Bureau of Prisons, 1972.

Koba Associates. *Summary report: Phase I assessment of coeducational corrections.* National Institute of Law Enforcement and Criminal Justice, Washington, DC, 1977.

Lambiotte, J. *Sex role differentiation in a cocorrectional setting.* Unpublished Masters Thesis, Department of Sociology, University of California at Santa Barbara, 1977.

Patrick, J. *Doing time: An ethnography of a cocorrectional institution.* Unpublished report, U.S. Bureau of Prisons, 1976.

Ross, J., & Heffernan, E. Women in a coed joint. *Quarterly Journal of Corrections,* 1977, *1,* 24-28.

Ruback, B. The sexually integrated prison: A legal and policy evaluation. *American Journal of Criminal Law,* 1975, *3,* 310-330.

Smykla, J. O. *Cocorrections: A case study of a coed federal prison.* Washington, DC: University Press of America, 1978a.

Smykla, J. O. *Measuring the impact of a coed federal correctional institution by perception of the inmates.* Unpublished research proposal, Research Grants Committee, University of Alabama, 1978b.

Chapter 8

THE DEVELOPMENT OF A SCALE TO ASSESS INMATE AND STAFF ATTITUDES TOWARD CO-CORRECTIONS

Helene Enid Cavior
Stanley H. Cohen

Co-corrections is relatively new in the Federal Bureau of Prisons. The first institution to become co-correctional was the Kennedy Center. In July 1971, women were admitted to this previously all-male institution; however, the Kennedy Center reverted to an all-male institution in July 1975.

At the time of this study, there were four co-correctional Federal Correctional Institutions (FCIs): One is for young adults (Pleasanton, California) and three are for adults (Fort Worth, Texas, Lexington, Kentucky, and Terminal Island, California). Terminal Island, historically, was two institutions—a male and a separate female facility. In 1975 some of its activities were combined. The other institutions were co-correctional since their opening. In July 1977 the Bureau of Prisons decided to convert the FCIs at Pleasanton and Terminal Island to single-sex institutions. This decision resulted from the need to equalize the inmate populations of several institutions in the western part of the country.

The original reasons for the transition to co-correctional institutions involved several factors: cost-effectiveness, normalization of the institutional environ-ment, and improved rehabilitation (see Karacki et al., 1972). Notwithstanding the validity of these factors, co-correction is now a reality, and in order to understand its impact on corrections, it is important to be aware of the reactions of the people who must deal with it daily.

This chapter reports three programmatic studies: (1) the development of an instrument to measure staff and inmate attitudes toward co-corrections; (2) a replication of this study at the same institution 13 months later; and (3) a series of comparisons using this same measure among co-correctional and all-male FCIs. The focus of this paper is empirical rather than theoretical. Because there was no literature on co-corrections when the study was begun, hy-potheses were generated afterwards from the research by Heffernan and Krippel (1975), which was not available at the time this study was planned.

Such a scale should prove useful in planning staff training and inmate orientation, as an index of individual satisfaction and/or adjustment, and as a measure of the effect of a switch to or from co-corrections. In general, this scale would *not* be appropriate for evaluating the effective-ness of co-corrections.

STUDY 1: INSTRUMENT DEVELOPMENT

The Likert method of attitude scale construction was used in this study (Edwards, 1957). A list of issues underlying a person's attitude toward co-corrections was generated by the researchers based on discussions with staff who had daily contact with inmates at a co-correctional institution. The list included such issues as sexuality, considerations of custody, discipline, and program, rehabilitative benefits, normalizations of the environment, social adjustment, and release adjustment.

For each issue, several Likert-type statements were constructed—38 in all. However, many of the items did encompass more than one issue. Each item was associated with a five-point rating scale (1 = strongly disagree to 5 = strongly agree). Of the 38 items, one-half stated positive attitudes and one-half negative attitudes. Table 8-1 lists these statements and their direction of scoring. The items were ordered to avoid sequences of items on the same issue, and they were worded to reflect approximately a fifth grade reading level and to take into account institutional vernacular.

Method

SETTING. All subjects were drawn from the population of staff and inmates at FCI Lexington, which is a medium-security federal prison for male and female adult offenders. There were 334 staff (65.3% male) and 530 inmates (71.9% male) in the institution at the time of the study (February 1975).

SUBJECTS. A total of 659 individuals returned completed questionnaires: 238 staff members[1] (67.4% male) and 398 inmates (68.4% male). The mean age of inmates in the sample was 34.4 years with a standard deviation of 10.7 years; the mean age of the staff in the sample was 41.4 years with a standard deviation of 9.9 years.

PROCEDURE. The attitude scale, along with several demographic questions, was distributed to staff and inmates during a three-day testing period by nine individuals representing the Office of Research of the Federal Bureau of Prisons. Respondents were also asked to rank in importance 11 aspects of institutional programs and environment: furloughs, work release, study release, coed institution, friendly staff-inmate relationships, good medical care, good food, good academic/vocational training programs, presence of a

Table 8-1 Items on Co-corrections Opinion Survey and Scoring Direction

_+_ 1. *There is less homosexuality among men in coed institutions than all-male institutions.

_–_ 2. Staff watch residents' day-to-day behavior more closely in coed institutions.

_–_ 3. A staff member and a resident of opposite sexes should never be alone together anyplace in the institution.

_+_ 4. Residents in coed institutions are more concerned with personal hygiene than in all-male or all-female institutions.

_+_ 5. *Homosexual assaults among women occur less frequently in coed than all-female institutions.

_+_ 6. *Coed institutions have fewer discipline problems than all-male or all-female institutions.

_–_ 7. When men and women are in the same institution it is only natural that they will try to have sexual relations whenever they can.

_–_ 8. Doing time in coed institutions is easy time.

_–_ 9. A woman is under a lot of pressure at coed institutions to get a boyfriend or walk partner.

_+_ 10. *There is more swearing in all-male and all-female institutions than in coed institutions.

_+_ 11. *The advantages of coed institutions outweigh the problems arising from resident sexual behavior.

_–_ 12. When male and female residents are assigned to the same work area they would rather talk than work.

_–_ 13. Staff spend a lot of time in coed institutions making sure men and women do not have sexual relations.

_+_ 14. *There is less fighting in coed institutions than in all-male or all-female institutions.

_–_ 15. *There is just as much homosexuality among women in coed institutions as in all-female institutions.

_–_ 16. *Releasees from coed facilities are more likely to commit a new crime.

_+_ 17. Most male-female relationships among residents in coed institutions do not involve sexual relations.

_–_ 18. One institution cannot give adequate job training to both men and women since the jobs they usually fill are very different.

_–_ 19. A staff member and a resident of the opposite sexes must be very careful about what they say to each other.

± 20. *There are fewer assaults on staff in coed institutions than in all-male or all-female institutions.

± 21. *First offenders find it easier to adjust to prison life in coed institutions than in all-male or all-female institutions.

± 22. *Residents in coed institutions pay more attention to how they look and what they wear than in all-male or all-female institutions.

± 23. Residents in coed institutions do not spend as much time thinking about their mistakes as those in all-male or all-female institutions.

± 24. *Coed groups are a more effective way of dealing with residents' interpersonal problems than all-male or all-female groups.

± 25. A woman is under a lot of pressure to get a sexual partner in all-female institutions.

± 26. *Residents in coed institutions do not develop as much hostility toward society as those in all-female or all-male institutions.

± 27. Serving time in coed institutions is "too pleasant."

± 28. *Residents in coed institutions are more involved in institution programs than those in all-male or all-female institutions.

± 29. *Homosexual assaults among men occur less frequently in coed than in all-male institutions.

± 30. *Although there are some advantages of co-corrections, there are many more disadvantages.

± 31. *Prostitutes and pimps can earn a lot of money in coed institutions.

± 32. *The transition to the free society is easier from coed institutions than from all-male or all-female institutions.

± 33. It isn't fair to put men and women together in an institution where sex is prohibited.

± 34. It is easier to organize recreational activities in coed institutions than in all-male or all-female institutions.

± 35. Residents earn paroles sooner at coed institutions than in all-male or all-female institutions.

± 36. Residents in coed institutions would rather spend their time socializing than participating in counseling groups.

± 37. Society believes that it is not punishment to be in a coed institution.

± 38. There is more desire to escape from coed institutions than from all-male or all-female institutions.

---

*Items selected for final scale.

prison industry, contact with community volunteers, and effective counseling groups.

All staff and inmates had been told in advance about the survey and were encouraged by the warden to cooperate. Inmates and most staff were given the questionnaire in group sessions during which the researcher explained that the survey was concerned with their opinions about co-corrections. The rest of the staff completed the questionnaire on an individual basis and returned it at their convenience, either via mail or by depositing it in a box provided for this purpose. The questionnaire was read to nonreaders and was read in Spanish to Spanish-speaking inmates. The approximate time to complete the questionnaire was 15 minutes.

Results and Discussion

In the analysis presented below, approximately 5% of the sample failed to respond to one or more of the items. The number of observations used for each statistic was based on those observations that included complete data on the variables involved in that analysis. Thus the sample size varies somewhat (from 600 to 640) for each statistic.

Separate correlational matrices were computed for inmates, staff, and total sample for the 38 items in the questionnaire. A cluster analysis was performed on each matrix according to the method described by Hunter and Cohen (1969) and Hunter (1973). Their clustering procedure was adapted from Tryon and Baily (1970) and involves clustering items by their degree of interitem similarity. This procedure yielded one major cluster for each matrix. Only items which appeared in this cluster for all three matrices were selected for the final scale. This strategy ensured a scale that is applicable for both staff and inmates. Ten items did not appear in any of the clusters and ten items were not common to all three matrices.

The 18 items so selected are asterisked in Table 8-1. These items were as representative of the list of issues as were the initial pool of items. Although the content of the items in the cluster is diverse, the degree of intercorrelation among the items is uniform, suggesting that staff and inmates believe co-corrections have a generally positive or generally negative effect on several aspects of the prison experience.

Table 8-2 details correlations among the 18 items and the scale sum for the total sample. The interitem correlations ranged from 0.04 to 0.44. The KR-21 reliability coefficients for inmates and staff were 0.83 and 0.89 respectively; for males and females they were 0.85 and 0.85 respectively; and for the combined sample it was 0.86. These results indicate that the scale has a high degree of internal consistency.

It was hypothesized that a respondent's attitude toward co-corrections would be related to the importance assigned to "coed institution" on the rank-order question. The correlation between rank of coed institution and score on the co-corrections scale (on which a high score indicates a more favorable attitude) was 0.35, t (470) = 9.25, $p < 0.0001$. An F test for departure from linearity was not significant, and this indicated that the relationship between attitude and rank was essentially linear. These results can be viewed as providing one measure of convergent validity for the scale.

A least squares 2 × 2 factorial analysis of variance was used to compare respondents' attitude toward co-corrections as a function of sex and status. Inmates had a more positive average attitude toward co-corrections than staff (69.7 and 66.0 respectively, F (1,610) = 13.24, $p < 0.0003$, eta^2 = 0.02), although both groups responded favorably (the implied neutral point is 54) and the magnitude of the difference was small. This generally positive attitude toward co-corrections is consistent with anecdotal comments made by inmates and staff at the institution.

More important was a significant sex by status interaction (F (1,610) = 5.06, $p < 0.02$, eta^2 = 0.01), which is shown in Figure 8-1a. Tukey's HSD test for multiple comparisons among means indicated that male staff were less favorable

Table 8-2 Correlations among Test Items and Total Score

	Q1	Q5	Q6	Q10	Q11	Q14	Q15	Q16	Q20	Q21	Q22	Q24	Q26	Q28	Q29	Q30	Q31	Q32	Total
Q1		0.30	0.28	0.17	0.29	0.31	0.19	0.14	0.27	0.20	0.20	0.27	0.29	0.18	0.44	0.17	0.24	0.39	0.54
Q5			0.24	0.18	0.21	0.29	0.37	0.14	0.22	0.19	0.27	0.21	0.26	0.10	0.27	0.18	0.25	0.19	0.50
Q6				0.30	0.33	0.44	0.20	0.21	0.30	0.24	0.30	0.29	0.36	0.21	0.28	0.21	0.21	0.31	0.60
Q10					0.29	0.31	0.15	0.12	0.13	0.10	0.18	0.25	0.26	0.21	0.19	0.10	0.09	0.20	0.45
Q11						0.33	0.17	0.21	0.24	0.28	0.27	0.39	0.33	0.29	0.30	0.38	0.16	0.40	0.61
Q14							0.24	0.20	0.39	0.24	0.29	0.27	0.33	0.24	0.42	0.20	0.30	0.39	0.63
Q15								0.15	0.15	0.17	0.16	0.14	0.21	0.04	0.21	0.23	0.15	0.20	0.44
Q16									0.22	0.13	0.19	0.23	0.19	0.15	0.22	0.25	0.33	0.16	0.44
Q20										0.29	0.30	0.37	0.39	0.26	0.36	0.17	0.25	0.34	0.57
Q21											0.29	0.29	0.30	0.25	0.28	0.20	0.16	0.35	0.51
Q22												0.41	0.37	0.27	0.30	0.12	0.24	0.35	0.55
Q24													0.38	0.32	0.36	0.22	0.24	0.34	0.60
Q26														0.29	0.37	0.19	0.20	0.43	0.63
Q28															0.31	0.17	0.16	0.28	0.49
Q29																0.17	0.29	0.43	0.62
Q30																	0.27	0.26	0.48
Q31																		0.20	0.49
Q32																			0.63
Total																			

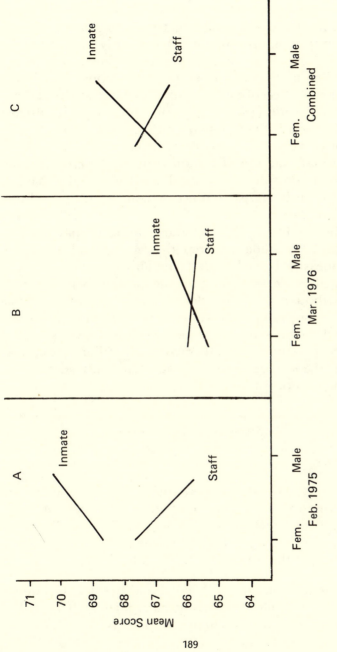

Figure 8-1 Attitudes on co-corrections at FCI Lexington by sex and status for (A) Time 1, (B) Time 2, and (C) combined over time.

than either male or female inmates ($p < 0.05$). None of the remaining comparisons were statistically significant. A status difference is not unexpected; inmates may be responding to the social aspect of co-corrections, that is, the normalizing effect of co-corrections. In contrast, the staff has to deal with supervision and control. What is more difficult to understand is that the status difference is found for men but not women. One possible explanation of this result is that the male staff might be more concerned than the female staff with controlling potential inmate sexual behavior. However, further research is necessary to determine if this is indeed the case.

The findings of this study indicate that the co-correctional attitude scale reported here is highly reliable when measured by the KR-21 reliability coefficients and correlated moderately with an independent validity measure. Although this study demonstrated that the scale has some convergent validity—that is, the relationship with the rank order item—the discriminant validity of the scale has yet to be investigated. In other words, we still must examine whether the scale can be differentiated from attitudes toward other aspects of corrections.

Study 2: A Replication

Method

SETTING.   All subjects were drawn from the Study 1 at FCI Lexington, Kentucky, 13 months later. There were 265 staff (66.0% male) who were asked to participate (the hospital staff was excluded) and 718 inmates (59.4% male) in the institution at the time of the study (March 1976).

SUBJECTS.   A total of 703 individuals participated in the study: 182 staff (66.5% male) and 521 inmates (49.9% male). The mean age of inmates in the sample was 32.0 years with a standard deviation of 11.3 years; the mean age of staff in the sample was 41.2 years with a standard deviation of 9.6 years. The decrease in the percentage of male inmates and the age of inmates from Study 1 can be attributed to an influx of younger women from the FCI for women at Alderson, West Virginia. Approximately 8.8% of the inmate population and 88.1% of the staff population were at the FCI at the time of Study 1.

PROCEDURE. The final version of the attitude scale along with the same demographic questions were administered to staff and inmates; the rank order question was omitted. All other procedural aspects of the study were the same as in Study 1.

Results and Discussion

Separate correlation matrices were computed again for inmates, staff, and the total sample for the 18 items in the scale. The interitem correlations were similar for both staff and inmates and also were comparable to those in the first study. The interitem correlations for the total sample ranged from 0.02 to 0.50; the KR-21 reliability coefficient was 0.83. These results indicate that the internal consistency found in the first study was replicated in this new sample.

A least squares $2 \times 2 \times 2$ factorial analysis of variance was used to compare the respondents' attitudes toward co-corrections as a function of sex, status, and time. This analysis indicated that respondents had a less favorable average attitude at Time 2 than at Time 1 (65.4 and 68.3 respectively, F (1,1309) = 15.77, $p < 0.0001$, eta^2 = 0.01). In addition, there was a significant status by time interaction: F (1,1309) = 5.17, $p < 0.02$, eta^2 = 0.01. Tukey's HSD test indicated that inmates at Time 1 had a more favorable attitude than inmates at Time 2 and staff at either time period (see Figures 8-1a and 8-1b).

A simple effects analysis controlling for time was performed to examine differences among the sex by status interaction cells from Time 1 to Time 2. These interactions are presented in Figure 8-1. The analysis revealed no significant effects at Time 2 and, as previously found, significant effects due to status ($p < 0.001$) and sex by status ($p < 0.05$) at Time 1. Tukey's HSD test indicated that the male inmate population at Time 1 had a less favorable attitude than the male inmate population at Time 2 ($p < 0.05$); the results for the female inmate population were in the same direction ($p < 0.10$).

One possible explanation for these changes is the difference in the inmate population from Time 1 to Time 2. A 35.5% increase in the inmate population (from 530 to 718) led to general conditions of overcrowding and the problems typically associated with it. Previous research on the effects of population density in general and specifically in prisons indicates that negative effects on attitude and other measures can be expected (see Dean, Pugh, & Gundersen, 1975; Griffitt & Veitch, 1971; McCain, Cox, & Baltes, 1976; and Megargee, 1977). Anecdotally, correctional workers generally believe that overcrowding leads to increased disciplinary problems and decreased morale. Thus the increased inmate population at Time 2 compared with Time 1 may have contributed to the less favorable attitude toward co-corrections observed as a function of time.

Another change occurred in the summer of 1975 when it became necessary to transfer from the FCI at Alderson, West Virginia, all women who were sentenced under the Youth Corrections Act. The influx at FCI Lexington of 96 women during a three-month period increased the female population by 95.3% (from 149 to 291) and lowered the average age of female inmates by approximately five years. (The average age of the female inmate sample decreased by four years.)

Although the effect of an age change or a change in the male/female inmate ratio is unknown, previous research

(Heffernan & Krippel, 1975) suggests that inmate age may be an important factor in the operation of a co-correctional institution. Anecdotally, staff believe that younger women are generally more difficult to work with and more prone to violate institutional rules, especially those rules related to the control of physical contact between inmates. Thus staff supervision and control of inmates, both qualitatively and quantitatively, undoubtedly changed, and this change may be related to the difference observed in inmate attitude toward co-corrections.

Finally, there was a 44.6% decrease in the percentage of inmates who were transferred to FCI Lexington from other federal institutions (from 63.2% to 53.0%). Previous research at a similar institution, the FCI in Fort Worth, Texas (Heffernan & Krippel, 1975), indicates that inmates' judgments of institutions and institutional programs depend on previous prison experience. It is likely that those committed initially to institutions with innovative programs judge them in an "absolute" sense or relative to the free community. These judgments seem to be harsher than those of inmates who have been transferred to institutions with innovative programs from those with more traditional programs. Members of this latter group, although they see the problems, tend to emphasize the "relative" benefits over more traditional institutions. Thus the sharp change in the ratio of transfers versus court commitments may have contributed to the less favorable attitude of inmates toward co-corrections at Time 2.

Another instrument, the Correctional Institutions Environment Scale, Form C (Moos, 1975), administered both times as part of the test battery, showed an overall trend (there are nine subscales) toward less positive inmate judgments of the institution at the two times (see Karacki & Prather, 1975a; Karacki & Prather, 1976). It is possible that the attitude toward co-corrections is affected by the general perception of the institution.

Study 3: Institutional Comparisons

Method

SETTING.   Subjects were drawn from three additional medium-security institutions. The FCI at Pleasanton, California, is for young adult female and male offenders. There were 143 staff (71.7% male) and 218 inmates (71.1% male) in the institution at the time of data collection (November 1975). The FCI at Englewood, Colorado, is for young adult male offenders. There were 195 staff (90.8% male) and 362 inmates in the institution at the time of data collection (December 1975). The FCI at Petersberg, Virginia, is also for young adult male offenders. There were 20 staff (85.0% male) and 232 inmates in the two living units where testing was done at the time of data collection (June 1975).

SUBJECTS.   A total of 1313 individuals participated in this study, including the individuals from FCI Lexington (Time 1).[2] At FCI Pleasanton there were 90 staff (67.8% male) and 130 inmates (67.7% male). The mean age of inmates was 22.2 years with a standard deviation of 2.8 years; the mean age of staff was 36.3 years with a standard deviation of 8.9 years. At FCI Englewood there were 93 male staff members[3] and 191 inmates. The average age of the male staff was 41.0 years with a standard deviation of 10.0 years, and the average age of inmates was 20.1 years with a standard deviation of 2.3 years. At FCI Petersberg there were 17 male staff members and 178 inmates. The average age of the staff was 36.2 years with a standard deviation of 10.8 years, and the average age of inmates was 22.8 years with a standard deviation of 2.3 years.

PROCEDURE.   The procedure was essentially the same as that in Study 2.

Results and Discussion

The following analyses involved selected comparisons: the two co-correctional institutions (FCI Lexington and FCI Pleasanton); females from these two institutions; and males from these two institutions and from two all-male institutions (FCI Englewood and FCI Petersberg). These analyses were performed to examine differences in inmate and staff attitudes on co-correctional versus single-sex institutions. It should be emphasized that the male analysis, but not the female analysis, includes respondents from single-sex institutions in addition to respondents from co-correctional institutions.

CO-CORRECTIONAL ANALYSIS. A $2 \times 2 \times 2$ least squares analysis of variance was used to analyze the attitude at co-correctional institutions as a function of institution, sex, and status. The FCI at Lexington had a more positive average attitude than that at FCI Pleasanton (68.3 and 64.7 respectively, $F(1,826) = 22.68$, $p < 0.0001$, eta^2 = 0.03), and inmates had a more positive average attitude than staff (69.4 and 64.1 respectively, $F(1,826) = 44.45$, $p < 0.0001$, eta^2 = 0.05).

More important is a significant institution-by-status interaction: $F(1,826) < 9.79$, $p < 0.002$, eta^2 = 0.01, which is graphed in Figure 8-2. The results of Tukey's HSD test indicated that the staff at FCI Pleasanton was significantly less favorable ($p < 0.05$) toward co-corrections than were the other three groups. In addition, the staff at FCI Lexington was significantly less favorable ($p < 0.05$) than inmates at FCI Lexington, but not less than those at FCI Pleasanton. Thus inmates' attitudes were similar across institutions, while the staff at Pleasanton had a less favorable attitude than that at Lexington.

The same factors that influence inmate attitude toward

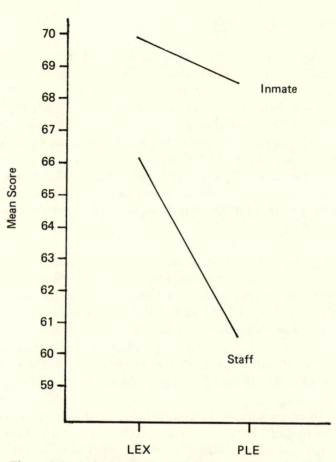

Figure 8-2 Attitudes on co-corrections among males and females by institution and status.

an institution are likely to influence staff attitudes as well. Thus the difference in inmate age at FCI Pleasanton and FCI Lexington (21.5 years versus 24.4 years) may have contributed to the difference in expressed attitude toward co-corrections between the two institutions. In addition, the previous work experiences of the staffs at the two institutions were different. Most of the staff at FCI Lexington at Time 1 came either from other federal institutions or from the hospital for drug abusers that previously occupied the facility. Thus they had other traditional programs to use as a comparison in judging the FCI. In contrast, a large number of the staff members at FCI Pleasanton were hired from the local community and had no previous experience in other institutions. Consequently, their judgments of the FCI and specifically of co-corrections were based on the problems they encountered and were not affected by the knowledge of problems in single-sex institutions.

Finally, the Correctional Institutions Environment Scale, administered at both institutions at the same time as the Co-corrections Opinion Survey, resulted in a consistently more favorable response by that staff at FCI Lexington than at FCI Pleasanton (see Karacki & Prather, 1975a; Karacki & Prather, 1975b). It is possible that this general response to the institutions influenced the attitude toward co-corrections.

As in Study 1, a significant interaction between sex and status was found: F (1,826) = 6.05, $p < 0.02$, eta^2 = 0.01; however, the effect can be attributed primarily to FCI Lexington.

FEMALE ANALYSIS.   Differences in females' average attitudes as a function of institution and status were analyzed by using a 2×2 least squares analysis of variance. As previously found, inmates had a more positive average attitude than staff (68.2 and 65.6 respectively, F (1,265) = 6.85, $p < 0.009$, eta^2 = 0.03), and FCI Lexington had a more favorable average attitude than FCI Pleasanton (68.2 and 64.3 respectively, F (1,265) = 9.97, $p < 0.002$, eta^2 = 0.04). Also, the institution-by-status interaction approached statistical significance ($p < 0.08$). The staff at Pleasanton had a less favorable average attitude (60.7) than the other three groups, which were similar to each other (range: 66.8 to 68.6).

MALE ANALYSIS.   Differences in males' attitudes as a function of institution and status were analyzed by using a 4×2 least squares analysis of variance. Again, inmates had a more

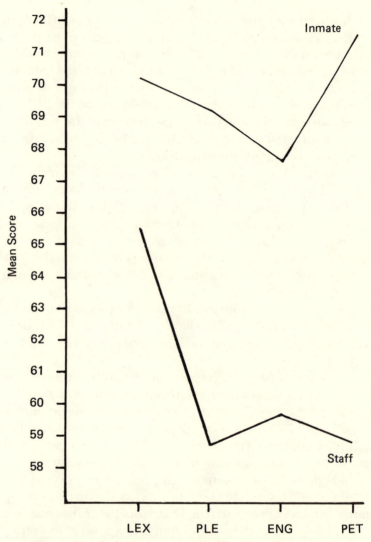

Figure 8-3   Attitudes on co-corrections among males by institution and status.

positive average attitude than staff (69.7 and 62.0 respectively, $F (1,1036) = 95.49$, $p < 0.0001$, eta^2 = 0.08). While differences among institutions were found ($F (3,1036) = 9.27$, $p < 0.0001$, eta^2 = 0.03), there was also a significant institution-by-status interaction: ($F (3,1036) = 4.24$, $p < 0.006$, eta^2 = 0.01, which is shown in Figure 8-3. The results of Tukey's HSD test indicated no differences among the staffs at the Pleasanton, Englewood, and Petersberg FCIs, and no differences among the inmates at all four institutions. The staff at FCI Lexington had a more favorable average attitude than all other staff groups ($p < 0.05$) and a less favorable average attitude than inmates at only FCI Petersberg ($p < 0.05$).

The difference in attitude toward co-corrections between male staff at FCI Lexington and male staff at FCIs Englewood and Petersberg is not surprising. Male staff members who have no previous experience working with female inmates in either a single-sex or a co-correctional institution often express reservations about doing it. They believe female inmates are difficult to work with and that in a co-correctional institution the inmates would be more interested in socializing than participating in institutional programs. The difference between FCIs Lexington and Pleasanton was also presented in Study 2, and the same interpretation would apply.

CONCLUSIONS

The results of Studies 1 and 2 indicate that the Co-correctional Opinion Survey is both reliable and stable and thus provides a tool for assessing both inmate and staff attitude toward co-corrections. The results of the three analyses that comprise Study 3 suggest several general conclusions.

Inmates tend to be more favorable toward co-corrections than staff; within institutions the status difference is statistically significant in all but one instance

(Lexington, Time 2). Status differences are not unexpected in institutions; inmates and staff have a different perspective—the "kept" versus the "keeper." Results of the Co-correctional Institutions Environment Scale, administered at several of the federal institutions, consistently yielded a more favorable attitude among staff toward the institution in general than among inmates.

It is generally expected that the staff, which is working hard to make the institution's programs a success, will express a more favorable attitude than inmates toward those programs. The reversal found with the Co-corrections Opinion Survey, in which inmates have a more favorable attitude than staff, may reflect the difference between a judgment of institutional programs per se compared with a "conceptual program" such as co-corrections. In other words, a favorable response to co-corrections is qualitatively different from judgments of concrete programs such as the counseling program, the education program, and so on.

The interaction between sex and status found in Study 1 (FCI Lexington, Time 1) was not replicated in the co-correctional institutions analysis in Study 3 for FCI Pleasanton (simple effects analysis), although the means for the four groups at FCI Pleasanton exhibited the same pattern as at FCI Lexington (groups ordered from high to low score are: male inmate, female inmate, female staff, and male staff). Further exploration into this result should be pursued at other co-correctional institutions.

Although differences between institutions were found in all three analyses that comprise Study 3, the consistent pattern of an interaction between institution and status is more important. This interaction was statistically significant in the co-correctional and male analyses. In all three analyses, the relatively favorable response of staff at FCI Lexington as compared with staff at the other institution(s) appears to "create" the interaction effect. Several possible reasons for this were discussed in the results section of Study

3, including the age of the inmate population, the overall attitude toward the institution as reflected in results of the Correctional Institutions Environment Scale, and prior work experiences of the staff. Further application of this scale at co-correctional FCIs which are similar in mission and program operation to FCI Lexington, at FCIs for women, and at FCIs for adult men is necessary before the institution-by-status interaction can be fully understood.

NOTES

1. All staff members employed at the institution were included in the survey because virtually all job roles involve daily interaction with inmates.
2. Time 1 was used to control for the length of time that the FCIs at Lexington and Pleasanton were operational.
3. The number of female staff members was too small to include in the analysis.

REFERENCES

Dean, L. M., Pugh, W. M., & Gunderson, E. J. Spacial and perceptual components of crowding: Effects on health and satisfaction. *Environment and Behavior,* 1975, *7,* 225-236.

Edwards, A. L. *Techniques of attitude scale construction.* New York: Appleton-Century, 1957.

Griffitt, W., & Veitch, R. Hot and crowded: The influence of population density and temperature on interpersonal affective behavior. *Journal of Personality and Social Psychology,* 1971, *17,* 92-98.

Heffernan, E., & Krippel, E. *Final report on research: Fort Worth Federal Correctional Institution: February, 1973-March, 1975.* Office of Research, Bureau of Prisons, Washington, DC 20537, 1975.

Hunter, J. E. Methods of recording the correlation matrix to facilitate visual inspection and preliminary cluster analysis. *Journal of Educational Measurement,* 1973, *10,* 51-61.

Hunter, J. E., & Cohen, S. H. PACKAGE: A system of computer routines for the analysis of correlational data. *Educational and Psychological Measurement,* 1969, *29,* 697-700.

Karacki, L., et al. *Going coed: A case study of the establishment of a coed program at a previously all male institution.* Office of Research, Bureau of Prisons, Washington, DC 20537, 1972.

Karacki, L., & Prather, J. *CIES profiles for Lexington, February 1975.* Office of Research, Bureau of Prisons, Washington, DC 20537, 1975a.

Karacki, L., & Prather, J. *CIES profiles for Pleasanton, November 1975.* Office of Research, Bureau of Prisons, Washington, DC 20537, 1975b.

Karacki, L., & Prather, J. *CIES profiles for Lexington, March 1976.* Office of Research, Bureau of Prisons, Washington, DC 20537, 1976.

McCain, G., Cox, V. C., & Baltes, P. B. Relationship between illness, complaints and degree of crowding in a prison environment. *Environment and Behavior,* 1976, *8,* 283–290.

Megargee, E. I. The association of population density, reduced space and uncomfortable temperatures with misconduct in a prison community. *American Journal of Community Psychology,* 1977.

Moos, R. H. *Evaluating correctional and community settings.* New York: John Wiley & Sons, 1975.

Tryon, R. C., & Bailey, D. E. *Cluster analysis.* New York: McGraw-Hill 1970.

Chapter 9

CO-CORRECTIONAL MODELS

James Ross
Esther Heffernan
James Sevick
Ford Johnson

In this chapter, each of three causal or logic models is outlined. It is stressed that each represents an actual operational model of co-corrections derived from activities observed in the field and discussions with those having responsibility for implementing programs. Each is an empirical, inductive model; however, in no institution was any model more than partially articulated, and in any given institution more than one model was operative. The underlying assumptions behind the models and their linkages to operating activities are an expression of the conceptions of co-corrections held by practitioners in existing coed institutions. After a discussion of the programmatic and nonprogrammatic models, the effects of the simultaneous presence of several models in a single institution are considered.

PROGRAMMATIC CO-CORRECTIONS

It became clear during site visits that co-corrections was seen as performing a positive function in the context of three general models of correctional practice operative within the institutions:

- Reintegration into the community
- Institutional control
- Therapy and treatment

Reintegration Model

The use of co-corrections in a reintegration model of corrections reflects efforts to use male-female interaction to "normalize" the institutional environment—to represent the fuller range of options normally available "in the free"—and, by being less "destructive" than traditional single-sex incarceration, to ease transition to, and reintegration into, the community after release. The function of co-corrections within the reintegration model—which has as its overall objectives the normalizing of the prison environment as far as possible to lessen the "destructiveness" of the prison experience and facilitate the re-entrance of the inmate into society—is seen as either maintaining or restoring in prison the option of interaction with the opposite sex and thereby effecting personal growth or preventing deterioration and "backsliding." Co-corrections here occurs in a context that stresses other normalizing aspects of institutional life, such as use of regular currency, inmate control over "rising time," etc., and is generally bolstered by a focus on community programming. The positive function of co-corrections in the reintegration model is based on several underlying assumptions that were articulated by persons directly involved in the planning and administration of institutions in which the model represented an "operational philosophy."

- The corrosive effects of traditional single-sex confinement impede postrelease adjustment and engender continued criminality.

- The deprivation of the full range of "normal" affectional relationships, which is associated with traditional single-sex incarceration, is the source of much institutional violence and predatory homosexuality.
- "Masculine" dominance roles and the violence associated with quarrels, triangles, etc., are undesirable in a prison·setting.
- Sexual relationships occur in prison, and preferably should be voluntary and heterosexual rather than coercive and situationally homosexual.

A brief overview of the policies and practices related to the use of co-corrections in the reintegration model will provide the basis for understanding the chain of assumptions it represents. The inputs to the reintegration model include an integrated staff and, ideally, an inmate population the composition of which reflects the range of attributes found in the "outside" world, particularly in terms of sex ratio. Control adequate to minimize predatory behavior is exercised, and, where possible, inmates with histories of assault are selected out and those displaying assaultive behavior within the institution transferred. At the same time, birth control is made available to limit pregnancies. The structured and unstructured interaction of male and female inmates is sometimes complemented, especially where the population is composed predominantly of one sex, by increasing the representation of the minority sex through disproportionate staff integration, furloughs, use of volunteers of both sexes, and community programs. Male-female interaction is seen as engendering a relational atmosphere in which the continuity or resumption of heterosexual options leads to low levels of violence and limited use of psychotropic medication. By transferring-in incarcerated spouses, the heterosexual options of married inmates unwilling to interact with persons of the opposite sex are restored; at the same time, to increase the likelihood of post-release marital stability, the program participation of "serious" couples is restricted if "outside" relationships are imperiled. A normalized atmosphere and heterosexual options are seen as leading, in turn, to a number of interacting phenomena: maintained or increased self-worth, improved appearance and grooming, improved staff and inmate morale, and increased postprison expectations.

The reintegration model of co-corrections anticipates the following outcomes: As a result of the presence of a more normal institutional environment, pressures for situational homosexual activity are minimized for first offenders; the resumption of heterosexual options for transfers from single-sex institutions provides a period of time for the redevelopment of heterosexual relational skills before release; some support is present for the continuation of marital bonds between incarcerated couples; and finally, the sexual options of protection cases, transferred-in because of the haven afforded by low levels of institutional violence, are protected. These outcomes provided by co-corrections contribute to reduced postrelease adjustment problems, which in turn reduce recidivism.

Institutional Control Model

The use of co-corrections in an institutional control model reflects the perceived value of the male-female interaction in normalizing the institutional environment, as in the reintegration model. The focus of the co-corrections institutional control model is on the power of the male-female interaction as a management tool in the reduction of institutional violence. The model is often found together with the reintegration model, because they both use the male-female interaction in shaping the institutional environment, despite the fact that many other input, process, and outcome elements differ between the two models. The institutional control model of co-corrections is based on the following underlying assumptions, which were most clearly articulated by those staff members in co-correctional institutions who were more directly responsible for institutional control.

- The deprivation of the full range of normal interactions with the opposite sex, which is associated with traditional single-sex incarceration, is a principal source of institutional violence, predatory homosexuality, and other problem behaviors.
- "Masculine" dominance roles and the violence associated with quarrels, triangles, etc., are undesirable in a prison setting.
- Sexual relationships, if they occur in prison, should preferably be voluntary and heterosexual rather than coercive and situationally homosexual.
- The presence of the opposite sex in an institutional setting provides a diversion that lessens institutional violence, predatory homosexuality, and other problem behaviors.

A brief overview will suggest both the differences and the similarities between the use of co-corrections in institutional control and in reintegration models and provide a framework for understanding the chain of assumptions it represents. The inputs to the institutional control model include an integrated staff, and an integrated inmate population, as heterogeneous as possible, containing a sufficiently visible representation of the minority sex to develop and maintain a normalized atmosphere, but not close enough to sexual parity to risk precipitating a battle of the sexes to "structure the situation." Control adequate to minimize predatory behavior is exercised, and population control effected through selection out of those with assaultive histories, transfer of those displaying assaultive behavior within the institution, and selective transfer for heterosexual intercourse or for pregnancies that occur within the institution. The structured and unstructured interaction of male and female inmates is sometimes complemented by increased representation of the minority sex through disproportionate line-staff integration, furloughs, use of volunteers of both sexes, and community programs. Male-female interaction leads to a less tense and crisis-oriented atmosphere and to a continuity or resumption of heterosexual options, which are reinforced by furloughs and community programs. The continuity or resumption of heterosexual options, improved appearance and grooming, and maintained or increased self-worth occur in interaction with each other and sustain a high level of inmate morale. Staff and inmate morale increases as a function of male-female interaction; staff in-service training, which explores and clarifies expected staff-inmate relationships; and the maintenance or increase of a sense of self-worth. At the same time, program participation by serious couples is restricted in order to achieve low emotional involvement between inmates, but has the inadvertent effect of threatening increased staff and inmate morale increases as a function of male-female inter-pregnancy, and assaultive behavior reinforces a low level of emotional involvement; and, should heterosexual options bring about a high level of "coupling," coed programming may be cut back to decrease the probability of emotional involvement. Low emotional involvement, availability of birth control, and selective use of transfer combine to limit pregnancy rates, although furloughs and community programs may increase the level of noninstitutional pregnancy. Low emotional involvement, a noninstitutionalized atmosphere, and the availability of heterosexual options yield a safe and manageable environment relatively free of sexual and sex-related violence.

Therapy Model

The function of co-corrections in a therapy model also involves use of the male-female interaction to normalize the institutional atmosphere, but with an eye less on the provision of the fuller range of options normally obtainable "outside," and more on the deliberate development of circumstances that allow "working with," and correction of, "sexually abnormal" attitudes and behaviors. The focus of the co-correctional therapy model is on the effects of the male-female interaction upon the development of an atmosphere that limits the necessity and frequency of exploitive behavior and on the reduction of evident or presumed sexual abnormalities, which are in turn presumed to be a direct or indirect cause of criminal behavior. The model is often found together with the reintegration model, even though they differ in selection criteria, means of population control, levels of control, function of program restrictions, and primary intended outcomes. The therapy model of co-corrections is based on the following underlying assumptions, which were outlined most frequently by administrators and treatment personnel in institutions with a history of providing a "therapeutic milieu."

- Much criminal behavior stems, directly or indirectly, from the absence of healthy relationships with the opposite sex or the inability to explore problems of sexual identification.
- Traditional single-sex incarceration has exacerbated the sexual abnormality of offenders by fostering development of homosexual and often violent subcultures.
- As undesirable as "masculine" dominance roles are in a prison setting, they must sometimes be tolerated if certain role changes are to be effected.
- Sexual relationships occur in prison and preferably

should be voluntary, nonexploitive, and heterosexual, or at least voluntary and nonexploitive rather than coercive and situationally homosexual.

- To achieve correction of sexually abnormal behaviors and attitudes, some "acting-out" behavior must be tolerated, and control policies must be constructed and implemented with discretion and sensitivity.

- Those inmates who have traditionally been the focus of sexual exploitation require a higher level of protection of sexual options than others.

A brief overview will suggest the complexities of using co-corrections in a therapy model. The inputs to the therapy model include an at least partially integrated staff, and an integrated inmate population, as heterogeneous as possible, containing a sufficiently visible number of the minority sex to provide a "therapeutic tool" for both sexes. The sexually abnormal—potentially to include prostitutes, sex offenders, and drug abusers whose criminality is presumed to derive from problems of sex identity—are intentionally overselected, and a differential control policy offers extra protection to males and females with histories of being sexually exploited while allowing levels of acting-out behavior sufficient to permit the therapeutic process to operate. The differential control policy and the policy of tolerating acting-out behavior require the implementation of staff in-service training. The resultant clarification of policy and increased understanding of the basis for policy lead to increased staff and inmate morale. The structured and unstructured interaction of male and female inmates brings about a more supportive atmosphere, which in turn facilitates the role of the structured and unstructured interaction of males and females, including a range of therapy modalities, in bringing about nonexploitive heterosexual relationships, a clarification of sex identity, and the perception of the opposite sex as "peers" and "co-workers." The restriction of program participation together by serious couples ordinarily occurs only when relationships are perceived as exploitive. The development of nonexploitive heterosexual relationships leads to development of heterosexual coping skills, the clarification of sex identity to increased self-acceptance, and the perception of the opposite sex as peers and co-workers to the reduction of sex-role stereotypes. The more supportive atmosphere increases self-worth, which combines with the development of heterosexual coping skills to effect changes in appearance and roles; at the same time, dress codes may mandate changes in appearance and interact with other variables to effect role changes. Changes in appearance and roles may inadvertently combine with the toleration of acting-out behavior to increase "therapeutic" pregnancies, i.e., those that may further contribute to a shift in sex identity. Changes in appearance and roles, development of heterosexual coping skills, increased self-acceptance, and reduced sex-role stereotypes combine to reduce postrelease adjustment problems and reduce recidivism.

NONPROGRAMMATIC CO-CORRECTIONS

While co-correctional relationships may be seen as integral components of correctional models involving reintegration, institutional control, and therapy, when co-corrections has been introduced into an institution where it was viewed not as a dimension of the institutional program but rather as a management problem, two approaches have been observed. Both focus on the presence of male-female interaction and attempt to minimize its effects on institutional life, but they vary in their approach to its control. When the major means for the control and limitation of interaction is through a combination of restrictions on contact, high levels of supervision or surveillance, and strict and severe disciplinary action, the management approach has been designated as a surveillance and sanction model. When the effort to minimize male-female inmate interaction occurs through the development of alternate relations by maximizing staff, local community, or family contacts, as well as work, educational and recreational activity that provides for alternate uses of time and attention, the term "alternate choice" has been chosen for the model.

Surveillance and Sanction Model

The co-corrections surveillance and sanction model emerges when system needs, especially economies in the use of staff and space, are perceived to shift an existing or planned single-sex institution into co-corrections. The focus of the surveillance and sanction model is on minimizing the effect of the presence of both sexes on operations and on allowing the system to fulfill its needs. The institutional control and surveillance and sanction models share intended outcomes: low rates of pregnancy, sexual and sex-related assault, and emotional involvement. However, the methods of population control in the surveillance and sanction model are more stringent than in any of the programmatic models. Institutional energies are marshaled, in the surveillance and sanction model, toward achievement of these outcomes, on the expectation that if problem behaviors related to pregnancy, assault, and emotional involvement can be minimized, the institution will have effectively functioned as a "depository" and system needs will have been served. This management model of co-corrections is based on the following underlying assumptions, articulated most frequently by administrators of institutions where decisions regarding the implementation of co-corrections were made substantially at the system level.

- The presence of both male and female inmates in the same institution poses a management problem that must be tolerated in the interest of system-level goals.
- Standard prison operations should not be altered by the presence of the opposite sex.
- Sexual relations will occur in prison unless a high level of external controls is present.
- Because of the higher probability that staff will condone heterosexual relationships, staff sanctions must be as high as inmate sanctions, if "operations as normal" are to be maintained.
- Priority implementation of external controls will allow maintenance of normal operations.

A brief overview of the elements of this model will provide the basis for the chain of assumptions it represents. The trigger for the surveillance and sanction model is the existence of one or more system needs and the expected impact of housing male and female prisoners under the same roof. In order to minimize problem behaviors and maintain normal operations, and in the absence of any perceived benefit to be derived from allowing full contact between inmates, a limited contact policy is formulated. On the assumption that external controls are required, the decision to permit limited contact leads to control through high surveillance and heavy sanctions. High surveillance may take several forms: facility modification, increases in supervisory staff either out of complement or from additional positions, or movement restrictions. Heavy sanctions are reflected primarily in population control through transfer for contact violations, although sanctions against staff are also heavy, especially when staff are perceived to put inmates in "embarassing positions" by failing to maintain low inmate-inmate or staff-inmate emotional involvement. Through the priority implementation of control policy, it is expected that low rates of pregnancy, sexual and sex-related assault, and emotional involvement will result, and that thereby system needs will be served.

The achievement of system needs, however, may be counterindicated by the occurrence of certain unintended effects of adopting a surveillance and sanction model of co-corrections. Implementation of movement restrictions may lead to dual programs for each sex and intensify the perceived need for increased supervisory staff. If increases in supervisory staff are taken out of the existing staff, programs may have to be further modified. Program modifications and heavy inmate sanctions may decrease inmate morale and lead to disturbances. The increase of supervisory staff, heavy staff sanctions, and the presence or threat of disturbances may decrease staff morale. Decreased staff morale may lead to a high rate of staff turnover. Several factors may lead to increased per capita costs: facility modification, new supervisory staff positions, dual programs, and high staff turnover. Increased per capita costs may be counter to the fulfillment of system-level needs; moreover, transferring inmates who violate contact regulations, and thereby becoming more "selective" an institution, may also be counter to fulfilling system-level needs for flexible population placement.

Alternate Choice Model

The co-correctional alternate choice model, like the surveillance and sanction model, emerges when an institution is perceived to be "dumped" into co-corrections in the interest of system-level needs. The model arises less as a conscious management strategy to control problem behavior and more as an alternate route for reaching system goals that inmates and line staff urge highly controlled institutions to adopt. It reflects the assumption that full contact is manageable, given sufficient options, without high surveillance and heavy sanctions. This model generally arises within the context of, and in reaction to, the surveillance and sanction model, and contends that the goals of the surveillance and sanction model can be reached without sustaining the associated costs. This model of co-corrections is based on the following underlying assumptions, which were expressed most consistently by lower line and staff personnel and, from another perspective, by inmates.

- The presence of both male and female inmates in the same institution poses a management problem that must be tolerated in the interest of system-level goals.
- Standard prison operations need not be altered by the presence of the opposite sex.
- Sexual relations are normal and inevitable, but a prison requires a minimum of external controls to limit their occurrence.
- Sexual relations between inmates are more appropriately limited by providing alternate means to "keep busy" and the opportunity for alternate relationships, which support personal internal controls.

A brief overview of the elements of the alternate choice model will provide the basis for the chain of assumptions it represents. The trigger for the alternate choice model is the same as that for the surveillance and sanction model: the expectation within the system that system-level needs can be served by housing male and female inmates in a designated institution. In order to minimize problem behavior and maintain normal operations, and in the face of perceived or anticipated counterproductive effects of directing institutional resources toward surveillance and sanctions, a non-restrictive contact policy is adopted. On the assumption that sufficient options will allow the institution to accomplish its intended outcomes, the decision to permit inmate contact leads to the implementation of alternate means of control, which are presented by, or to, inmates as alternate choices. These choices include alternate relationships, alternate uses of time, alternate income sources, selective surveillance and sanctions for coercive relationships, and birth control. Alternate relationships (furloughs and visitation, community programs, and staff-inmate relationships) and alternate uses of time (educational options, full work assignments, and broad recreational options) are expected to yield low emotional involvement between inmates. Alternate uses of time, alternate income sources (industrial and educational pay), birth control, and low emotional involvement are expected to result in low pregnancy rates. Selective surveillance and sanctions (for assault, and with uniform sanctions for both males and females and for both homosexual and heterosexual relations), alternate income sources, and low emotional involvement are expected to bring about low frequencies of sexual or sex-related assault. Implementation of staff in-service training to work through and clarify co-correctional policies is expected to increase staff morale, fostered by the encouragement of staff-inmate relationships as one more alternate relationship. The levels of emotional involvement between inmates, pregnancy, and sexual or sex-related assault are expected to be as low as or lower than those produced through exclusive use of surveillance and sanctions. By obtaining its intended outcomes, the alternate choice model is expected to serve system needs. The costs associated with the delivery of alternate uses of time (educational options, full work assignments, and recreational options) and alternate income sources (industrial and educational pay) are expected to be lower than the fiscal and human costs associated with the surveillance and sanction model of co-corrections. Moreover, the delivery of a relatively high level of programs to keep inmates "busy" and prevent "just sittin' around and thinkin' about sex" may secondarily result in the development of community contacts, employable skills, a bank account, and other tangible and intangible assets that may, after release, lead to reduced criminal activity.

PROGRAMMATIC AND NONPROGRAMMATIC CO-CORRECTIONS

The above presentation and discussion of programmatic and nonprogrammatic models of co-corrections suggested some of the points at which given models are either compatible or in conflict. Each of these models was present and operative, in varying degrees, in each existing co-correctional institution. Although a single model often predominated, no one model was unanimously espoused and no model was fully articulated. Under ordinary conditions, the several models generally "coexisted" with each other and "everything flowed," despite the "state of tension" prevailing among the divergent processes and objectives represented in the models.

Day-to-day operations were often perceived differently as a function of different conceptions of co-corrections. The day-to-day operations of a given institution might very well be interpreted within selected models by different sectors of an institution: for example, within an institutional control framework by the central office, within the alternate choice model by the line staff, on the premises of normalization and reintegration by the administration, and in terms of therapy by the treatment staff. However, while the division of labor might have influenced what functions co-corrections was presumed to serve, it was also evident that within each level of an institution and each person taking part in an institution's life, a measure of ambivalence existed about the model or models within which the institution was addressing operational issues and formulating expectations. From this ambiguity emerged divergent policies, wide ranges in the level of policy implementation, inconsistent modes of action, and heated debates about both actual and ideal policies, programs, and objectives. This ambiguity was reflected in such basic questions as: Do we actually house a highly selected inmate population or a typical one? Are we selecting-out inmates with certain characteristics, and how uniformly? How long do we and should we "work with" someone who finds it difficult to abide by "the rule" of co-corrections? Do we and should we tolerate acting-out behavior? Are we concerned more with the special requirements of a population in need of rehabilitation, the reduction of destructive aspects of incarceration, or neither of these?

Such interplay among divergent policies and expectations was observed to wreak havoc with institutional life in an imperceptible, insidious way, "like arsenic." Occasionally the presence of divergent models was reported to surface dramatically, making it clear that even identical words—words such as "normalization"—held several different theoretical and operational meanings within the same institutional community. In other words, there were generally not one, but several, programs related to co-corrections in the same institution.

Part II

THE FEMALE OFFENDER IN COED PRISON

Chapter 10

SEX ROLE DIFFERENTIATION IN A CO-CORRECTIONAL SETTING

Joellen Lambiotte

"Normalizing" Impact of Co-corrections

The aim of this study was to confirm whether or not a co-correctional institution would maintain the traditional social division between the sexes, specifically in relation to women. If prisons are microcosms of society, what one would generally expect to discover about the dynamic between the sexes in a co-correctional setting is that it duplicates the societal roles of the sexes.

Even though inmates at Pleasanton, California, are deviant in other aspects, the learning of appropriate sex roles is a very basic aspect of the socialization process that occurs at an early age. Sex roles are considered natural and thus accepted without question by many people. One might even expect this setting to accentuate the usual dynamic, since the relatively closed system would seem to offer little support for deviation from group norms. Furthermore, possibilities for withdrawal, which essentially means retiring to one's own room, are severely limited at Pleasanton, as the following comments indicate:

> It's hard to find any privacy in here. Someone is always knocking at your door, and if you don't open it they act like they are going to knock it down. (male resident)

> There's not that much space in here. You're never able to get away by yourself. (male resident)

> At _____ when you wanted to be alone, you could spend a whole day by yourself. That's not possible here. (female resident)

Female staff and male staff and residents (22)* note the more "normal" behavior that arises in the co-correctional institution. More "normal" behavior here means that homosexuality is considerably diminished, that social behavior (physical appearance, manners, etc.) improves, and that violence is reduced. It may be that co-corrections and the resulting coed relationship act as a conservative and stabilizing force.

> I think that it (co-corrections) helps them with their female identity. You know, having men around, and lots of them. There's not as much homosexuality. (female staff member)

> It [co-corrections] cuts down on the homosexual problems. There might be some, but it's not so open as you would have at an all-female or all-male institution. It's generally a more relaxed atmosphere. (female staff member)

> The women have a lot to do with mellowing the place out. (two male residents)

> The females are in here to make it closer to the streets. (male resident)

> They've learned how to dress, and the women have learned how to do their hair, which they didn't do before. The men

---

*Throughout this chapter the numbers in parentheses indicate the number of residents or staff in the specific sample being discussed.

> are more gentle and the women may be more gentle too. (male staff member)

> It makes for a much mellower environment. There's not as much homosexuality. (male staff member)

The coed relationship—having a coed partner—is a central feature of the co-correctional institution. Regardless of whether or not you are part of a couple, it touches and affects numerous aspects of your life. As is typical of the larger society, the relationships are exclusive, although the exclusiveness is often of a serial nature. This exclusiveness is manifested in a couple's behavior: Any free time when women and men can be together is spent with one's coed partner; and it's clear that women know whom a man is calling for at the women's unit, because the woman is notified before the man has to say a word. In addition to these observations, most comments from residents (26) indicate that relationships are exclusive:

> I'm his woman. He's my man. (female resident)

> I would ask someone to dance, but the girls that are here are with their men. (male resident)

> People are involved with their girl friends and boy friends here and they stick like glue. (female resident)

Only one resident had a different point of view:

> People here share a lot, and I don't want to do that. There are about four or five women that share different men.

Exclusiveness pertains to the relationship in the institution and does not affect relationships with spouses or lovers on the outside. Specific couples usually stay together for several months. Even though remaining together upon release may be discussed, it usually does not happen. And such permanency does not seem to be a genuine expectation.

> Most people don't stay together. Out of all the couples now, probably only _____ and _____, _____ and _____, and _____ and _____ will stay together when they hit the streets. (female resident)

> We've been together for three or four months, and in here that's a long time. (female resident)

As stated before, being feminine or masculine is necessary if each sex is to be successful in finding its place in the world. In our society women receive their primary identity and reinforcement from their activities in the family, while men receive their primary identity and reinforcement from their activities in production (Benston, 1971; Holter, 1970; Mitchell, 1973; Polatnick, 1974; Rowbotham, 1974; Weitzman, 1975). What women and men do and feel at Pleasanton duplicates this division.

Women in the family are expected to behave passively—to accept and adapt to the current structure of society. Men, however, are expected to change this structure through their role in production (Firestone, 1972; Holter, 1970; Rowbotham, 1974). Residents' initial reactions (29) to me demonstrate these characteristics. Women did not question my presence. If they did ask me what I was doing, they left it at that and did not pursue matters further.

> A woman resident asked me if I was a resident who had come from _____. I said no. She left without questioning me further about what I was doing there.

> I ate lunch with two residents, male and female, and a female staff member. The woman resident ate her lunch and said nothing.
> The male resident asked, "What are you doing here?"
> "I'm doing a study of co-corrections."
> "Does that mean that you are going to be doing interviews with residents?"
> "Not formal interviews, but I will be talking to both residents and staff."
> "Well, what do you think of this place from what you've seen?"

"I haven't really been here long enough to form an opinion."

"Well, I guess that's true."

He then proceeded to tell me what he thought of the place.

Two male residents and one female resident were in the research office while I was typing notes. Both men asked what I was doing and if they could see the notes. The woman said nothing.

A black female resident asked me what I was doing. Before I could answer, another black female resident said, "Oh, she's a researcher." The subject was dropped.

Two male residents were talking, then they noticed me:

"Hey, there's a new face around here."

"No, she's not in."

They picked up their conversation again, but after a couple of minutes one inmate said, "Well, what do you do here?"

"I'm doing a study of co-corrections."

He then began a 10-minute critique of Pleasanton and the co-correctional concept.

Another male resident asked me:

"What do you do here?"

"I'm doing a study of co-corrections."

"What do you think of the place?"

"I haven't had time to form an opinion."

"Yeah, well, I've been here a couple of months, and . . ."

Because women receive their primary identity and reinforcement from their role in the family, they achieve self-realization through other people—usually through their husband and children if they have them (Bardwick & Douvan, 1971; Freeman, 1971; Rossi, 1972). Hence, the women residents focus their energies on their men and their relationships. Comments from residents (6) and staff (9), and observations (6) involving residents (9) are an indication of this focus:

A woman resident told a staff member that she had finished her work assignment so that she could be with her coed partner. She received a "shot" for lying about finishing her work assignment.

A woman resident entered a male unit without authorization and received a "shot" for being in an unauthorized area. She wanted to talk to her coed partner, with whom she was fighting. He refused to leave the unit to talk to her.

Since this is a coed institution, I think that we have a problem getting the women involved personally in individual programs that exclude male residents. The female residents only want to involve themselves in activities that include male residents. (female staff member)

I know from working in a female institution that the coed environment really detracts from women being involved. (female staff member)

The women aren't here tonight. They're probably out coeding. (female resident)

The women don't have much organized activity. They're pretty much entertaining the men. (male staff member)

Say, I wish I could get this meeting over with. It's taking time away from my coeding. (female resident)

The women here are simply into doing their time and being with somebody that's nice. (female resident)

This is the worst [women's] unit for getting people organized and getting anything done. No one is doing anything for themselves in here because so much energy is directed outside toward the compound and the men. (female resident)

When in the few cases (3) that I know of, women residents decided not to focus their energies on men, they retreated into the women's unit. There, to some degree, they avoid interaction with men.

MALE ABILITY TO DEFINE SOCIETAL STRUCTURE

Partially because of their role in the sphere of production, men are better able than women to define the structure of society. They, more than women, control the means of producing it (Firestone, 1972; Holter, 1970; Rowbotham, 1974). This dynamic continues at Pleasanton in a reduced manner. Imprisonment imposes certain limitations not found in the larger society. Because both women and men are so accustomed to male definition of situations, male residents are able to define the female residents' relationship to them through labeling, verbal harrassment, violation of women's physical space, the right to initiate relationships, and their leadership of programs. Evidence of this dominance is provided in comments from residents (25) and observations (15) involving residents (54).

> There was one woman that was with three different guys in the first three weeks that she was here, but she's settled down because people talked to her. (male resident)

> If a woman is with one guy one week and another guy the next week and another guy the next week, she's looked at as something other than a woman, as a whore, because of her association with different guys. (female resident)

> No, they're not together. She's too good for him. She's too good for everyone here. (2 male residents referring to a woman resident who refused to become involved with anyone in any way other than a friendly one)

> I'm having trouble with a guy right now that I thought understood that we were good friends. I hang around with one of the fags now because it just creates less trouble. (female resident)

> I just stay in the unit and go out to work or eat. The guys call me square because I won't get involved with anyone. (female resident)

> We don't understand why you're going to something like that or why you would want to get off by yourself to talk about it. (male residents responding to the idea of a woman's sexuality class)

> We're the ones who are discriminated against, not women. Why do we want to have a class on that? (male residents responding to the idea of a women and law class)

> After an initial experience I realized that being with one guy
> was not for me. I retreated into the [women's] unit with my
> books. (female resident)

> I was with one guy for a while, and it was just too much of
> a hassle so I broke that off. Now I spend my time in the
> [women's] unit, except for going to work or to meals. (female
> resident)

> My girl friend and I were talking at lunch, and this guy came
> and sat down. We got up and left and told him that we wanted
> to talk alone, but he wouldn't take no for an answer. So we
> ended up going into one of the bathrooms to get away from
> him. (female resident)

The men's ability to define relationships is facilitated
by their right to initiate (Bernard, 1971; Henley and
Freeman, 1975). In this process the "stronger" men succeed
at the expense of the "weaker" men. That men initiate
relationships is based on observations (17) and comments
from staff (1) and residents (4).

> The weaker guys who can't take the scene at night withdraw
> to the unit. (male resident)

> When there started being more men than women, a lot of the
> men went back into the unit. This is a competitive situation
> and a lot of the guys can't take it. (male resident)

> It will be better if we house him in the unit next to the wo-
> men's unit so that other men won't have a chance to come on
> to her. Otherwise we'll have fights. (male staff member dis-
> cussing housing assignment of married couple)

> Men call at the women's unit for women.

> This other guy and I were sitting at the table in the cafeteria at
> lunch and she walks up and says what her name is and asks if
> she can sit down. It totally blew me out. (male resident's
> response to deviation from acceptable pattern)

Another way in which male residents control the means
of producing the social structure, or defining the situation,
is through their leadership of programs.

A number of transactional analysis groups, both single-sex and coed, hold regular meetings. The introductory TA class required for all of those who want to participate in the program is led by two male residents and the male unit manager of the male TA unit. Only people who are advanced in TA can lead the class, and all of these people are male.

Initially both men and women were allowed to join the Jaycees, and women were instrumental in its inception. Men eventually assumed leadership. A female resident explained this takeover by citing loss of interest among the women and the dictator types in the group.

There aren't any women in there [the Jaycees award presentation] but there are women in the group. Primarily it's a men's organization. Women aren't allowed much. (male resident)

An exception to this pattern was the position of editor of the newspaper, which was held by a black woman.

ROLES AND CHARACTERISTICS OF THE SEXES

Holter, Mitchell, and Rowbotham, among others, argue that women are primarily responsible for the maintenance of the family. At the same time they are subordinate to their husbands (Benston, 1971; Mitchell, 1973; Polatnick, 1974; Rowbotham, 1974). At Pleasanton women residents are perceived as playing "maintenance" and "subordinate" roles both in heterosexual relationships on the outside and in coed relationships.[1] *Maintenance* here means that women are responsible for the emotional stability, the solidarity, and the tasks of the relationship. This conclusion emerges from the comments of residents (24) and staff (3) and from observations (6).

He doesn't want me to work. I don't want to either, but while we're setting up I'll work some little factory job or something. I want to stay home with my kids and educate them there. (female resident)

Doing a man's hair or his nails is a sign of loving him. When a wife cooks a man's meals, cleans the house, does his laundry, it's the same thing. (female resident)

Wives are for husbands to take care of. Women should give 80% in any relationship. (male resident)

I'm not going to follow my ol' lady around. This relationship is her life and she should fight for me and follow me. (male resident)

She was accepted into the program but her husband wanted her to stay in the area so that she would be close to him. She did stay. (female resident)

Most of the women are concerned with being shipped here to coed with a boy friend. It's sad because most of the people they won't ever see again. (male staff member)

At Pleasanton *subordinate* means that women are seen as less than men and thus should defer to them. This concept is reflected in the comments of residents (10) and staff (7) and in observations (1).

You can sit down and talk about something, but the husband always has the right to override the wife's veto. (male resident)

Every woman is looking for a master. (male resident)

The men here run you through all sorts of games. They say you're a woman so you do this. You walk three feet behind me. That's extreme but you know what I mean. (female resident)

In some cases women have been used by the men. They're dependent on and influenced by men. They don't have the oomph to say, "Hey, I'm not doing it." (male staff member)

From what I've seen, a lot of the women, especially the ones that I've been in close contact with, are used to being in the woman subject role. They should try and stand on their own two feet and not get pushed around. (female staff member)

A female resident who knew what she wanted and made her own decisions was told by her coed partner that she was trying to be the man in the relationship.

Female residents (40), in speaking of female and male relationships in the institution, consistently emphasize the personal dynamics of the relationships. That is, they speak of the comfort that women derive from companionship and more involved relationships with the men, and about the conflicts created by the men and female-male relationships. Personal dynamics are a significant aspect of the mainten-ance of relationships. Relationships are spoken of by the women as totalities. Within the family, too, women perceive personal dynamics or expressive dynamics as an essential aspect (Bardwick & Douvan, 1971; Holter, 1970).

> I liked _____ better. You were busier. Here the men create a lot of problems for the women. (female resident)

> In a place without men, you don't get involved with men and have them and interpersonal relationships messing up your life. (female resident)

> Having the men here can be bad because he and I have gotten really involved and he's going to leave, which will make it hard for me. (female resident)

> You can have a full relationship with someone in here, if they ship in someone that you like. (female resident)

In contrast, a man's perspective is found in the following statement:

> Just a couple of weeks ago that girl slit up the other one's face and it was over *nothing* [my emphasis] except their boy friends. (male resident)

In commenting about relationships in the institution, male staff and residents (42) emphasize the sexual aspects of these relationships in contrast to the expressive emphasis of the female residents. Women are seen primarily as sexual beings reflecting their reproductive and sexual role in the larger society (Mitchell, 1973; Phelps, 1975).

We're like walking vaginas to the men (female resident)

I have a wife and two kids at home and it's really hard to do time with these women in here. I have to watch all these people kissing and the girls teasing you. (male resident)

I'd rather smoke dope than be around the women. I don't want to be around women if I can't make love to them. (male resident)

They throw these guys in here with all of these women and most of them haven't been around women for a while. What do they expect them to do? (male staff member)

It's good to have the women in here. The other alternative is to set up some kind of traveling whorehouse down near the back gate and the government isn't going to do that. (male staff member)

The women residents' reproductive potential serves as a crucial indicator of co-correctional failure, if not its success. Women are expected to avoid becoming pregnant. That birth control is made widely available to women is evidence of this proscription and of where the responsibility for pregnancy and birth control lies. A male department head phrased it this way:

The official position is that only women on furlough status have access to birth control, but virtually any woman who requests it can have it. (male staff member)

Additional evidence is provided in the following comments:

The rumor is that _____ closed because of too many pregnancies. (female staff member and male staff member)

She got pregnant so they shipped her. (female resident)

Things have been pretty good here. Out of the three or four pregnancies that we've had, there's one that may have been conceived within the institution, but we let that pass. (male staff member)

Women, if they have sexual contact, are the ones that are going to pay for it because of the pregnancy factor. The man doesn't pay for it in a sense. The woman does. (male staff member)

Our program is much more successful than _____. They've had umpteen pregnancies and we've had only one. (male staff member)

One woman's account demonstrates the fear of pregnancy among women residents. The rationale behind the fear, accurate or not, is that they will be transferred if conception is believed to have occurred in the institution.

We can show this [the interview demonstrating that conception could not have occurred in the institution] to the warden and he'll see that you got pregnant on your furlough, and it'll be okay then. (female resident)

This is an area requiring further exploration, but this example does not seem to be an isolated one. The woman involved did not have a coed partner and had withdrawn to the women's unit. If her account was seriously questioned, one can only assume that women having coed partners would be even more seriously questioned.

That an important area for women is reproduction is also demonstrated by the mandatory attendance once required of women in the human sexuality class.

It was started as a birth control class and the men just weren't allowed. (male staff member)

Originally the sexuality class was mandatory for women residents. The staff thought it was great for the men to go too. (female staff member)

The sexuality class seemed necessary for the women. Most of them had children that they couldn't support in the community, as well as venereal disease. (male staff member)

In the larger society, a crucial goal for women is winning a husband and raising a family, and thus affirming their physical beauty (Bardwick & Douvan, 1971;

Brun-Gulbrandsen, 1967; Holter, 1970; Weisstein, 1971; Weitzman, 1975). Attractiveness remains an asset for the women residents at Pleasanton, both in their own eyes and in the eyes of others. This attitude is reflected in the comments of female (21) and male (14) residents, in the comments of female (13) and male (17) staff members, and in observations (5).

> When she [a woman resident] first came in she was political and into a feminist thing. Now she's starting to dress and look more feminine. She's starting to come around. (male staff member)

> He and I were laughing about how our standards have really gone down around here. We just got a new woman inmate and not only is she pregnant, she's ugly! (two male staff members)

> When I was in the county jail, I got pushed into a fight. I was sitting on the bed with my legs curled up and was going to push her back with them. But then she pulled a shank and I decided I didn't want to do that. She could have cut my legs and I already have enough scars on my legs. (female resident)

> My ol' man just sent me a picture of himself and wants a picture of me. I've got to lose some weight before I do that, before I go home or he won't want anything to do with me. (female resident)

> Being locked up with all women puts the weight on you because you start not to care about how you're going to look because no one is going to see you. (female resident)

> A woman resident said, "oh, fuck," when she missed a pool shot. A woman staff member who was watching chided her by saying, "You don't look very pretty when you talk like that."

> Women really let themselves go in an all-female institution. They look pretty bad. (male resident) They gain weight. They don't fix their hair. (female staff member)

> Men's appearance doesn't change very much. I mean, what do they have to do? Even if they have really long hair, they usually don't have to do anything with it. Women do stop a lot of the violent behavior of the men. (male resident)

The first women that came in here were great. They had big tits, nice bodies, but we've gone downhill since. (male resident)

If you're a good-looking woman here and you put up a good front, you'll go a long way. (male resident)

She's [his coed partner] doing some sit-ups that she needs to do. She's getting fat so I'm making her do them. (male resident)

Participation in recreational activities demonstrates the division of women and men along the lines of family and production. In general, women are passive spectators while men are active participants. Women (5) who do participate regularly in recreational activities are involved in individual games of paddleball, occasional relay races, and jogging. The only team activity that they participate in is volleyball, unlike the men who have formed intramural teams. This reflects women's activity in the family and men's activity in production (Lever, 1976; Rowbotham, 1974). It emerges from the comments of residents (5) and staff (9) and from observations (24).

The men like to participate in intramurals. The women have been the [recreational] area where we've been the weakest. The men are not too hard to motivate. Periodically we have women that come out and play with the men in a coed game, but it's nothing competitive. (female staff member)

The men seem to participate more in rec activities than the women do, although the women have been given the opportunity to participate in all aspects of rec activity within this institution but have failed to involve themselves. (female staff member)

It's harder to motivate the women to participate in activities than it is the men. The men are more apt to go out and involve themselves in rec activities. (male staff member)

The nucleus of women that participates [in recreational activities] is so small that I probably know all of them by first name. They want to be spectators. (male staff member)

> They don't seem to have much organized activity. There are some unit-related activities that they're involved in, but they have no teams and they're not involved in the athletic leagues. (male staff member)

> It wouldn't hurt the girls to get out here and play basketball, but they don't do it. (male resident)

> We tried to get a softball team together, but the women were afraid of the ball. (female resident)

> Even as spectators the male residents are active. During the women's volleyball games they shout and make comments.

PATRONAGE

In some cases (8) male residents behave protectively toward female residents. *Protective* here implies that these women are to be respected and that their reputation and physical being are to be defended. In all cases the woman deserving protection is the male's coed partner, and this pattern reflects the patronage system that exists in female-male relationships. In payment for the services women provide in the family, they win protection from other men and the larger society (Rowbotham, 1974).

> At first she was doing hard time but now she's happy because I protect her and take good care of her. (male resident)

> The male resident said he was fighting to protect his girl friend, who was being sprayed by the hose.

> He really watches the physical contact with me. He doesn't want people to ever get the idea that we're doing it. (female resident)

> The blacks run this place. They travel in groups and know they're not going to get busted. They'll pinch your ol' lady on the ass and there's nothing you can do about it. (male resident)

MORAL EXPECTATIONS OF WOMEN

In general, the women residents at Pleasanton are not

considered "decent women" (male staff member). This labeling does not arise solely from their status as incarcerated women—as might be expected considering the role of women in the larger society. Women are responsible for the moral standards of the family and society and thus should not commit crimes. Criminal behavior is more accepted for men who are responsible for production, which may require criminal behavior at times (Brun-Gulbrandsen, 1967; Burkhart, 1973; Holter, 1970). Incarceration was taken as evidence of the immorality of criminality among women in at least three cases, but I never heard a similar negative characterization of male inmates.

> Some of the guys won't have anything to do with the women here because they think they're bad girls. Look, they got busted. No young lady had any business being involved in that. (male resident)

> Being in prison has got to be a lot worse for women. I'm embarrassed about being in jail, but society reacts more negatively to a woman being in prison. (male resident)

> The girls in here are pigs because no decent woman does something to get herself thrown in jail. (male resident)

Another factor is women's behavior in the institution that does not adhere to the behavioral patterns expected of those who, as socializers of children, should maintain the moral standards of the family and society (Holter, 1970). That woman is considered responsible for maintaining moral standards is demonstrated directly in comments of residents (23) and staff (13), and indirectly in comments of residents and staff and in observations of objections made to behavior that violates woman's task of maintaining moral standards. These objections concerned the *sexual* behavior (residents 17, staff 33, observations 10), *manipulative* behavior (residents 6, staff 24, observations 13), and *interracial* behavior (residents 9, staff 6, observations 4) of the women residents.

Typical comments directly demonstrating women's responsibility for the maintenance of moral standards include the following:

> This chick and I nearly got a shot the other night because the male officer thought there was sexual stuff going on. If one of us gets a shot, both of us do. (male resident) Well, aren't you both to blame? (observer) No, she is. (male resident)

> I had my wife declared an unfit mother. She is more into dope than she is kids. My mother has them now but I'll have them when I get back out on the streets. (male resident)

> I liked things a lot better when he was with _____. Now that he is with this other woman, they are always hugging and kissing in front of everyone. (female staff member)

> The women just let those guys maul them. I guess they must believe what they're telling them. Women who let guys do that to them in front of everyone just aren't nice. (female staff member)

> I caught them getting down but I went to _____ and spoke for the guy. I felt sorry for him. What do they expect these guys to do. They throw them in here with all these women and they haven't been around women in a while. There aren't many decent women around here. (male staff member)

The sexual behavior that violates women's role as maintainers of moral standards consists of their perceived attempts to purposefully excite the men. Typical comments and observations demonstrating the perception of women as tempting objects include the following:

> And the response to women being able to untie their bathing suits on the sun deck was: What about those poor guys? (male staff member)

> There aren't that many decent women around here and they rub against the guys and tease them. (male staff member)

> I've got a wife at home and I have to watch these people kissing on each other and the girls teasing you. And believe me, the girls around here do tease you. (male resident)

They put it [the women] right in front of you and you're not supposed to do anything. (male resident)

They decided not to make it [the weight room] coed because the women have sometimes used their muscles where men can see things. (female resident)

I think _____ is frustrated about being in here with women. When I worked at _____ the guys would tell me that they would rather have all the staff be male because just seeing a woman was hard for them. (female staff member)

You have to be careful of what you wear, because if you wear anything like a halter top or something like that, they [the men] think that's an open invitation. (female resident)

The women are basically a temptation. They [the men] get themselves into more trouble. [female staff member]

Typical comments pertaining to manipulative behavior include the following:

Time is harder for men than for women. Women can manipulate people and will kiss ass to get what they want. I can do that with both males and females. (female resident)

Women can't snow another woman like they can a man. Women will just sidle right up to a man. A lot of women feel that way about the counselors in our unit. (female resident)

This is the best deal that the women here have gotten—four men to a woman. Most of the women here wouldn't be noticed on the streets, and they really use the situation to get something. (2 male residents)

To a lot of these girls this place has got to be a utopia. Out on the streets there's lots of young ladies. Here the situation is reversed. And they'll use it—they'll say that I think I'll go after this guy this week because he's got commissary or this one because he's got a stereo. (male resident)

I'm really jealous and she does things to make me more so. (male resident)

You might not want to be over at the women's unit at night. It's really treacherous at times. Women [residents] have the last say [here] just because they're a little bit more cunning and shrewd. (male staff member)

Some of the women we have here come from a background that taught them to use their feminine ways to create problems for some of the guys, but that's something the guys are going to have to face anyhow, so it's good that they have it here. (male staff member)

If you say no to them [women], usually what happens is that they go into an emotional thing and they start screaming and cursing and crying. It's usually with a male. (female staff member)

There's a group of people around here who love to instigate trouble. They sort of stay behind the scenes. (female staff member referring to women residents)

Another manifestation of violation of woman's role as the guardian of moral standards is the frequent association of white women with black men. Although there were other racially mixed couples (Indian-black, Chicano-black, white-Chicano), comments on their associations were never made. A very noticeable number of couples paired a white woman with a black man. At any one time during the summer, there were 10 to 15 such couples. In contrast, there were only two to 15 couples in which both the woman and the man were black. The following comments are typical reactions to black-white relationships:

All the women in this institution are pigs. They can't all be, but there's something wrong because of this black-white thing. I'm for people doing what they want, but there's too much of it to be normal. (male resident)

I wouldn't touch a bitch that's been with a black dude. (male resident)

I can't stand to see those women with those black baboons. (male resident)

The black guys call the white women snow or white bitch. They're just interested in turning them on to heroin or using them. They talk about black women with a lot more respect. (male resident)

There's a lot of tension here, partially because some of these guys can't get ready for the blacks with the whites. (male staff member)

The black males seem to be extremely attracted to the white females. This has been a big problem and has caused a lot of jealousy from the white men. There's a lot of hostility there. (female staff member)

The white women are with the black men here. The white guys really don't want anything to do with these women here. (male staff member)

BLACK WOMEN'S VIOLATION OF EXPECTATIONS OF WOMEN

If any one group of women is considered "bad" women it is the black women. Their behavior in particular violates what society expects of women. Instead of behaving passively or adaptively, they behave in a loud, obscene, challenging, and assertive manner. Unlike the other female residents who form bonds with one or two other women—reflecting woman's traditional socially isolated position in the family—the black women form a more organized group. This pattern is seen in instances (57) of loud, challenging, and organized behavior among the black women:

The blacks playing cards had the radio tuned to soul music at high volume. They turned it up even more. The correctional officer on the unit started screaming at them, "Turn it down. Just because you're deaf doesn't mean that everyone else is." The officer turned to me and said, "They don't listen to anything you say until you get violent."

Ten women and a correctional officer were sitting in the lobby of the women's unit before town hall. The correctional officer told them about the new policy on physical contact. One black woman said, "What do they put the men in here for if you can't kiss and you can't fuck."

I've really gotten to hate blacks here. They're really loud. Some of them are so noisy and boisterous. (female resident in reference to black women in the unit)

Another black woman walked into the unit before town hall saying, "I hate fucking town hall." Then she looked around to see if anyone had heard her.

Four black women walked into the unit immediately before town hall saying, "Let's sit by the window where we can make some noise."

Challenging or assertive behavior is typified by the following instances:

The staff member directing town hall was sitting on the pool table. A black woman interrupted the flow of conversation and screamed, "You're always yelling at us about abusing things in here but you're sitting on our pool table and unbalancing it." The staff member got off the pool table.

I see the black women intimidate them [the white women] over and over again and they just back off. (female staff member)

In town hall one of the unit staff began to give the results of a report that a woman resident had been assigned to do the previous week. A black woman shouted out from the group, "Why don't you let her do it?" He did.

In the midst of a discussion in town hall about using the institutional laundry, a black woman said, "Let's get on with something else. It's going to be the way you want it to be." The staff member chairing the meeting said, "So we agree." The black woman said, "No, we don't agree, but it's going to be the way you want it to be."

Typical instances of organized behavior among the black can also be cited:

I call the black women "the group." The white women don't do that. They're much more likely to pair off with one person and stand with them. (female staff member)

The black women here do stick together, and I admire that because other people around here don't do that. (female resident)

A black woman and a Chicano woman were playing cards. Another black woman wanted to play. The black woman said, "You're full of shit. You can play but we don't want your man coming over here in five minutes and you getting up and saying you have to leave."

We have something going here [in the women's unit] now that was there at first but now is very evident—a black power group. (male staff member)

In contrast, the other women are more divided because they do not associate with women outside of their small circle of one or two, and/or because of their association with men (43 instances).

The reason that you have trouble talking to women is that you are a woman. There are just a few women here that I am close to. There's a confidence thing and I always seem to run into the wrong woman. (female resident who spends her time with her coed partner and with two other female residents)

She doesn't do anything with girls. Maybe I shouldn't have gotten involved with the girls on the unit. With the way some of them are, no one should. (female resident)

Wish there was a place where coed sexes could sit and watch TV. I get real tired of being around a bunch of bitches. (female resident)

Most of the women in here are girls. It's only in the last couple of months that I've gotten any mind stimulation. I would rather be with the opposite sex. That's the way I am and always have been. (female resident)

She was my best friend. You know, the person that you spend your time with when you're not with your ol' man. (female resident)

I really spend a lot more time with the men because they know what's happening. (female resident)

No, I'm not going to lunch unless they let him [her coed partner] out. He's been locked up since Saturday and this is Tuesday. I've been over there until 9 PM every night, which is as late as they'll let me stay. (female resident)

CONCLUSION

In most areas, the sex role structure at Pleasanton duplicates the social division between the sexes in society both in behavior and behavioral norms and in adherence to traditional societal sexual standards. However, what female residents do and feel reflects their primary identification with the family, while what male residents do and feel reflects their primary identification with production. These processes are most clearly seen in the coed relationships.

Thus we see most women residents focusing their energies on men and their coed relationships and being responsible for the maintenance and personal or expressive dynamics of these relationships. Women in the external society, too, are responsible for nurturing and maintaining human beings—their men and children—in the family. Serving as a retreat from the world of production, the family is a place of comfort, love, and tenderness, of personal dynamics for which women are primarily responsible (Benston, 1971; Rowbotham, 1974).

Male residents at Pleasanton are better able than female residents to define the nature of relationships. Even though the general structure of the men's lives is controlled by institutional factors, they control the way in which female residents relate to them through labeling, verbal harrassment, violation of women's physical space, initiation of relationships, and leadership. Heffernan (1974) and Karacki, Cavior, and Kennedy (1972) note a similar pattern at Fort Worth and Kennedy Youth Center respectively. This dominance is similar to that evinced in families in the external society (Holter, 1970; Rowbotham, 1974).

Women residents are valued for their sexuality and attractiveness. The value placed on these natural attributes reflects the value society places on woman's natural functioning within the family (Mitchell, 1973). Attractiveness is crucial for women, because they must attract and hold men to validate themselves as women. Transitory and relative as it may be, women's beauty is a valuable bargaining point (Bardwick & Douvan, 1971; Brun-Gulbrandsen, 1967; Holter, 1970; Weisstein, 1971; Weitzman, 1975.) This is especially true in prison, where a woman's physical appearance may be her one remaining asset.

The labeling that occurs when women residents do not conform to society's standards of moral behavior also results from woman's role in the family. As socializers of children, women must maintain the moral standards of the family and society (Holter, 1970). Women residents who excite men or who participate in interracial coupling are perceived as deviating from their role as upholders of morality. In our society, only men possess the right to experiment with sex. In a broader sense they possess the right to experience and knowledge, which are both assets in the productive sphere. Women do not have this right (Holter, 1970). Heffernan also notes this phenomenon at Fort Worth, where male residents were known to think of female residents as a "pretty bad lot" (Heffernan, 1975, p. 42). The distrust created by women's perceived manipulative actions corroborates this view of women at Pleasanton.

The behavior of black female residents in particular violates society's expectations of women. In comparison to other women in the institution, the black women are assertive and organized. This difference can be partly explained by the reality that black women face in our society. Survival has required independence and aggressiveness, while conformance to society's expectations of women has required dependency and passivity. Black women are caught in a double bind.

Finally, the co-correctional setting, in its duplication of the sex role structure of the larger society, does provide one aspect of normalization. In terms of sex roles, the co-correctional prison is very consistent with the life-style and social interaction of the community. It also seems that co-corrections enhances the degree of social control held by the staff. The inmates' focus on the coed relationship seems to be a factor in decreasing organized disruptive behavior in the institution.

NOTE

1. Comments concerning outside heterosexual relationships are appropriate in that the dynamics of the coed relationship seem to reflect the dynamics of the residents' heterosexual relationships on the outside.

REFERENCES

Bardwick, J. & Douvan, E. Ambivalence: The socialization of women. In V. Gornick & B. K. Moran (Eds.), *Woman in sexist society*. New York: Basic Books, 1971.

Bart, P. Depression in middle-aged women. In V. Gornick & B. K. Moran (Eds.), *Woman in sexist society*. New York: Basic Books, 1971.

Benston, M. The political economy of women's liberation. In M. Garskoff (Ed.), *Roles women play*. Belmont, CA: Brooks/Cole Publishing, 1971.

Bernard, J. What do you mean "the sexes"? In C. F. Epstein & W. Goode (Eds.), *The other half*. Englewood Cliffs, NJ: Prentice-Hall, 1971.

Brofenbrenner, U. Some familial antecedents of responsibility and leadership in adolescents. In L. Petrullo & B. M. Bass (Eds.), *Leadership and interpersonal behavior*. New York: Holt, Rinehart, and Winston, 1961.

Brun-Gulbrandsen, S. Sex roles and the socialization process. In E. Dahlstrom (Ed.), *The changing roles of men and women*. Boston: Beacon Press, 1967.

Burkhart, K. *Women in prison*. Garden City, NY: Doubleday & Co., 1973.

Firestone, S. *The dialectic of sex*. New York: Bantam Books, 1972.

Freeman, J. The social construction of the second sex. In M. Garskoff (Ed.), *Roles women play*. Belmont, CA: Brooks/Cole Publishing, 1971.

Giallombardo, R. *Society of women*. New York: John Wiley & Sons, 1966.

Glazer-Malbin, N. & Warhrer, H. *Woman in a man-made world*. Chicago: Rand McNally, 1973.

Hacker, H. Women as a minority group. In B. Roszak & T. Roszak (Eds.), *Masculine/feminine*. New York: Harper & Row, 1969.

Heffernan, E. *Final report on research*. Unpublished Bureau of Prisons report. Bureau of Prisons, 1975.

Heffernan, E. *Interim report on research*. Unpublished institutional report. Fort Worth Federal Correctional Institution, 1974.

Henley, N., and Freeman, J. The sexual politics of interpersonal behavior. In J. Freeman (Ed.) *Women: A feminist perspective*. Palo Alto, CA: Mayfield Publishing, 1975.

Holter, H. *Sex roles and social structure*. Oslo: Universitetsforlaget, 1970.

Karacki, L., Minor, J. A., Cavior, H. E., & Kennedy, B. *Going coed: A case study of the establishment of a coed program at a previously all-male institution*. Unpublished institutional report. Kennedy Youth Center, 1972.

Ladner, J. *Tomorrow's tomorrow*. Garden City, NY: Doubleday, 1972.

Lever, J. Sex differences in the games children play. *Social Problems*, 1976, *23*, 478-487.

Mitchell, J. *Woman's estate*. New York: Vintage Books, 1973.

Phelps, L. Female sexual alienation. In J. Freeman (Ed.), *Women: A feminist perspective*. Palo Alto, CA: Mayfield Publishing, 1975.

Polatnick, M. Why men don't rear children. *Berkeley Journal of Sociology*, 1974, *18*, 45-79.

Rossi, A. Sex equality: The beginnings of ideology. In C. Safilios-Rothschild (Ed.), *Toward a sociology of women*. Lexington, MA: Xerox Publishing, 1972.

Rowbotham, S. *Woman's consciousness, man's world*, Baltimore, MD: Pelican Books, 1974.

U. S. Bureau of Prisons. *Pleasanton master plan*. Federal Correctional Institution at Pleasanton, California. No date.

Ward, D. & Kassebaum, G. *Women's prison*. Chicago: Aldine Publishing, 1965.

Weisstein, N. Psychology constructs the female. In M. Garskoff (Ed.), *Roles women play*. Belmont, CA: Brooks/Cole Publishing, 1971.

Weitzman, L. J. Sex-role socialization. In J. Freeman (Ed.), *Women: A feminist perspective*. Palo Alto, CA: Mayfield Publishing, 1975.

Chapter 11

WOMEN IN A COED JOINT

James G. Ross
Esther Heffernan

The coeducational correctional institution has been commonly viewed, since the opening of the first coed institutions in 1971, as an alternative to "the women's correctional institution." The National Advisory Commission on Criminal Justice Standards and Goals (1973), for example, discussed co-corrections in terms of women offenders. The Commission did mention the potential therapeutic effects of co-corrections as "an invaluable tool for exploring and dealing with social and emotional problems related to identity conflicts that many offenders experience." Nevertheless, the Commission's expectations for co-corrections focused primarily on outcomes unrelated to the presence and interaction of male and female prisoners in the same institution. The Commission's strong endorsement was premised more on (1) increased diversification and flexibility of program offerings, and equal program access for males and females; and (2) expanded career ladders for women, who were previously often "boxed into" the single state women's institution, as correctional staff. Indeed, LEAA's support under the auspices of the National Evaluation Program of a Phase I Assessment of coeducational correctional institutions was prompted in part by programmatic interest in forms of incarceration affecting the female offender.

In many respects, conceptualization of co-corrections as an alternative to "the women's correctional institution" may be justified. A disproportionately large percentage of female offenders are housed in coed institutions. Recent compilations by the Bureau of Prisons show that 997 females and 2,077 males, or 58.1% of female federal prisoners and 7.5% of male prisoners, occupy coed institutions (U.S. Bureau of Prisons, 1977).

Although these figures will be reduced by the imminent withdrawal of two federal institutions from co-corrections, similarly disproportionate percentages of the female population are found in state coed institutions. According to Ross, Heffernan, Sevick, and Johnson (1977f), 1,232 females and 2,377 males are in state coed institutions, which represents 9.7% of the female and 0.53% of the male state prison populations. In addition, of the 11 single-sex state institutions that have been converted to co-correctional status, seven have been women's institutions.

In other respects, analysis of co-corrections solely in terms of the female offender is not justified. Just as there are more men incarcerated than women, more men than women occupy coed institutions, although this difference is marginal on the state level. The very definition of co-correctional institution requires that a facility be "an adult institution, the major purpose of which is the custody of sentenced felons, under a single institutional administration, having one or more programs areas in which *male and female inmates are present and in interaction.*"

Finally, the perceived role of co-corrections as an intervention promising positive effects either on institutional functioning or on the lives of both male and female inmates is demonstrated by the range of programmatic expectations associated with the concept. Among these expectations, some of which have been articulated more in relation to one sex than the other, have been:

- Reduction of the dehumanizing and destructive aspects of confinement by allowing continuity or resumption of heterosexual relationships.
- Reduction of institutional control problems through the weakening of disruptive homosexual systems, reduction of predatory homosexual activity, lessening of assaultive behavior and the diversion of inmate interests and activities.
- Protection of inmates likely to be involved in "trouble" if they were in a predominantly same-sex institution.
- Provision of an additional tool for creating a more normal, less institutionalized atmosphere.
- Expansion of treatment potentials for working with inmates having "sexual problems," and development of positive heterosexual relationships and coping skills.
- Cushioning the shock of adjustment for releases by reducing the number and intensity of adjustments to be made.

While each of these expectations can be applied to inmates of either sex, it would seem that certain anticipated outcomes are linked more to one or the other sex. For example, more comments have been made about "turning around" female inmates who had been playing the male role in female institutions, than about males ceasing to play the "macho" role. Similarly, "protection of inmates likely to be involved in trouble" may apply more to the transfer of individual males into a co-correctional institution (but also more to the transfer of groups of females).

Finally, the anticipated reduction of institutional control problems may be related primarily to the reduction of assaultive and disruptive male behavior, although it may also be true that women are sometimes introduced to an institution precisely for the purpose of achieving institutional control, or "rounding out rough corners."

The previous discussion should make it evident that although the impact of co-corrections on women's institutions and the lives of female inmates is a major issue, a larger framework comprised of other anticipated co-correctional outcomes must be kept in mind, even when it is not directly examined. Extensive considerations will not be given to other intended outcomes associated with "going coed," particularly to nonprogrammatic objectives, that is, reasons for implementing a coed institution related to achieving system level needs for efficient utilization of space, staff, and programs. Nor will the political environment that influences the continuity of programs, especially those instituted to serve the system economy, be taken heavily into account. The ensuing discussion of co-correctional impacts revolves instead around three areas: institutional change, heterosexual relations, and effects on relations beyond heterosexual ones. General descriptive information, suggested research designs, and bibliographic materials can be found in other sources (Ross, Heffernan, Sevick, & Johnson, 1977a; 1977b; 1977c; 1977d; 1977e; 1977f).

INSTITUTIONAL CHANGE

The introduction of inmates of the opposite sex to a previously single-sex institution, and the opening of a new institution as coed, have been observed to produce changes in the actual and traditionally accepted realities of institutional life. Six issues will be discussed: single-sex sentencing, housing, security level, women's programs, women's jobs, and health care.

Single-Sex Sentencing

While the implementation of co-corrections has had little impact on the availability of single-sex sentencing alternatives for males, the process of integration has generally reduced the options for female offenders. Not only in the seven states where a women's institution was used for co-corrections, but even in most other states, where men's and other noncorrectional institutions have been used for co-corrections, women have not had the alternative of single-sex incarceration that men have had. However, the two states that most recently moved into co-corrections— Tennessee and Indiana—are the notable exceptions to this rule, because co-corrections has emerged for women as an alternative to being housed in a women's institution.

In the federal system, although there are some single-sex sentencing alternatives, most women live in coed facilities because of the shortage of single-sex options. The imminent end of co-correctional status at two federal facilities—Terminal Island and Pleasanton—will significantly reduce the percentage of inmates, especially women, in coed institutions, and will provide a single-sex sentencing alternative on the West Coast for federal women offenders.

Housing

The actual process of integration has generally been accompanied by housing shifts, either to achieve physical separation or to increase the opportunities for interaction with the opposite sex. Other factors have precipitated housing shifts: changes, including reversals, of sex ratios; needs for increased security in certain units; experimentation with coeducational therapy programs; and general population pressures. Related to housing shifts have been changes in the number and location of dining facilities, partitioning of toilet facilities, and other elementary physical adjustments.

Male and female inmates live in physically separate housing—either in different buildings or in cottages—at most institutions. In one federal institution most of the women live on what is virtually a separate compound. Actual inmate living space in coed institutions includes private rooms, semi-private rooms, open dorms, several types of cubicles, and makeshift space in the halls. With a few exceptions, the two sexes receive similar quarters. Women may be more crowded than men because of recent shifts in sex ratios, but efforts to provide greater privacy to women have generally been evident.

Security Level

Although the nominal security level in most institutions has remained the same after "going coed," the actual security level of many has been modified. Actual increases in security level were implemented by a combination of the following measures: the locking of previously open gates; installation of additional security fences, or an initial one, either as a psychological barrier or to control traffic; use of gate houses to search visitors and strip-search inmates returning from the community; performance of strip-searches not only upon re-entry and for "probable cause," but at random; development of central security systems; installation of mass lighting; use of inmate ID cards.

Security shifts have often been paralleled by shifts in staff responsibilities for levels of contact between inmates, restrictions on movement, and other such matters. However, it appears that such security shifts and adjustments in staff responsibility stem not from anything inherent in the coeducational setting, but from two other factors that are often closely related: decisions about how the setting is to be managed, and system-level modifications in programs and activities.

It appears that increases in security may be closely related to efforts to "overmanage" the setting, through extensive prohibitions of either physical or social contact between inmates. Moreover, administrators have been quick to note that such changes have not generally been made because the co-correctional setting was necessarily "out of control," but precisely as a result of system-level adjustments, which may be disproportionately affected by the coed institution.

The adjustments—often spoken of as "increasing accountability" or "catching up with good correctional practice"—have often led to a shift in the focus of control, and to the impression among inmates that "it's coed in name only," but not truly coed. At the same time, it often leads to the impression among staff that "caution creeps in, and this is what the time calls for. In five or six years, we'll be back to more creative strategies."

Women's Programs

It appears that the introduction of co-corrections has infrequently decreased the availability of traditional women's programs. Even in the few institutions where a case could be made that some women's programs had been lost, there appears to be a general increase in the availability and range of academic and vocational education programs, while a traditional women's program, like cosmetology, is attracting male inmates. The increased numbers of "male-geared" programs may be partly a function of inmates' choices of the more desirable types of institutional activity, but they are also closely related to administrative decisions about the allocation of limited program funds and a need to provide alternate activities, particularly to keep the potentially more disruptive male population "busy."

Women's Jobs

Women in coed institutions have often complained that males introduced to a women's institution have "taken over all our best jobs" within the institutional structure. Where this is true, it may be partly related to custodial decisions to restrict certain difficult-to-supervise jobs to inmates of one sex. This observed loss in job opportunities is often compensated for by an increase in opportunities for participation in prison industries, and by receipt of "good industrial pay."

Ironically, the loss of "women's jobs" may also extend to female administrative staff. In the changeover to co-correctional status, no previously male or noncorrectional institution has been placed in the hands of a female administrator. However, several women's institutions previously under female administrators have been subsequently administered by male superintendents. This raises questions about the appropriate administration of a coed institution, and about the need to keep the highest positions in the correctional system open to women.

Health Care

When female inmates are introduced to an institution that lacks experience with a female population, questions may arise about changes in the types of illnesses to be treated, appropriate prenatal care procedures, and other matters. Frequently, such questions are articulated in terms of the impact of women on the allocation of health care resources that were initially budgeted on the basis of the needs of male prisoners.

Birth control measures for women were accessible at all coed institutions. At only one institution did inmates strongly complain that birth control was difficult to obtain. In most institutions only birth control pills were generally available, but IUDs were also occasionally provided. The official rationale for the availability of birth control involved some notion of "protecting the women's health" and of providing the right to contraception to those on furlough. However, many staff members at visited institutions regarded the official purpose of birth control as "subterfuge," stating that the "real reason" was that "we can't be everywhere" and "every women has a right to protection."

Pregnancy rates, which were distinguished on the basis of possible institutional and noninstitutional contacts, were regularly available at federal institutions, but were infrequently available at state institutions. State institutions also seemed less willing to discuss issues of pregnancy, and careful guidelines on and protections against abortions seemed to be lacking in some institutions. Abortions seemed to be available to women at most coed institutions, although the openness with which they were performed, the amount and nature of previous counseling provided, the sources of financial support, and the services provided to a woman afterwards varied widely.

Prenatal care was available at all institutions. Indeed, most of the institutions had learned to deal with pregnancies before the inauguration of co-corrections. But the quality of prenatal care seemed to vary not only in terms of the importance with which the staff regarded these services, but also in terms of the emotional support provided. While no institution regularly allowed babies to remain at the institution for any great time after birth, most institutions with furlough policies have arranged for home furloughs to allow the mother to place the child.

HETEROSEXUAL RELATIONS

The opportunity to resume or continue relationships with members of the opposite sex has had predictable impact on the types of institutional relationships developing in coed institutions. The major issues related to heterosexual relations are the level of integration, normalization to "street behavior," and "going both ways." Each of these areas requires further, more systematic investigation.

Level of Integration

The extent to which a shift toward heterosexual relations was observed seemed to depend on how much the sexes were truly integrated. The actual level of integration involves notions of the sex ratio, parity of both the age range and distribution between the sexes, mixture of the sexes in programs, levels of social and physical contact permitted, and equality of security levels for both sexes. The movement toward resumption or continuity of heterosexual relations was often observed to be affected by shifts in any of these critical dimensions of the level of integration.

Paralleling both reduction in the times and places during which interaction is permitted and modifications in the quality of "true" unstructured interaction have been shifts back toward more "traditionally acceptable" adaptive sexual relations. Similar shifts toward or away from heterosexual relations have accompanied changes in other critical dimensions.

Normalization to "Street Behavior"

Particularly during the formative period of co-correctional program implementation, rumors have arisen about "back-sliding" toward the normal "street behavior" that led to incarceration. Especially while security and housing adjustment have been in process, rumors have flown wild about resumption of "pimping" and "prostitution." In at least one institution, this phenomenon has been viewed as part of the resumption of the "gang structure" that previously existed outside. Although some of this kind of activity is clearly present in coed institutions, as in society, there is little evidence that this phenomenon is widespread.

"Going Both Ways"

Particularly when the level of integration between male and female inmates is low or declining, but also in fully integrated institutions, there has been a continuation of homosexual relationships between women for supportive purposes and of heterosexual relations for financial purposes. Partly because of the frequent absence of means to obtain financial self-reliance within the prison, many female inmates have been observed to "play the men for suckers to get them to buy things, and then they have someone at the cottage."

A female inmate at one institution stated that "a lot of womens messes with the women in cottages and with the mens outside. One reasons is they is bisexual. Another reason is they go out and collect from the men and come back and share with their people. The fem, the frail woman, goes out and collects." Similar patterns of relating to the opposite sex by day and the same sex by night have not been generally observed among male inmates. However, the high numbers of known male homosexuals as protection cases, coupled with the reduction in opportunities for heterosexual contact during evening hours, has led to somewhat similar behavior patterns among some males.

EFFECTS OF RELATIONS BEYOND HETEROSEXUAL ONES

Closely related to, but conceptually different from observed shifts in heterosexuality are other relations that go beyond the heterosexual, including power struggles, family patterns, and role structure. The discussion below should be considered exploratory; further investigation is needed.

Power Struggles

In several institutions, power struggles develop between the "stud broads" and elements of the male population, especially those regarded as "pimps." The "turning around" of women who have been involved in female homosexual relationships implies shifts in the power position of the male partner, of the woman who has been "turned around," and most importantly of those key females in the pre-existing social structure who do not turn around, but instead dig in their heels.

The resolution of such power struggles probably depends largely on the prevailing integration level, as well as on the physical separation of housing, and even on the opportunities for both sexes to participate in institutional decision making. According to male inmates at one institution, males had earlier been harassed and physically abused by "stud broads," but over the course of time an accomodation had been reached.

Family Patterns

A version of family dependency roles in women's institutions has been described by Giallombardo (1966), Heffernan (1972), and Ward and Kassebaum (1965). Such family networks are considered to fill needs for affection and protection and to serve economic, social, and recreational functions. These constellations involve both the development and sustaining of nuclear family relationships, and also more extended kinship ties.

The introduction of co-corrections to a pre-existing female correctional community raises questions regarding the continuation of such volitional relationships, even when males are present. Although men may generally be perceived as a threat to family networks, and although they provide alternative means to serve many of the functions served by the family, family behavior has not decreased in all institutions after the introduction of males to an all-female institution. Indeed, in at least one institution the female "fathers" reportedly reacted to the male presence by intensifying the family network to something more extended and visible.

Role Structure

Closely related to the development of nuclear families in women's institutions is the adoption of the full range of societal sex-role behaviors found on "the outside." In a women's institution, both traditional female and traditional male roles are frequently displayed by women. When men are introduced to a female institution, many of the roles occupied by women are expropriated by men, and the opportunities for nontraditional sex-role development by women are reduced. This reduction is reflected in the perception that pressures on women to resume traditional relational roles emerge (Lambiotte, 1977), even while the co-correctional setting may expand work opportunities.

In conclusion, co-corrections appear to have a number of potential implications for institutional change and the relations of female offenders to both men and women. Because the first systematic investigations of co-corrections are only now being initiated (Burkhead, Cavior, & Mabli, 1977), further research on the effects of co-correction is suggested. The differential effects of co-corrections on women in the criminal justice system must be carefully explored.

REFERENCES

Burkhead, J.D., Cavior, H.E., & Mabli, G.A. Comparison of two approaches to incarceration: Co-correctional and single-sex institutions. Unpublished research proposal. U.S. Bureau of Prisons, 1977.

Giallombardo, R. *Society of women: A study of a women's prison*. New York: John Wiley and Sons, 1966.

Heffernan, E. *Making it in prison: The square, the cool and the life*. New York: Wiley Interscience, 1972.

Lambiotte, J. *Sex-role differentiation in a co-correctional setting*. Unpublished master's thesis, University of California at Santa Barbara, 1977.

National Advisory Commission on Criminal Justice Standards and Goals. *Corrections*. Washington, DC: Law Enforcement Assistance Administration, 1973.

Ross, J.G., Heffernan, E., Savick, J.R., & Johnson, F.T. *Issues paper: Phase I evaluation of coeducational corrections*. Washington, DC: Koba Associates, 1977a. Available on loan from the National Criminal Justice Reference Service.

Ross, J.G., Heffernan, E., Savick, J.R., & Johnson, F.T. *Frameworks paper: Phase I assessment of coeducational corrections*. Washington, DC: Koba Associates, 1977b. Available on loan from the National Criminal Justice Reference Service.

Ross, J.G., Heffernan, E., Sevick, J.R., & Johnson, F.T. *Knowledge assessment of coeducational corrections*. Washington, DC: Koba Associates, 1977c. Available on loan from the National Criminal Justice Reference Service.

Ross, J.G., Heffernan, E., Sevick, J.R., & Johnson, F.T. *Phase II design: Phase I assessment of coeducational corrections*. Washington, DC: Koba Associates, 1977d. Available on loan from the National Criminal Justice Reference Service.

Ross, J.G., Heffernan, E., Sevick, J.R., & Johnson, F.T. *Single institution evaluation design: Phase I assessment of coeducational corrections*. Washington, DC: Koba Associates, 1977e. Available on loan from the National Criminal Justice Reference Service.

Ross, J.G., Heffernan, E., Sevick, J.R., & Johnson, F.T. *Summary report: Phase I assessment of coeducational corrections*. Washington, DC: Law Enforcement Assistance Administration, 1977f. Available from the National Criminal Justice Reference Service or the U.S. Government Printing Office.

U. S. Bureau of Prisons. *Monday morning highlights*, May 9, 1977.

Ward, D.A., & Kassebaum, G.G. *Women's prison: Sex and social structure*. Chicago: Aldine, 1965.

Chapter 12

TWO LOSERS DON'T MAKE A WINNER

The Case Against the Co-correctional Institution

Jacqueline K. Crawford

Periodically a program is introduced into the corrections scene and given a great deal of fanfare as an innovation that will have a salutary impact on those inmates fortunate enough to be exposed to it. Such has been the case with the co-correctional institution.

Placing male and female offenders in the same institution was introduced a few years ago (actually reintroduced— the idea was around over a century ago) because it was believed that this would establish an atmosphere more closely related to normal community living and would result in a more smoothly functioning institution that would have a beneficial impact on the process of trying to change the behavior patterns of the offenders. There are many uninformed and misinformed individuals who believe this program will work and will make a useful contribution. But to date, no evaluation has been conducted to give us definite data on the impact of living in a co-correctional institution. However, based on the informal information I have gathered about the operation of co-correctional institutions, and based on my experience with incarcerated female felons, I am opposed to the further implementation of these experiments.

For a number of years American society has had a larger number of females than males in its total population. On the other hand, for reasons we all know, women comprise only a very small percentage of the clients in the criminal justice system, and in the final analysis only about 3 in every 100 persons sentenced to a federal or state correctional facility are women. Because they make up such a small portion of the institutionalized population, female prisoners have tended to be given last priority in the scheme of correctional planning and programming.

Anyone familiar with the history of corrections knows that programs for women have traditionally been watered down versions of activities that have been tried in men's institutions. Only in the past few years has there been a determined effort to design programs specifically to meet the unique needs of today's female offender. I believe that the co-correctional institution (which will generally have a population that is disproportionately male) will destroy any separate programming for the female and will attempt to force the small number of incarcerated females into programs designed to meet the needs of the much larger number of male prisoners. The need for special programs to meet the unique needs of the female offender has been well documented, and I fear there is small probability that these special programs will be maintained in a setting that is not strictly female oriented.

I am also dubious of the effectiveness or even of the ability of co-correctional institutions to serve the needs of female offenders, because women who are institutionalized have generally been exploited by men in their lives. The co-correctional institution may well be the setting for a continuation of this demeaning experience. This will be true especially if women are in a minority and if the programmatic structure of the institution does not meet the special needs of the women confined there.

Much of the problem in this setting can be ascribed to the fact that the men who are institutionalized are predominantly from that portion of society that maintains the most traditional relationships with women. Hence, even if exploitation is not a material fact, it will in all probability show in the male inmates' attitudes, and as a result they will continue to put down women. I have seen this sort of dominance when women merely maintained a relationship with a man through correspondence, and I am confident that the effect would be even more pronounced in a co-correctional setting.

I have not been able to find statistical data to support my contention, but it has been my experience that when both a man and a woman are incarcerated for the joint commission of an offense, and then reunite after their release, the woman soon returns to the institution. What I am saying is that two losers don't make a winner. The relationship of male loser and female loser creates an environment that tends to reinforce negative attitudes. If this is true in the "real" world in a normal environment, would it not be even more magnified in the artificial setting of a co-correctional institution?

It is my contention that convicted females who are sent into confinement need a protracted period of time away from men. This gives them ample opportunity to discover their own identity, to come to a realistic understanding of their responsibilities, and to cope with the fact that they are going to have to meet these responsibilities by themselves and through their own resources. The average incarcerated female is very much concerned about her children and about how these children are going to be cared for. A portion of the programming that prepares her for release is designed to allow her to come to grips with these problems and to face realistically her future responsibilities.

The incarcerated female is generally an extremely dependent individual. This dependence usually had a male orientation before her incarceration and is frequently related to the reason she is in prison. Placing the female offender in a co-correctional institution will in all probability allow these attitudes of dependency to continue. The danger I see in this is that the woman will never learn to become self-reliant in the co-correctional setting, and upon her release she will probably seek out another male upon whom she will become dependent.

The insecurity of the incarcerated female will manifest itself in many ways. Generally this insecurity has been demonstrated in the free world by her failure, or inability, to be content with one man. Insecurity and dependency are reflected by the woman's need to have more than one man "paying attention" to her. If this is true outside, would it not also be true within a co-correctional institution? Very frequently the incarcerated female is indiscreet in her correspondence and feels a strong need to send letters to and receive letters from several males. If this indiscretion is exhibited in correspondence, I can readily assume what would happen in the co-correctional institution where the population would have many more men than women—men from whom she could seek personal attention.

Traditionally women's institutions have not been as well financed as men's institutions. However, with their small populations they have been able to maintain informality in their housing, feeding arrangements, and programming. This relaxed atmosphere in the physical aspects of female institutions has always been considered one of the most positive parts of their operation. To increase the population several fold and to add men to the population will require many more rules and will destroy this relaxed informality. This will detract considerably from the type of living arrangements that have been one of the biggest advantages women's institutions have had over their male counterparts.

We are told that women need to identify with men when preparing to return to society. I have already mentioned the unhealthy dependency that most convicted females have had with males in their lives, and I do not believe it needs to be continued in a co-correctional institution. I do not deny the desirability of identification with the opposite sex and of the need for the reinforcement of positive behavior by members of the opposite sex, but I believe this will not be accomplished by using as examples men who are demonstrated failures.

I believe we can best meet the need for male identity figures by allowing the women to have contact with men who have shown that they can successfully cope with the stresses of life, probably best represented by carefully selected men who serve as staff and professional employees in the women's institution.

In addition, there is an intense need for women to be allowed to live with their children. The vast majority of incarcerated women have children who are completely dependent on them. Most of these women have very strong feelings that they have failed their children and that their children will slip away from them while they are in prison.

At the Nebraska Center for Women we have found that the Mother Off-Spring Life Development (MOLD) Program has been extremely beneficial to the incarcerated female. This program allows male children up to age seven and female children up to age 16 to spend several days a month living in the institution with their mother. The attitudes and behavior of all of the women in the institution improves dramatically while children are on campus, and I cannot help but wonder whether a mother-child institution may not be a better living arrangement than a co-correctional institution. Certainly it would establish a positive mother-child relationship that could be the first step in preventing another generation of violators. All the co-correctional institution seems to offer at this time is the possibility that behavior may be better and that homosexuality may be reduced.

I must ask whether homosexuality has really been reduced in co-correctional institutions. Is it not very possible that the "look but don't touch" rule of the co-correctional institution may be extremely stimulating to people who have demonstrated a lack of self-discipline, and might this not be so frustrating that it could increase homosexual behavior?

In addition to the sexual frustration of the inmate that might arise because of the necessary "look but don't touch" rule, there is the strong possibility that suspicion will arise in the minds of the husbands or wives of the residents of a co-correctional institution. Many of these marriages will already be severely strained by the incarceration of one mate and by the resulting financial, social, and emotional strains this causes for the marriage partner in the free world. In many instances the free mate will have strong feelings of animosity, and placing their husband or wife in a co-correctional institution may exaggerate these feelings to a point where it ruptures the marriage. From this perspective, the co-correctional institution may be counterproductive when it comes to providing stability for the inmate about to return to the free world.

One must also consider that the stresses and strains caused by sexual frustrations may well be detrimental to the programmatic planning designed for any given inmate. If an inmate, married or single, finds himself or herself strongly attracted to a member of the opposite sex but can make no advances or is afraid of developing feelings of guilt because of a mate outside, will this not make the treatment process more difficult to accomplish?

The questions that have been posed here and the adverse comments that have been made are not intended to argue that we should banish the co-correctional institution forever. Rather, I believe we should systematically seek answers to these and other unasked questions before we commit ourselves to unverified operations. After careful planning and small-scale testing, we may discover much more significant information than is presently available.

From the perspective of a superintendent of a women's facility, I believe the existing co-correctional institutions are detrimental to women's programs. Some co-correctional institutions are being operated for economical reasons or because men's institutions are becoming overcrowded. One gets a very strong impression—even though it cannot be verified—that institutions are being sexually integrated to please male egos or to smooth out the operation of men's institutions, and not to meet the unique and special needs of the female offender. Only when we become completely aware of these special needs and the manner in which they must be served will we be able to assist the incarcerated female offender. The co-correctional institutions, as they are presently designed, do not seem to hold any promise to provide that assistance.

Chapter 13

THE ERA AND COED PRISONS

Ralph R. Arditi
Frederick Goldberg
M. Martha Hartle
John H. Peters
William R. Phelphs

Ratification of the Equal Rights Amendment would require sexually integrated prisons which incorporate, wherever feasible, the best aspects of previously segregated institutions. Such a system would dictate changes in many aspects of prison life and administration.

Obviously, those treatment differences that result from economies of scale would be eliminated automatically by the integration of the institutions. For example, men and women would have equal access to medical facilities and religious programs provided at a particular institution. The problem of remoteness would be similarly eliminated: Although a given facility might still be remotely situated, the men and women sent there would be equally disadvantaged. Many other problems would not, however, be solved by the simple act of integration.

THE CLASSIFICATION PROCESS

When a state maintains only one institution for all male offenders and none for its female felons, the process of integration would be relatively straightforward: All offenders would be housed in that one institution. However, in those states where different institutions are presently set aside for different categories of male offenders, the classification process would have to be revised to accommodate women on an equal basis. The ERA would require that the classification standards employed be objective and sexually neutral in both application and effect.

Because of the vastly greater number of men sentenced to confinement, the application of a sexually neutral classification scheme would raise certain problems. There is some danger that application of such a sexually neutral scheme would result in grossly unequal treatment for some women. For example, in a particular state system, a female inmate might find herself one of only two or three women in an "integrated" population with hundreds of men. Such gross numerical disparity might run afoul of the Eighth Ammendment prohibition against cruel and unusual punishment, the inmate's right of privacy, and her right to equal protection of the laws. Balancing these rights in urgent situations, the courts might allow a woman to choose not to be confined in a particular institution. Incarcerating at least five or 10 women in each institution should, however, provide sufficient female companionship without significantly hindering the process of integration.

THE PHYSICAL ENVIRONMENT

In terms of physical facilities and the general prison environment, most women now receive better treatment than their male counterparts. The ERA would eliminate this difference by subjecting both men and women to the same physical surroundings in sexually integrated institutions. Ideally, the equalization would be up to the level presently enjoyed by the women. But in most states, this would require either renovation of almost all existing male institutions, or construction of all new facilities designed to meet the high standards now found in most female prisons. Again, if the state faces an economic roadblock to equalization *up* to a certain level, the ERA would tolerate equalization *down* to a lower, more economically feasible level.

As discussed above, sexual integration of the nation's correctional institutions need not result in heterosexual cohabitation, since the constitutional right to individualized privacy would probably require the authorities to provide sexually separate facilities for disrobing, sleeping, and performing personal functions. Although the degree to which these facilities would have to be separated in order to meet constitutional requirements is not precisely defined, a state would probably be permitted to look to "societal mores" in interpreting the right to privacy in public institutions.

REHABILITATION

Under the ERA the current disparity in both the quantity and quality of rehabilitative programs available to men and women would have to be eliminated. Since the ERA also requires the integration of institutions, however, such equalization should not increase costs. The Amendment would not require that every institution in a state offer identical rehabilitative programs, but rather only that both sexes within any given institution be provided equal access to all programs within that institution. Assignments to prison industries and other work details would also have to be made on a sexually neutral basis.

CONCLUSION

Patterns of sexual discrimination exist throughout the prison system of the United States. Every state exhibits differences related to both scale and sexual stereotypes in the treatment of its male and female offenders. The discrimination involved in differential treatment varies considerably, but substantial discrimination against both men and women is widespread.

The Fourteenth Amendment has done little to eliminate these patterns of sexual discrimination, and it does not seem likely that it will bring about significant reform. But ratification of the proposed Equal Rights Amendment should require that, within certain constitutional limitations, the nation's prisons should be integrated to ensure equality of treatment for both men and women.

Part III

ANNOTATED BIBLIOGRAPHY ON COED PRISON

This bibliography, which began as a modest effort to pull together what I thought were very few published sources on adult coed prisons, grew very rapidly to reach its present size. Part of this growth was due to the uncovering of sources buried in a wide range of places, especially in the Federal Bureau of Prisons, and much of the growth is due to the increased attention which this topic is receiving. The reader will note that the oldest reference date is 1972—an indication of the rapid spread of interest in adult coed prisons. References here *do not* duplicate the papers in this volume.

My goal has been to compile this information in a very general form. Each item is annotated and arranged by author's name. The topics include various dimensions of adult coed prisons. I do not claim that the bibliography is comprehensive. To the best of my knowledge, it includes references beyond a few found in popular magazines that would be helpful to administrators, researchers, and teaching faculty interested in the adult coed prison.

With papers and reports that are unpublished, I have tried to provide the addresses of the authors.

Anderson, David C. Co-corrections. *Corrections Magazine*, 1978, *4*, 33-41. This article is a journalistic account of the history, rationales, and current coed institutions in the United States. The author interviews inmates, staff, and top administrators of the Federal Bureau of Prisons. The author concludes that in spite of the potential trouble caused by going coed, it has worked in a few places.

The story of co-corrections revolves around a few central themes. At the coed FCI Fort Worth, co-corrections began because the Federal Bureau of Prisons needed a place to put a busload of tough ladies from the FCI Alderson, West Virginia. A second theme is the policy on physical contact. At coed FCI Fort Worth, a couple may hold hands or put their arms around each other; at coed FCI Lexington, they may only hold hands. A third theme concerns how co-corrections fits into the field of corrections as a whole. Officials say co-correction is one part of a larger picture, but sex remains a constant preoccupation. A fourth theme is the administration of a coed prison. The warden at FCI Fort Worth says his task is to impose a more structured routine on the old spirit of mutuality. Another warden prefers older inmates for co-corrections. A final theme concerns the advantages of co-corrections for inmates, especially the opportunity to experience something other than an exploitive relation with the other sex.

Baunach, Phyllis Jo, and Murton, Thomas O. Women in Prison—An Awakening Minority. *Crime and Corrections*, 1973, *1*, 4-12.

The authors provide an overview of the current plight of the female prisoner. There are approximately 30,000 women serving prison sentences in the United States. The increases in female criminality and the problems caused by a growing female inmate population are explored first. Prison conditions in female institutions in Georgia, South Carolina, Illinois, and Iowa are described, and the wide range of prison types is thus demonstrated. Little-publicized strikes and riots by female inmates to protest prison conditions are also described. Innovations such as the coed prison, inmate councils, and allowing female prisoners to keep their babies while in prison are discussed, and their consequences on female offenders are explored.

Benedict, P. E., Brewer, C., Matthews, J., Polhemus, J., Schwartz, S., Suss, L. C., Teicholz, R., Thomas, D., Tuemmler, J., Tweedy, A., and Wilkins, C. The Effects of a Coeducational Facility: A Continued Analysis. Unpublished Masters Thesis, Boston University, 1976.

Brandon, N., Carson, B., Disenhof, S., Eden, A., Gurtler, R., Lipps, B., Menkel, S., and Williams, L. A Study in a Coeducational Correctional Facility: Differential Effects of Psychotherapy and Other Programs. Unpublished Masters Thesis, Boston University, 1977.

Burkhead, John D. Preliminary Summary of Follow-up Study. January 1, 1975–July 31, 1975. Federal Correctional Institution, Lexington, Kentucky (no date, around 1975).

> In an effort to assess the recidivism rate of former inmates of coed FCI Lexington while on parole, a questionnaire was mailed to U.S. Probation Officers supervising 263 inmates released to their custody from January 1, 1975 through July 31, 1975.
>
> Ninety-five percent (249) of the questionnaires were returned; 207 (83.1%) of the subjects included in this follow-up study were considered "successful" while on parole because they had not had their parole revoked or received a new sentence of 60 days or longer. The average ages of the recidivist and nonrecidivist were 35 and 38 respectively. This finding would appear to support the notion that criminals mature out of their deviant behavior patterns. The 207 nonrecidivists averaged 314 days of supervision, and the 42 recidivists averaged 202 days of supervision. This would suggest that the first year after release from prison is a critical time for many inmates. A second follow-up study is in progress.

Burkhead, John D. Physical Contact Violations at FCI, Lexington. A paper presented at the Bureau of Prisons Conference on Confinement of Female Offenders, March 1978. Copies available from John Minor, Bureau of Prisons, 320 First Street, NW, Washington, DC 20534.

> Burkhead reports on physical contact violations at FCI Lexington, Kentucky, from February 1974 through December 1977. He found that men had fewer incident reports (83) than women (197). One reason for this difference was that women were more involved in homosexuality (82 reports) than were men (4 reports).
>
> The number of incident reports increased from a low of 12 in 1974 to 123 in 1977. During 1975 and 1976 there were 66 and 79 reports respectively. The big jump in 1977 can be attributed to violations for kissing, which had not been written up the year before. Kissing accounted for 60 of the 123 violations. Under heterosexual violations, intercourse resulted in 29 reports for women, 7 for men; 30 women and 29 men were found in a compromising situation. Most of the homosexual violations involved women found in bed together.
>
> Most heterosexual contact violations and the four male homosexual violations were referred to the Institution Discipline Committee, whereas only 23% of the female homosexual violations were so reported.

Cavior, Helene Enid. A Survey of Student Reaction to a Coed Federal Youth Institution. Unpublished report, Federal Bureau of Prisons, October 1972.

> Cavior surveyed 183 of the 209 males and 17 of the 18 females on their

attitudes about the coed program at the Kennedy Youth Center, Morgantown, West Virginia (now known as the FCI Morgantown) two months after its initiation. The survey shows that female and male residents at KYC support the coed concept. In two male units, however, the socialized subcultural inmates and the inadequate, immature inmates felt that the coed program had increased the problems of daily living. Cavior says realistically, however, that any population change as drastic as that from a one-sex to a coed institution can be expected to cause apprehension and to result in a somewhat pessimistic attitude.

Cavior, Helene Enid. The Results of a Rank-Order Question Which Included Cocorrections. Unpublished report, Federal Bureau of Prisons, February 1975.

As part of Cavior and Cohen's "The Development of a Scale to Assess Resident and Staff Attitude Toward Co-corrections" (Chapter 8), staff and residents at the coed Federal Correctional Institution in Lexington, Kentucky, were asked to rank-order eleven items from most important (1) to least important (11). There were 614 questionnaires distributed to 198 staff members and 394 inmates; 426 of the questionnaires returned were usable, 148 from the staff and 278 from inmates.

Averages of the rank order were computed for female and male inmates and staff. These means were then ordered from most to least important and assigned ranks from 1 to 11. Results show that female and male inmates ranked the 11 items in essentially the same order. Female and male staff also ranked the 11 items similarly, though differently from the inmates. The greatest sources of disagreement concern furloughs, which residents ranked 1 and staff ranked 7, and effective counseling, which inmates ranked 10 and staff ranked 2. Coed programming was seen as relatively unimportant by both inmates (rank 8) and staff (rank 9). Of the four groups, female inmates assigned the highest rank (6) to coed programming.

Cavior, Helene Enid. Ethnographic Evidence for Three Positive Aspects of Co-Corrections: Normalization, Inmate Sexuality, and Inmate Violence. A paper presented at the Bureau of Prisons' Conference on Confinement of Female Offenders, March 1978. Copies available from John Minor, Bureau of Prisons, 320 First Street NW, Washington, DC 20534.

Cavior examines the results of two ethnographies of FCI Pleasanton (Lambiotte, 1977, and Smykla, 1978) as they related to three issues: normalization, inmate sexuality, and inmate violence. She reports that both ethnographies agreed that FCI Pleasanton achieved a more normal environment than is typically found in institutions. Heterosexual relationships are continued, and they reduce the predatory homosexuality and inmate violence that is exacerbated by the presence and interaction of both sexes.

Consad Research Corporation. *Bureau of Prisons Female and Co-correctional Addict Client Outcome Evaluation.* Pittsburgh: Consad Research Corporation, 1975.

Eaton, Travis. Opening Up Legitimate Opportunities in a Co-correctional Institution. Copies available from author, Department of Sociology, North Texas University, no date.

Albert K. Cohen (ASR, 1965) has suggested the possibility of four responses toward deviance. He believed that deviance may (1) open up legitimate opportunities, (2) close off legitimate opportunities, (3) open up illegitimate opportunities, or (4) close off illegitimate opportunities. Responses 1 and 4 may be classified as positive responses because they tend to discourage further deviance, while responses 2 and 3 are negative because they would encourage more deviance. Although incarceration of deviants may (and most often does) lead to all four response patterns, the goal of most prisons would be toward the positive responses. Response 4 might be thought of as a passive reaction, since the mere fact of imprisonment itself would tend to close off illegitimate opportunities. However, response 1 would be an active response because it would force the prison personnel to pursue a direct line of action in order to open up legitimate opportunities for the prisoners.

The Fort Worth FCI is one prison which seems to be responding in this positive, active manner. Through direct observation and personal interviews with various FCI participants (including the warden, social workers, staff psychologists, and numerous prisoners or "residents"), the author was able to delineate at least three areas in which the FCI opens up legitimate opportunities to those who are imprisoned: (1) the co-correctional setting—both males and females are housed in the same facility and allowed contact with each other; (2) mutuality—the residents are encouraged to work mutually with the prison staff to determine their program of activities at FCI; and (3) community relationships—residents are permitted to participate in community functions in various ways, and, at the same time, community citizens are invited to share in the activities of the prison. This type of positive, active response to deviance seems to be consistent with general prison reform measures offered in recent years by professionals within the field.

Evans, Don. Prison and Conjugal Visiting in Mexico. A paper presented at the annual Southern Conference on Corrections held at Florida State University, Tallahassee, Florida, 1975.

The author believes that conjugal visits and coed prison environments are valuable in maintaining family stability and emotional stability among inmates. Such considerations are important in promoting rehabilitation and in facilitating readjustment to society. The Mexican experience is said to indicate that such policies compensate more than adequately for primitive facilities. Overall resistance to such policies in the United States is said to result from general ignorance about the nature and effects of such policies, and from a determination to retain the punitive aspects of corrections, even at the expense of rehabilitation.

Folts, Ed. Staff and Their Attitudes: A Study of Employees at a Coeducational Correctional Institution. Unpublished Master's thesis, University of Alabama, 1979.

The author contends that the staff's understanding of personality development and the ability to work with people determines the success or failure of the program. He analyzes 55 staff interviews conducted at the coed Federal Correctional Institution at Pleasanton, California. Using independent measures of sex, age, length of time employed in the Bureau of Prisons, and education, he discusses issues like program clarity (mission, methods, and evaluation), and attitudes toward inmates, their jobs, and co-corrections. The study is also important for the statistical comparisons it draws with similar staff interview data collected at the coed Fort Worth Federal Correctional Institution by Heffernan and Krippel.

Grossman, Bud, Gengler, Lou, Markley, Carlson, Norman, and McDannell, Ken. Wardens' Summary. A paper presented at the Bureau of Prisons' Conference on Confinement of Female Offenders, March 1978. Copies available from John Minor, Bureau of Prisons, 320 First Street NW, Washington, DC 20534.

Grossman enumerates several advantages of co-corrections: quality medical care for women; reduction of homosexuality; housing alternatives for weak males; placing women closer to their homes; improved self-esteem; normalization; and "down the road relief on programs for men and women." Grossman makes several follow-up recommendations:

- develop standards for co-correctional institutions;
- develop a training program for staff at co-correctional institutions;
- include co-correctional staff training at staff training centers;
- develop inmate selection criteria for co-correctional designations;
- standardize policy statements on co-corrections;

- develop a transfer policy for physical contact violations;
- develop standards for staffing patterns and ratios of men to women;
- develop an inmate orientation program on sex education, planned parenthood, and other related topics;
- develop physical facility standards;
- develop guidelines for inmate community involvement, especially town furloughs.

Warden Gengler writes that "Co-corrections is a fact of life and is a viable component of corrections for a select group of prisoners and staff. The population of such a facility should be not only male and female, but also a mix of the young and old, healthy and ill, educated and non-educated." Although some of the severest critics are a BOP staff, Gengler points out that he has a low turnover and very high application rates. He also calls for research on staff turnover and the need for unit management in a co-correctional setting, and he asks for a definition of "normalization."

In the same paper, Markley observes that "Co-correctional institutions are rewards for inmates." Such institutions give women greater opportunities to maintain family ties.

McDannell writes that at FCI Pleasanton he is dealing with the issue of community placement of infants. At Pleasanton there are women mechanical services crews, a strong vocational training program, and a large number of female correctional officers.

Director Norman Carlson closed the conference saying he had "no intention to phase out co-corrections." He sees co-corrections operating within the framework of safe, humane institutions and in an environment that facilitates inmate change. He believes that co-correction has reduced sexual assault and homosexual activity. It has created a more normal environment than a penitentiary, and it has provided a broad range of programs for both sexes.

Hawthorne, Jimmy. Family Planning and OB/GYN Services at Lexington. A paper presented at the Bureau of Prisons' Conference on Confinement of Female Offenders, March 1978. Copies available from John Minor, Bureau of Prisons, 320 First Street NW, Washington, DC 20534.

According to Hawthorne, the pill is the most commonly used birth control method. The number of women taking the pill or using birth control measures has decreased from 17% in 1974 to 11% in 1977. Women realize that the pill has serious side effects. Moreover, they believe that the staff will watch them more closely if they are on the pill. During the period from February 1974 through January 1977, there were 25 pregnancies resulting from intercourse at FCI Lexington. During the same period, 34 of 114 pregnancies were aborted. Of the 25 at Lexington, 60% were aborted. Hawthorne emphasizes the "normal" atmosphere at FCI Lexington, saying that "treating men and women helps recruit good medical staff."

Heffernan, Esther. Co-corrections: Some questions to be asked. In *Proceedings of the Tenth Annual Interagency Workshop of the Institute of Contemporary Corrections and the Behavioral Sciences*. Huntsville, Texas: Sam Houston State University, June 1975.

Heffernan, Esther, and Krippel, Elizabeth. Final Report on Research: Fort Worth FCI. Unpublished report, Federal Bureau of Prisons, Washington DC, 1975.

One of the most extensive studies of co-corrections to date, this is a two-year research project conducted at the coed Fort Worth Federal Co-correctional Institution. Heffernan and Krippel examined co-corrections at Fort Worth, a medium-security, open institution housing a population heterogeneous in race, age, offense type, and sex, and with an explicit correctional philosophy of "mutuality" and "community engagement." Their tasks at FCI Fort Worth were twofold: first, to develop a descriptive analysis of the internal characteristics, relationships, and structures of control at FCI Fort Worth; and second, to explore the question of the degree to which Fort Worth's approaches to co-corrections can be reproduced in other institutional settings.

The large amount of data in their report defies summary here, so it will suffice to say that for their first task, the authors use a typology of inmates' styles of adapting to prison that was developed in Heffernan's previous research at the DC Reformatory for Women. These three adaptive styles are called "square," "cool," and "in the life." In a random sample of the Fort Worth inmate population, the authors categorized 14% as "squares" (first time commitments), 55% as "in the life" (the majority of all prison populations, characterized by contacts with juvenile justice system, early entry into correctional institutions, drugs, ordinary job skills, and a sense of prison as a way of life), and 30% as "street people," which developed as a special category at FCI Fort Worth to account for high-risk offenders usually involved with violations of the narcotic laws or drug-related crimes and with a large number of arrests. The authors found no "cools" in the Fort Worth population. Data were collected on differences in program participation and disciplinary levels and rates between the two sexes, and some comparative data on recidivism were used.

Heffernan and Krippel also saw that they had to identify issues in institutional planning if the research done at Fort Worth was to be relevant for institutions with diverse programs and backgrounds. The possible inter-relations among these components, including co-corrections, involve the applicability of co-correctional philosophy, questions about staff recruitment and background, appropriate staff-to-inmate ratios, inmate population criteria and inmate sex ratios, distribution of inmates in institutional programs, rates of admission and release, security levels, and relations with the community.

Holley, Charles. An Evaluation of Inmates Assigned to a Transactional Analysis Program Using a Multidimensional Scaling Technique: An Exploratory Study. Fort Worth Correctional Institution, Fort Worth, Texas, no date.

The purpose of this study was to determine whether prisoners enrolled in an introductory transactional analysis (TA) course change their relative locations (i.e., Euclidean distances) in respect to selected adjectives used as stimulus words, during the period that they are assigned to the program. Further, given that a change does occur, the study aimed to assess the direction of the change in regard to course objectives.

By interpreting changes between the distances of the data plots of administrations 2 and 3, the authors reached the following conclusion: While assigned to the TA course, two subjects moved in a direction prescribed by the course objectives, two subjects did not greatly alter their positions in one direction or the other, and three subjects moved in a direction opposite to that prescribed by the course objectives.

The program appears to have been successful with some prisoners and unsuccessful with others. Since some subjects are moving away from the course objectives, something may be occurring during this period that exerts a stronger influence on these prisoners than the TA course. Another possibility is that the program simply may not be effective for some residents. An extension of the present project would be to isolate this latter possibility. This could be done by identifying the demographic and attributive variables associated with the successful and unsuccessful subjects. A prediction equation could then be developed to assign those prisoners to the class that could be expected to benefit from the exposure. Non-assigned prisoners could be enrolled in alternative programs.

The multidimensional scaling technique appears to have identified those subjects who benefit from the TA course as well as those who do not. With sufficient replication (or a slightly altered methodology) to provide a statistically adequate sample size, this knowledge

could be related to idiographic variables of the appropriately categorized subjects for the purpose of predicting "success." Longer-term
evaluation would be necessary to ensure validity of the prediction
equation as well as empirical validation of the multidimensional
ratings.

Holley, Charles, and Mabli, Jerome. Short-Itis—A Pre-release Phenomenon in Prison. Copies available from the Research Office, Fort Worth
Federal Correctional Institution, Fort Worth, Texas, no date.

The primary purpose of this project was to determine the existence,
or nonexistence, of "short-itis"—a transient situational stress dis-
order in prisoners during the 3 months immediately preceding
release from incarceration. A secondary purpose was tentatively to
identify some of the attributes associated with prisoners' susceptibil-
ity to the malady. Both subjective and objective data were gathered
and analyzed in making the determinations.

"Short-itis" does indeed seem to be an identifiable phenomenon.
The evidence is quite convincing in this regard, and goes even further
by tentatively identifying various contributory factors that need to be
investigated in a more in-depth manner.

For instance, young female inmates seem to be more susceptible
than other inmates. Is this a result of their background? Is it due to the
effects of the socialization process? Is it caused by staff attitude and
treatment? The specific antecedent variables must be identified and
the proportion of variance attributable to each one must be determined. Furthermore, it is evident that there are variables over which
the rehabilitation facility has manipulative control and, equally
important, over which it has no control. The success of any program
developed to counter "short-itis" will be limited by the number of
variables that institutions can control.

To put this interactive proposition in more concrete terms, if the
institutional factors negatively combine in an additive fashion (for
example, "authoritarian" team plus lack of peer support), the prognosis for successfully coping with the "short" period would appear to
be very poor. The question becomes whether or not the impact of
positive idiographic variables can offset institutional variables. If
either (but not both) institutional or individual variables were positive, the prognosis of successfully coping with "short-itis" would be a
toss-up, and intervening treatment could be of value.

There is, perhaps, a more fundamental issue involved. Should
"short-itis" be eliminated? It is conceivable that this period of anxiety
"energizes" the residents and thus prepares them for entry into the
free world. If this were true, the phenomenon might be beneficial. In
addition, it may be that this period affords that opportunity for the

staff to determine if the inmate can "take the pressure." The underlying assumption is that the inmate's success in coping with "short-itis" is indicative of his or her ability to cope with the outside world. These assumptions must of course be empirically validated. A partial methodology for such validation would be to perform follow-up studies on subsamples of released inmates who had exhibited varying amounts of "short-itis."

Given our assumptions that "short-itis" is a deleterious side effect of imprisonment and that it exists in a large number of residents, the authors offer the following recommendations: (1) that additional research on "short-itis" be conducted to develop a predictive equation to identify those residents susceptible to the malady; (2) that a counseling program be developed for susceptible inmates and that it be mandatory for this group and voluntary for all others (this program would be an ideal position for student interns); (3) that an ongoing evaluation be conducted for this "short-itis" program. (This evaluation would include the follow-up studies previously mentioned).

In summary, this study found that "short-itis" does indeed exist in prisons as a form of acute anxiety, and that it occurs primarily in subpopulations associated with certain identifiable attributes and certain management policies. The condition can (and quite often does) result in serious and deleterious consequences for the inmate and for the prison. It is believed, however, that the condition is susceptible to treatment and that existing prerelease programs should be broadened to deal with this problem.

Huston, William. Results of Co-corrections Survey. Division of Corrections, Department of Health and Social Services, State of Alaska, Pouch H-03, Juneau, Alaska, March 8, 1978.

William Huston, Director of the Division of Corrections in Alaska, surveyed the 50 United States for their views on co-corrections. Thirty-eight (80%) of the states responded, and 66% of the states responding took a neutral stand on coed prisons. Most said they did not have enough experience with coed prisons to form an enlightened opinion. Ten of the 38 responses (26%) were ideologically opposed to sexually integrated facilities. Three states (8%) announced they were in favor of the concept. States which at one time operated coed prisons but have since reverted back to one-sex prisons opined that coed prisons are difficult to administer and less practicable than sexually segregated facilities. A bibliography on sexually integrated corrections is also included.

Jenkins, O. C. Statistical Summary—Incident Reports. A paper presented at the Bureau of Prisons' Conference on Confinement of Female Offenders, March 1978. Copies available from John Minor, Bureau of Prisons, 320 First Street NW, Washington, DC 20534.

Jenkins offers a statistical summary comparing incident reports from Federal Correctional Institutions at Alderson (West Virginia), Lexington (Kentucky), Fort Worth (Texas), and Seagoville (Texas) from July through October 1977. Generally, co-correctional institutions had higher numbers of reports than did the single-sex institutions. Jenkins writes that incident reports reflect staff behavior as well as inmate behavior, and that attitudes toward certain behaviors, institutional practices, and amount of supervision all affect the number of incident reports as well as actual inmate infractions.

Judd, Barbara Geist. The Effect of the Length of Imprisonment Upon Learned Helplessness. 1977. Copies available from the author, Psychology Department, Southern Methodist University, Dallas, Texas.

This study assessed the hypothesis that prisoners initially react with anxiety, followed by hostility or rebellion, and finally depression during progressive stages of their imprisonment. A total of 58 female inmates responded to the Multiple Affect Adjective Checklist (General Form), the Beck Depression Inventory, and the SMU Activity Questionnaire (purported to be a self-report behavioral measure of depression).

Results indicated that length of imprisonment was not correlated with anxiety, hostility, or depression on the Multiple Affect Checklist and the Beck Depression Inventory. Arguing with staff and other inmates and length of imprisonment were significantly correlated ($p < 0.01$). Depressed subjects were found to participate less in group activities ($p < 0.05$) and more in nongroup activities ($p < 0.001$). Probation violators tended to be more depressed ($p < 0.05$).

Karacki, Loren. Kennedy Youth Center Student Response to a Coed Questionnaire. Unpublished report. Federal Bureau of Prisons, October 1972.

Questionnaires were distributed to 20 males and 21 females at the Kennedy Youth Center to tap their attitudes on the coed program there. The sample was selected to ensure representation by living units and race within living units. Overall, the residents responded favorably to the coed program. Inmates were also quite liberal regarding the amount of contact they felt they should have with the other sex and what they consider to be appropriate standards of dress. On some issues, however, there were differences between males and females. The young women were generally inclined to take more liberal stances and to voice more criticism of their current situation at KYC. For instance, they were more likely than males to say that no disciplinary action should be taken when an inmate of the other sex is found in one's room, or when two inmates are found in the sexual act. Karacki also reports that more females than males felt that the staff at KYC was "uptight" about the coed setting and that females were more severely disciplined than males.

Mabli, Jerry. Single Sex Co-corrections Comparison on the Basic Social Climate CIES Scale. A paper presented at the Bureau of Prisons' Conference on Confinement of Female Offenders, March 1978. Copies available from John Minor, Bureau of Prisons, 320 First Street NW, Washington, DC 20534.

Mabli evaluates co-corrections on the basis of a Correctional Institutions Environment Scale (CIES) administered at the Federal Correctional Institutions at Fort Worth, Texas, Alderson, West Virginia, Lexington, Kentucky, and Seagoville, Texas. The CIES measures an institution's social climate as perceived by staff and inmates. Inmates at Fort Worth (women and men) scored higher than other inmates in the categories of involvement, support, autonomy, practical orientation, personal problem orientation, and clarity. Alderson inmates (all women) scored highest on expressiveness, Lexington (women and men) on staff control, and Seagoville (all men) on order and organizations. According to Dr. Mabli, the CIES results "will substantiate that co-correctional institutions do have a place in the Prison System as a result of their unique capacity to provide a humane, nearly 'normal,' safe environment."

McCollum, Sylvia, and Hambrick, Margaret. Program Issues. A paper presented at the Bureau of Prisons' Conference on Confinement of Female Offenders, March 1978. Copies available from John Minor, Bureau of Prisons, 320 First Street NW, Washington, DC 20534.

The authors contend that the small number of women in prison affects the variety of programs offered, and although co-correctional institutions increase these offerings, participation by women does not increase. Nontraditional vocational training programs have been offered to women, but they have not been successful. McCollum writes, "It is not realistic to assume that women will adopt nontraditional roles without strong incentives and support.

It is difficult for women to assume nontraditional roles in traditional—that is, prison—environments. Only 2.7% of the women are enrolled in vocational training programs compared to 10.2% of the men. However, in social education programs, women are becoming more involved than men. The authors stress that women in prison need to learn status occupation trades, receive decent pay, and acquire socialization and coping skills.

Mebane, Bette G. Differential Life History Factors Among Incarcerated

Offenders. Unpublished PhD Dissertation, North Texas State University, 1976.

This study was designed to be the first step in an empirical investigation of the female offender, using biographical information. It is the goal of the research eventually to be able to predict probable criminal activity among women.

The most readily delineated group for study consisted of female prisoners. The purpose of the study was to determine whether factor clusters representative of women in prison could be produced. Specific objectives were to organize descriptive biographical information of incarcerated women and to correlate biodata results with important current and postincarceration events.

A group of 314 women—173 in a federal prison and 141 in a state prison—completed life history questionnaires. Their responses provided objective, descriptive data about them. Separate and unique factors were produced from the federal prisoner sample; the first factor—recognition of cultural norms—accounted for 72% of the total variance. The state prison sample produced eight factors; the first of these factors—marital history and discord—accounted for only 5% of the total variance.

The factors indicate a pronounced desire for home life, family life, and stability—all of high cultural value. There is also a large inconsistency between statements about goals and behavior, with an impoverishment of ideas, plans, and the actions designed to achieve stated objectives.

For the federal sample, multiple linear regression models were derived and were found to be significantly related to various aspects of pre- and postincarceration events and behavior. These models could not be cross-validated on the state sample.

The regression analysis identified specific variables such as age, race, and occupational choice, and assessed their relationship to problem behaviors, for example, disciplinary reports. A limited number of significant relationships were found. The communality in response style suggests that an atypical pattern or "set" exists, and that measures can be developed to identify it. But the data are not clear enough to limn a behaviorally valid category of deviancy that could define incarcerated females by their bias in responding to BIB item content.

This study makes it clear that merely labeling behavior as criminal—connoting a deviant class of behavior—is highly inexact in identifying it. The female offender cannot yet be defined in the same way as a person suffering from depression, hypochondriasis, or schizophrenia—that is, by distinctive response groupings. Although this study made many inroads, generating descriptive factors and significant behavioral/life history correlates, incarcerated female offenders as a class cannot yet be identified by responses that make up a valid category of behavior.

Miller, Ervin. Female Property Offenders. Copies available from author, Department of Sociology, University of Texas, Arlington, Texas, 1976.
Because of the lack of research on female criminality and because the number of females involved in property offense has risen over the past several years, a small-scale exploratory study was conducted at FCI Fort Worth. The study was conducted with the cooperation of 10 female residents who were interviewed about their life histories. The concept of subjective career was used as the theoretical framework, and efforts were made to identify career contingencies that consistently emerged in the 10 interviews.

Career contingencies can most simply be described as events in an individual's life that are interpreted as turning points, in that they change one's outlook and motivate the person to behave in a particular manner. Five such contingencies were identified in the present study: (1) Interaction with agents of social control, most often during adolescence, such as police, probation officers, and juvenile courts. (2) Forming a dependence on males or peers as a result of conflict in the family between the parents and child or between the parents in the future offender's family. (3) Attachment to an older age peer group. This factor was identified because several residents discussed association with people older than themselves once they got out "on to the street." (4) Loss of a male companion or spouse on whom the woman was in some way dependent, as a result of his incarceration or the couple's separation. (5) Interaction with the FBI in the period after arrest, a reflection of the Bureau's tactic of "offering deals" to those who will "snitch" on others. This last contingency does not explain the behavior that resulted in the present incarceration but may hold implications for future behavior to the extent that the resident interprets her present situation as a result of her not cooperating with the FBI.

Nacci, Peter. Sexual Assault Study. A paper presented at the Bureau of Prisons' Conference on Confinement of Female Offenders, March 1978. Copies available from John Minor, Bureau of Prisons, 320 First Street NW, Washington, DC 20534.
Nacci attempts to assess the level of safety in institutions and the effects on homosexuality in co-correctional institutions. He uses levels of victimization and predation as indices of institutional safety. His results indicate that co-correction reduces homosexuality. Nacci

believes that co-correction is a trade-off because it does "reduce violence and sexual assaults even though pressures for heterosexual activity exist between men and women."

Patrick, Jane. Doing Time: An Ethnography of a Co-correctional Institution. Unpublished paper, Federal Bureau of Prisons, May 13, 1976.

This ethnography was written as a senior project in an anthropology course. The institution studied is the coed Federal Correctional Institution at Fort Worth, Texas. The author discusses the relative importance of "community engagement" between FCI Fort Worth and the local community as a component of "normalization." The author also provides descriptive data on the "stages" inmates at Fort Worth pass through, from reception to their "merry-go-round" (a term referring to collecting signatures and getting ready for release).

Descriptive data are also provided on the question of whether inmate programs are largely intended to please the staff and parole board. The author also discusses the relative isolation inmates feel during their incarceration and suggests that "community engagement" is helpful in minimizing or reducing this deprivation. That FCI Fort Worth is coed, she concludes, helps create an environment similar to the outside world and instills in residents a sense of responsibility and self-respect.

Prison Education: The College of Santa Fe and the New Mexico Penitentiary Approach. College of Santa Fe, Sante Fe, New Mexico, 1975.

This report describes major ongoing coeducational programs at the New Mexico Penitentiary with emphasis on the college credit program of the College of Santa Fe. The report also describes an evaluative conference on educational issues.

The New Mexico Penitentiary, whose facilities are briefly reviewed in the report, sponsors four major educational programs: a vocational program, an adult basic education program at elementary and secondary school levels, a college preparatory program which includes counseling support (Project Newgate), and a college credit program leading to associate and baccalaureate degrees for inmates and parolees. The last program named is offered by the College of Santa Fe.

This report also covers the discussions and deliberations of 65 professionals and laypersons at a conference on prison education held at Santa Fe in May 1975. Some of topics examined were the response to the College of Santa Fe program, the parole board's view of education as rehabilitation, future directions for course content emphasis, societal implications of a broadly based law education program, and the role of technical-vocational prison education. The appendixes include the legislation enacted in Illinois that made the state department of corrections an independent school district.

Ross, James, Heffernan, E., Sevick, J., and Johnson, F. Framework Paper: Phase I Assessment of Coeducational Corrections. National Institute of Law Enforcement and Criminal Justice, LEAA, September 23, 1977.

This paper develops generalized causal flows in the form of logic models for both programmatic and nonprogrammatic models of co-corrections. It synthesizes the elements of the several causal flows and presents a measurement model, or general framework, applicable across the universe of co-correctional institutions. The synthesized measurement model serves as an "envelope" in which to identify measurement points and potential measures for each of these states. The final chapter briefly discusses the applicability of the measurement model to specific programmatic and nonprogrammatic models, and to individual institutions.

Ross, James, Heffernan, E., Sevick, J., and Johnson, F. Single Institution Evaluation Design: Phase I Assessment of Coeducational Corrections. National Institute of Law Enforcement and Criminal Justice, LEAA, September 23, 1977.

The authors develop an evaluation design focusing on the co-correctional aspects of a given institutional program and assuming the presence of the basic managerial data necessary for the monitoring of any institution. Seven variables are thought to play critical roles in the development of any given co-correctional program. As independent variables they should be considered and controlled for in either cross-institutional comparisons or before-after comparisons within the institution.

The seven variables are (1) capacity of the institution, (2) sex ratio of both inmates and staff, (3) racial (and ethnic) ratios within and between the sexes, (4) size of staff and inmate composition, (5) security levels, (6) age range, and (7) program types. Additional variables to be considered when the measurement involves individual behavior changes are offense type, previous institutionalization, educational level, employment history, disciplinary record, marital status, time in sentence, drug and alcohol dependence, and salient factor score.

Five models of co-corrections are presented (reintegration, institutional control, therapy, surveillance, and alternate choice), and the authors suggest that many of the anticipated outcomes are similar among the five models, and that many of their measurements are identical. However, the priority of relationships of the outcomes to each other would vary from institution to institution.

Ross, James, Heffernan, E., Sevick, J., and Johnson, F. Phase II Evaluation Design: Phase I Assessment of Coeducational Corrections. National Institute of Law Enforcement and Criminal Justice, LEEA, September 23, 1977.

This report is an appendix to the following Knowledge Assessment, which arrays existing information on the synthesized measurement model developed in the Frameworks Paper. It is presumed that the reader of this report is familiar with, or has access to, at least the Summary Report, which consolidates the first four reports from the Phase 1 Assessment of co-corrections. The research issues discussed in this report as potential areas for further evaluation involve improvements in the data base and data collection procedures; the costs of co-corrections; the effects of co-corrections on the institutional program; the impacts of co-corrections on postrelease behavior; and development of a model institution. Each of these issues is discussed in terms of the importance and methods of obtaining more conclusive evaluative data on co-corrections, as well as in terms of cost and feasibility, to the extent that these can be estimated. Finally, several ways of redefining co-corrections within a broader systemic and evaluative context are presented for potential future study.

Ross, James, Heffernan, E., Sevick, J., and Johnson, F. Knowledge Assessment: Phase I Assessment of Coeducational Corrections. National Institute of Law Enforcement and Criminal Justice, LEAA, September 23, 1977.

This report traces the emergence of co-corrections and describes the characteristics of visited institutions at a single point in time, as well as changes occurring over time. It also estimates the future growth rate of the concept. The report compares co-correctional policy with actual operations.

Another chapter presents the major research problems related to the evaluation of co-corrections; reviews past and present co-correctional research designs; arrays existing knowledge about outcomes and impacts on the measurement model; and assesses ongoing research. Final chapters expand on the synthesized measurement model by considering the obtainability of primary and secondary data for each of the measurement points in the model. The concluding chapters also suggest several potential designs for filling gaps in knowledge about co-corrections and end with conclusions and recommendations.

Ross, James, Heffernan, E., Sevick, J., and Johnson, F. Issues Paper: Phase I Assessment of Coeducational Corrections. National Institute of Law Enforcement and Criminal Justice, LEAA, September 23, 1977.

This paper presents, in modified catalog form, the range of issues associated with the concept of coeducational correctional institutions. Because of the recent development and relative authenticity of published information about co-corrections, much discussion of its anticipated effects has been either conjectural, representing hopes and fears rather than direct experience, or "gut" level impression, rather than the product of systematic observation. Such issues, raised through discussion with experts, have been included in this paper, because their articulation plays an important role in a fuller understanding of the concept. This paper conveys a preliminary understanding of the breadth of perspectives impinging on several questions: How innovative are coed prisons? What functions do they serve? What are their unanticipated consequences? What problems exist in implementing coed prisons?

Smykla, John Ortiz. The Humanity of Coed Prisons. *Columns*, Fall 1978.
This short article proposes that there is a relationship between the quality of prison life and recidivism. The author cites early coed prison studies that describe the improved conditions of coed prisons and summarizes what we know about preliminary recidivism in this field. He contends that the absence of homosexual prison violence and other assaultive behaviors, including racial groupings, and reductions in psychological medication—together with the advantages of sexual integration that accrue to inmates and staff— contribute to recidivism data showing that from 70% to over 90% of the inmates released from coed prisons remain in the community. Smykla does not directly attribute this success to sexual integration but to a package of prison programs centered around co-correction.

Smykla, John Ortiz. *Co-corrections: A Case Study of a Coed Federal Prison.* Washington, DC: University Press of America, Second Edition, 1979.
This is a seven-month participant observation study conducted at the coed FCI at Pleasanton, California. In the first part of the book, the author establishes the framework for the participant observation study in phenomenology and the history of coed prisons. Details of the process leading up to the study are discussed.

In the second half of the book the author examines more closely issues related to sex, the inmate underlife, and communication in a coed prison. In the area of sexual adaptation by inmates in a coed prison, the author finds that about 90% of the inmates at Pleasanton consider themselves heterosexually oriented and engage in heterosexual activity in prison. The remaining 10% consider themselves homosexual with some accommodations to bisexuality. In the area of violence in a coed prison, the author reports that no incidents of predatory homosexual activity, assaults, racial or ethnic violence, or heterosexual assaults occur at Pleasanton. The presence of the other sex, in addition to a host of other factors, accounts for this lack of violence.

Finally, the author reports that communication between staff and inmates is not reserved to an elite few, as reported in other prison literature. Pleasanton does not follow the traditional model of "do your own time, don't talk with staff." On the contrary, staff-inmate communication at Pleasanton is quite frequent and highly visible. Communication between staff and inmates takes three forms: formal arrangements between staff and inmates, informal contacts, and open communication resulting from a lack of inmate pressure groups.

Smykla, John Ortiz. Theory, Practice and Research in Sexually Integrated Prisons. A paper presented at the Mid-South Sociological Association Meetings, November 1978, Jackson, Mississippi. Copies available from the author, Criminal Justice Program, University of Alabama, University, Alabama 35486.

Because coed prisons have passed relatively unnoticed in the criminal justice literature, the author surveys the literature on co-corrections. He finds that descriptive studies on coed prisons are plenty, but planned evaluative efforts are absent. The author reviews the descriptive studies done in this field, details what happened to evaluative research planned in this field, and concludes with a summary of 10 problems and issues encountered in conducting research in co-corrections. The paper also includes a discussion of the theoretic rationales for going coed.

Smykla, John Ortiz. Homosexuality in a Coed Joint. Unpublished paper, 1978. Available from the author at the Criminal Justice Program, University of Alabama, University, Alabama 35486.

The author reports that coed prison is successful in reducing and almost eliminating predatory and violent homosexuality. What that research has not done, however, is explain and then compare the sources and meanings of homosexuality that emerge in coed prison with the sources and meanings of homosexuality in our one-sex prisons. And neither does that literature discuss the unintended negative effects of "going coed" on homosexual identity.

Homosexuality among women in coed prison is not as reduced as homosexuality among men. There are several reasons for this: first, women come into coed prison carrying with them the pre-prison experience of subservient relations with men on the outside. Inside the coed prison women do not get the special assistance they need to overcome this dependency. Men, then, continue to validate their masculine egos.

A second reason for higher rates of homosexuality among women in coed prison is a sex role stereotype that has wrongly led us to accept as universal truth that men are satisfied by the act of physical release but that women need more emotional attachment. This disregard for women's feelings and pressure on women to "satisfy" men, but not for men to satisfy women, leaves women returning to their living unit to find satisfaction with other women.

A third explanation is that the extent of homosexuality depends on the level of integration of female and male inmates. Where the ratio of women to men is low or declining, we find that homosexual relationships between women continue or resume for supportive purposes, and that heterosexual relations meet financial ends.

Smykla also finds a similarity between the sources and meanings of homosexuality among women in coed prison and that recorded in all women's prisons. He observes a family-style network of homosexual dependency roles among women in coed prison. This same kind of family-style homosexual network has been reported among women in an all-women's prison. The functions of homosexuality in these situations are also similar: affection, protection, recreation, socialization, maintenance of submission and dominance, and economics.

Homosexuality among men in coed prison does not develop along the divisible lines of active and aggressive (wolf and punk) found in all men's prisons. Instead, in coed prison, since heterosexual relations are emphasized, most men are involved with women and the number of homosexuals is small. Among this small homosexual group, sexual activity is consensual, nonpredatory, and nonviolent. This male homosexual alliance primarily meets emotional and recreational needs. Protection and economic ends are not among its major functions, as they are in all-men's prisons.

Smykla also speculates on the effects of sexual integration on homosexual identity. He asks whether the "look but don't touch rule" of coed prison frustrates inmates, and whether this frustration might not increase homosexual behavior. The developing homosexual identity is also affected by other factors in coed prison: power struggles between female studbroads (daddy types) and male inmates over "turning around" women who have been involved in homosexual relationships; the tightening up or intensifying of the family-style network after the introduction of males to an all-female institution; and, when women are "turned around," their reversion to passive dependency roles.

Smykla, John Ortiz. The Impact of Co-Corrections. In Sherwood Zimmerman and Harold Miller (Eds.), *Crossroads in Corrections: Designing Policy for the 80's*. Cincinnati, Ohio: Anderson Publishing Co., 1980.

    The author surveys the literature on co-corrections and co-correction decision makers, administrators, and wardens for their definitions of "success" in co-corrections. Co-correctional programs are found to be measured in many ways: normalization, recidivism, community engagement, resumption of heterosexual contact, self-esteem, improved hygiene, improved social skills and communication with inmates of the other sex, reintegration ideals, economics, protection, and constitutional safeguards.

    He finds that data are available to support just about any contention in co-corrections. The problem lies in the vague and ambitious ways administrators go about attaining their goal and in whether they seek measures of their own effectiveness. Smykla contends that co-correction is drifting in a dismal darkness shielded from "publics" that could aid in its development. The author also opines that co-correction is suffering from a lack of a research perspective, created in part by lingering shibboleths holding that one-sex prisons are the prisoners' natural lot.

Smykla, John Ortiz. Coed Corrections in the United States: A Look at Theory, Operations, and Research Issues. *Howard Journal of Penology and Crime Prevention*, 1979 *18*,44–53.

    Using the volumes of data collected by Koba Associates in their assessment of coeducational correctional institutions in the United States and his own research in co-corrections, the author discusses the precedents for "going coed" in the United States; the rationales for coed corrections; the theoretical issues that constitute the basic hypotheses about the effects of sexuality integrated prisons; and the operational and evaluative issues that result from "going coed." The author's purpose is not to evaluate coed corrections but rather to bring the issues into the open so that others can study them more closely and perhaps employ them in evaluative research.

Smykla, John Ortiz. Sexual Oppression of Women in Coed Prison: Notes on the Myth of Equal Treatment. Unpublished paper. Available from the author at the Criminal Justice Program, University of Alabama, University, Alabama 35476.

    This paper asks if female prisoners in coed prison are less the subject of paternal differential treatment than their counterparts in all-women prisons. A survey of the literature on coed prisons seems to refute the state's contention that coed prisons are solving the sexist problems that have plagued the women's prison system for a hundred years. The paper concludes that coed prisons are masking the inequality in false benevolence and new pastel cloaks of kindness.

Teddie, Sallie, and Shelden, Terry. Prisoner Attitudes Toward Death and Dying as It Relates to Their Incarceration. Fort Worth Federal Correctional Institution, Fort Worth, Texas, 1977.

In reviewing the variables that might be related to attitudes toward dying in prison, family ties seemed to be relevant. Therefore attitudes of the total population of the 46 who completed the questionnaire were viewed in relation to family ties.

Nineteen of the residents, comprising 41.3% of the total population, had strong ties, while 23 or 50% had weak ties. No data are available for the remaining 8.7%.

Of those who said they were not afraid to die in prison, there was no difference between those who had weak and those who had strong ties; five respondents (38.5%) in each group gave this response. The remaining 23% had no family ties.

Among the residents who were fearful of dying in prison, those with weak family ties, 10 (58.8%), outnumbered those with strong ties, 6 (35.3%). One had no family ties.

None of the residents without family ties felt that a social stigma might be attached to dying in prison. There was very little difference in this area between those with strong ties (6 or 46.2%), and those with weak ties (7 or 53.8%).

In the total population, regardless of strength of family ties, 17 (36.95%) of the total were fearful and 13 (28.26%) of the total felt that there was a stigma attached to such a death. So a total of 65.21% expressed fear and felt that death in prison was shameful.

A brief review of the response themes seems to indicate that the following ideas are frequently mentioned:

1. Many cited happiness as a key ingredient in their philosophy of life.

2. A large group of residents said they would learn from mistakes and not repeat unhappy experiences.

3. A majority believed in life after death, heaven and hell.

4. All of those residents who had experienced the deaths of others in prison had strong, well-defined feelings about it.

5. Many members of the group who had been exposed to dying in prison denied having given much thought to their dying in prison.

6. Many residents expressed a fear of dying in prison because of shame, inadequate care, or being alone.

The indications are that the surface has just been scratched in surveying attitudes about death and dying in prison. Some responses indicated that acceptable surface feelings are currently being expressed, while many more feelings, strong feelings, lie beneath the surface.

The survey findings indicate that the Bureau of Prisons might take some steps that would enable staff, residents, and family to cope with the impending death of an incarcerated offender.

1. The institution could transfer residents who are expected to die before release to a facility near their next of kin.

2. Special arrangements could be made for daily family visits.

3. Group sessions should be conducted for residents whose illness is terminal. These groups should discuss death and dying. They should be conducted by a leader who is sensitive to verbal and nonverbal expression. The group leader should be extensively trained—for example, a psychiatrist, clinical psychologist, or social worker.

4. Follow-up studies should be conducted at institutions that provide extensive medical care for prisoners. The facility at Springfield, Missouri, could be an excellent place for continued study.

United States Bureau of Prisons. Summary—NARA Program Evaluation. Fort Worth Federal Correctional Institution, Fort Worth, Texas, July 1975.

The effectiveness of the small group as a significant part of NARA programming at FCI Fort Worth was evaluated. The drug risk questionnaire—a modification of the Kogan-Wallach Choice Dilemma Scale—was administered twice at four-month intervals. The questionnaire presented 10 real-life situations; five of the items were related to achievement (for example school and business) and not to drugs, while the remaining five items dealt with taking risks in drug-related or criminal situations.

On the basis of considerable previous research, the drug risk questionnaire was viewed as a measure of an attitude toward risk, and it was assumed that the NARA program should affect these attitudes. Residents were first asked to personally evaluate and come to their own decision about each item. They were then asked to discuss each item in a small group and to reach a unanimous group consensus.

It was predicted that upon entering the program a resident's level of risk taking would be relatively high on drug-related items, and low on the non-drug items. These levels would reverse themselves as a function of the program. It was also predicted that for drug-related items the pressure of the peer group would show increasingly greater influence on the decisions made, so that groups would exhibit less risk taking than individuals. With the nondrug issues it was predicted that individuals would endorse greater risks in the group than they would when responding as individuals. These predictions were supported by strong trends. It can be tentatively concluded that the NARA program is facilitating a shift in expressed attitudes toward criminality and drug abuse from one of high risk to one that is more consistent with program goals and socially accepted values.

United States Bureau of Prisons. STAR (Alcoholism) Unit In-Service Training. Copies available from the Research Office, Fort Worth Federal Correctional Institution, Fort Worth, Texas, 1975.

This follow-up is the result of a need to determine how ex-residents function once they leave the STAR unit of FCI Fort Worth. Since the unit began in January 1972, it has released 168 men from its program. The present study was conducted by telephoning parole officers, who were asked to respond to a questionnaire. Usable data were gathered on 27 of the 35 subject sample.

Results showed that the releasees studied had an estimated success rate of 81.5%. The small size and unrepresentativeness of the sample prevent any definite conclusions from being made, but the results can be used to highlight areas that need future work. One such area is the need for a more effective system of record keeping, which would allow all residents to be followed up after their release. The second area involves future follow-up to validate the trends in the present work and to develop methods to evaluate the relative effectiveness of institutional programs.

United States Bureau of Prisons. Work/Study Release Evaluation. Copies available from Research Office, Fort Worth Federal Correctional Institution, Fort Worth, Texas, 1975.

The Work/Study Release program at FCI Fort Worth offers the resident education, training, and the opportunity to save money to aid in his or her readjustment to the community. The program provides the individual with "real life" situations in which to demonstrate responsibility in handling productive community involvement. The motivation and responsibility are entrusted to the resident, whose own efforts determine success.

As a very rough estimate of the ability of residents to handle the responsibilities associated with work and study release, data on the last six months of this program (October 1974 through March 1975) were collected. In addition to the usual "anecdotal" support for program success, it was found that only 13% of the 152 residents assigned to this program had to be removed by the unit teams during this half-year period.

United States Bureau of Prisons. Co-corrections Conference Summary. January 26, 1977. Bureau of Prisons, 320 First Street NW, Washington, DC 20534.

The U.S. Bureau of Prisons conducted a co-corrections conference for federal administrators involved with coed Federal Correctional Institutions. The purpose of the conference was to review the Bureau's experience with co-corrections, its current status and viability, and its future.

After a brief discussion of the history of co-corrections in the Federal Bureau of Prisons, the issues of "public" and "visibility" were examined. The conference concluded that co-correction is not a panaceas, and that it is not appropriate to give it a "visibility" higher than a balance of its advantages and disadvantages warrants.

Generalities about the "public" were considered. The conference identified at least seven "publics" to consider: judges—most supportive; law enforcement—predictably critical; press—neutral to supportive; inmates' families—normally supportive; staff—quite variable depending on consistent discipline in any given institution; civic groups—generally positive; and volunteers—quite supportive. Generalities about the public vary considerably from one geographical region to another, and this variation suggests that in future planning for co-corrections, it is advisable to pick a "winning" location.

The conferees identified the following advantages of co-correction: predatory homosexuality is virtually nonexistent; homosexuality among women is significantly reduced; racial and cultural grouping is virtually nonexistent; the convict code is less evident; assaultive behavior toward inmates and staff is reduced; co-correction actually tends to make staff more alert to the need for supervision; the use of psychological medication is reduced; co-correction maintains social skills; releasees from coed prison are doing well; and co-correction assists in the recruitment and upward mobility for women.

They also identified several disadvantages; public skepticism; risk of pregnancy; possibility of inappropriate staff involvement with inmates. It was also felt that co-corrections might lead the staff toward an attitude of general permissiveness rather than high expectation and discipline, and that co-corrections may decrease program options for women. The conferees pointed out the difficulty of separating the effects of co-corrections from those of other factors in the institution.

United States Bureau of Prisons. FCI Fort Worth Recidivism Study Summary. Fort Worth Federal Correctional Institution, Fort Worth, Texas, 1977.

This report is part of an ongoing research project to determine the rate of "success" among FCI Fort Worth releasees. Success is defined as the avoidance of parole violations and new convictions resulting in incarceration for longer than 60 days for a period of two years following release.

The expected (baseline) success rate was calculated from the Salient Factor Score. This score is the index used by U.S. Parole Commission and ranges from 0 through 11, with higher scores indicating greater probability of post-release success. The average Salient Factor Score for the federal prison system for 1970 was 5.26. Scores of a random sample of 202 individuals released from FCI Fort Worth from 1972 through 1974 averaged 5.85.

Based on Parole Commission data, the hypothetical projected success rate of the 202 FCI Fort Worth releasees would be 70.5%. The actual success rate of the sample is 80%. This result tends to indicate that FCI Fort Worth releasees may be more successful than would be predicted on the basis of Bureau-wide baseline data. Of course, more extensive research is needed before firm conclusions can be drawn about the Fort Worth success rate, but these data are quite impressive.

United States Bureau of Prisons. Therapeutic Community Outcome Evaluation. Copies available from Research Office, Fort Worth Federal Correctional Institution, Fort Worth, Texas, no date.

Thirty former male residents of the Therapeutic Community at Fort Worth were the basis of a follow-up study. Each releasee was evaluated by his probation officer in the areas of employment, involvement with drugs and alcohol, and criminal activity. In-depth personal interviews were conducted with a subsample of releasees.

Although average time since release was only about nine months, 70% of the releasees wiere reported to be completely free from drug use and similarly high percentages were employed and avoiding criminal activity.

Age, time spent in the Therapeutic Community, and time out in the free world were also considered in relation to the above-mentioned variables. The results indicated that younger men seemed to manifest more difficulties in their postrelease adjustment, and that the time from six months to one year after release appears to be the most difficult period of adjustment.

Vanier Center for Women. An Evaluation of Co-correctional Recreational Programs. Unpublished report, December, 1975.

INDEX